FORKS IN THE ROAD

*A Story of a Pittsburgh Native, His Youth,
World War II Experiences and his
Accomplishments in the Field of Retailing*

By C. Mel Eiben

Printed in the United States of America.

ISBN: 978-1-59571-164-9

Library of Congress Control Number: 2006937041

Word Association Publishers
205 Fifth Avenue
Tarentum, Pennsylvania 15084
www.wordassociation.com
1-800-827-7903

For my parents, Frank and Leona, who gave me love, guidance and discipline in equal measure while allowing me the freedom to find my own way in life.

CONTENTS

FOREWORD
A Voice from the Past

In July 2002, during my 79th year on Earth, I received a phone call from "a voice from the past," a guy in the jewelry business in Pittsburgh, Pennsylvania, named Mel Eiben. Mel and I were once close friends when we attended Duquesne University in the early 1940s. I also knew Mel as a fellow Naval Officer during World War II, but before that random call more than 50 years later, I hadn't talked to or seen him since then. The reason Mel called me was to tell me that he decided to write and publish his memoirs and wanted my help in recalling some of the details of our experiences together in college, the Navy, and during the war.

I remembered Mel as a pleasant, soft-spoken personality, slender, well-groomed, wore clothes well, and with his beloved Winnie, loved to dance, and he was very good at it—somewhat of a Fred Astaire type. But my initial reaction to his phone call was a certain puzzlement about his intention to write a book because insofar as I knew, he had no training, experience, or aptitude for writing. So, with those kinds of credentials, why should Mel Eiben, my age and just turning into his octogenarian years think he was capable of writing and publishing a book? I even thought of the possibility of diplomatically suggesting that he forget about the proposed project and not introduce unnecessary complications to his life at an age when for most of us there are already plenty of other complications, either at hand or waiting in the wings.

But on nudging my memory further for additional recollections of Mel Eiben's character and qualities, I realized there was no point in trying to talk him out of something he had decided to attempt. His principal qualities as I recall them were a high degree of independence and initiative and a tendency toward audaciousness—to the point of brashness and daring—in undertaking tasks or projects just to prove he could do them and sometimes just for the hell of it. He unexpectedly dropped out of the Army Officers Training Program at Duquesne and signed on with the Naval Air Corps as a pilot trainee

With all his capacity to do the unusual in the Air Corps, it was decided by the Navy it was best he not be a pilot. The Navy found another part of the service he did qualify for. They trained him to be captain of an amphibious ship known as a landing craft tank or LCT. As the reader will see, while in the Navy during the war and preparing for sea duty and combat, Mel married his Winnie (in contrast to most of his contemporaries who waited until the end of the war and our return safe and sound to the States before mating up). He was also known to go trekking through the jungles of a remote South Pacific Island to find and introduce himself to the Sultan of Jolo (pronounced 'holo') the spiritual leader and mogul of the Moros, the fierce Muslim tribesmen who populate the islands of the Sulu Archipelago in the southern Philippines (this was one of those in the 'just for the hell of it' category). Then after the war, plunging into the series of merchandising business ventures, overcoming and bouncing back from setbacks, betrayals, and various other adversities, and today prospering in his upscale jewelry business in Pittsburgh.

What it all amounts to is that a minor obstacle such as lack of training or experience in writing is not going to deter Mel Eiben from writing his memoirs if Mel Eiben has decided he wants to write his memoirs. So with typical initiative and audacity, Mel undertook the project, composing and putting together the chapters covering his ancestry, his childhood, and as commanding officer of a U.S. Navy amphibious vessel— not to mention his post-war life in marriage, family and business. All in all, a worthy representative of the population group in this country that Tom Brokaw has publicized and honored as "The Greatest Generation."

Mel has titled his memoirs, "Forks in the Road." A competing title is a play on the wording and phonetics of Mel's current business card and stationery, "C. Mel Eiben Jewelers," transposed to simply, "See Mel Eiben," which is what the reader will experience in the pages to follow.

George Lake — March 2006

INTRODUCTION

There are many things in life over which we have no control, but quite often, certain situations present us with a choice. When we find ourselves at those life-altering "forks in the road," those times when we do have a choice, the direction we take indelibly affects the rest of our lives. That is why I chose this title for my book.

I had no idea how much writing my memoirs would cause me to reflect on the decisions I have made in my lifetime. As such, I became intrigued by how each choice I made, regardless of how insignificant it seemed at the time, led me to other life-altering decisions. It is amazing how important the small seeds of our existence and the little choices we make grow into a major part of our future and influence our paths in life. Early decisions we make, such as when to crawl, walk, and talk are our own choices, and when we make them, they become part of our future. Those basic choices may seem like small beginnings, but the forks in the road go on throughout our lives.

When I first considered penning my memoirs, I wondered if I had enough experiences to fill the pages, but sure enough, after six months of writing, I feared the book would be too long.

I initially began writing this book so that I could recount my experiences as the captain of a Landing Craft Tank during World War II. To me, the LCT is the forgotten ship of World War II. It is hard to find any book that has to do with amphibious ships at all. There are certainly endless stories about battleships, aircraft carriers, destroyers and small, fast PT boats. Writers hoping to sell many books probably see no excitement or glamour with the landing crafts. I intend to show to you that we did have an important role to play in winning this war, and I hope you will agree that my personal experiences as a captain of an LCT are worth reading.

My choices in life have been both good and bad, but one thing is constant with my decisions: I make them quickly. Though some seemed to turn out bad, many of them enhanced my future and led to other opportunities that were favorable. I have always been determined to excel in whichever activity I found myself, whether it was in sports, war, business, or writing my memoirs. As you read this, you may wonder why I mention an experience that seems insignificant. I assure you it is a seed of information that greatly affected my life at a future date.

While reading this book, I hope you will be caught up in daydreaming about your forks in the road. Perhaps you will recall experiences you thought you had forgotten and enjoy re-examining those memories as much as I have enjoyed remembering mine.

Perhaps in my lifetime I avoided the adage, "the only way not to make a mistake is to do nothing." I assure you, this is one of life's pitfalls I did not experience. I was never bored.

May the many aspects of my life be of interest to you.

ACKNOWLEDGEMENTS

To my friend, George Lake, whom I had not seen nor heard from since our chance encounter in the city of Zamboanga in the Philippines in the year 1945, I owe a huge debt of gratitude. George served on a landing craft infantry (LCI) during the war and supplied me with important time and place information in regard to the Pacific War Zone.

My heartfelt appreciation to Bill "Cookie" Miller who was the cook aboard ship. A series of unusual circumstances made it possible for Bill, whom I had not seen or heard from for 62 years, and me to spend an incredible weekend together. His detailed information regarding the name and rank of all the crewmembers and the major happenings aboard ship was invaluable to the content of the book.

I am grateful to Ralph Keenan,who also served on an LCI, and provided me with pictures and specifications of various amphibious ships which was helpful in writing the book.

It is with great appreciation I acknowledge the work of Chris Plendl, a dedicated and talented editor. Without Chris, this book would not have been possible. Her expertise, diligence and patience were unequaled.

Thanks to my neighbor, Fred Pement, for helping me

with historical facts and assuring me that all phases of my life would be of interest to the reader.

I would also like to thank my daughters, Suzi and Cindy, for helping me with the exact time and place of many events in our lives.

Finally, thanks to my friend P. J. Compton who continually encouraged me and typed my handwritten manuscript.

Like all endeavors in life, most accomplishments would be difficult without encouragement from associates and friends.

MY TRAVELS IN THE SERVICE

A train ride from Pittsburgh to Philadelphia started my career in the service. Little did I know that it was the beginning of 12 stops to 11 different cities by train and bus for a distance of 8,500 miles. Many of these locations had a bearing on how I became the captain of the ship known as Landing Craft Tank (LCT).

My last stop before going overseas was New Orleans. From this port I traveled by LST (Landing Ship Tank) through the Panama Canal and on to Manus Island in the Pacific. Once in command of the LCT I sailed to 10 different locations. All of these journies involved a distance traveled of 28,500 miles. The total of 37,000 miles of travel by land and sea is the equivalent of one and one-half times around the world.

CHAPTER 1
MANUS ISLAND

November 23, 1944. I was standing on the bridge of LST #778, a very large amphibious ship that was 345 feet long and displaced 4800 tons of water. Sitting on its deck was LCT #804, a 123-foot long, 142-ton Landing Craft Tank. I was Ensign C. Mel Eiben, captain of that LCT, with a crew of 12 men under my command.

Landing Ship Tank (LST)

"Cast off lines," the captain of the LST shouted and the ship glided out of New Orleans into the Gulf of Mexico. I did not know where we would end up. All I knew was that we were proceeding to Pearl Harbor. I had no idea where or when my LCT would be separated from the LST.

After more than a month at sea, we finally arrived at Pearl Harbor and continued to sail west from there. Shortly after leaving Pearl Harbor, the Executive Officer of the LST informed me that the captain wanted to see me in his quarters. At this meeting, he told me he was removing my LCT from the deck of the LST at Manus Island. There, we would part company.

February 11, 1945, 11 a.m. The Captain of LST-778 gave orders to drop anchor and secure the engine. I was at my destination, 10,300 miles from New Orleans. It seemed strange not to hear the engines humming and not to feel the motion of the ship under me after two and a half months at sea. The silence and the lack of a breeze were overwhelming. As I stood on the deck, looking out over the harbor in this hot, humid climate, a very uncomfortable feeling came over me. Just what fork in the road awaited me now? No question about it; all day I felt confused and very depressed.

I decided to find the executive officer, and ask him to arrange a meeting with the captain. I told the captain I was concerned about what I was to do after the launching. He was a standoffish type of individual, impressed with the importance of his command. He simply said his orders were to deliver me to this island. Once I was in the bay, it was my problem to figure out my assignment. He suggested I go ashore and find an authority who knew the reason for my being at this location.

That evening I had difficulty sleeping because I knew the next day I would have to face reality. At the age of twenty-one, I found my responsibilities suddenly awesome. I had 12 men under my command, and my decisions could mean life or death for all 13 of us. Three quarters of the men were older than I; two of them were over thirty-five. What was on their minds? I wondered if they were saying to themselves, "How can this young man possibly command a ship in a war zone and make major decisions for our survival?" From now on, all decisions were up to me, and I had no one to turn to for advice since I would be the only officer on board.

At 8 a.m., the captain told me he was going to commence removing my craft from the top of his ship. I asked, "How are you going to do this since there isn't a ship in the harbor with a large crane aboard?" The captain explained the procedure. In fact, as we were talking, I noticed the LST start to list. He was going to launch the LCT over the side of his ship when it reached a predetermined angle, which he accomplished by using water as ballast in a compartment on the starboard side of the ship. It was amazing, the extreme angle at which the LST finally came to rest. I was about to suggest that we find a bottle of champagne, tie a ribbon on it, and smash it over the bow of the LCT, but the captain seemed to be in too serious a mood for any frivolity, so I abandoned the idea.

I began to realize why the captain seemed concerned; his ship was at a tremendous angle. I wondered what would happen if one side of the LCT let loose faster than the other; I was sure much damage would occur. Was the angle of the ship constant from bow to stern to prevent this from happening? I asked him if he thought he could achieve this without serious problems. With a little disturbance in his voice he said, "How do I know? I never did this before, nor have I ever seen it done." He gave the command to release all fasteners at one time, and my LCT went splashing into the water. I was now in command of my own ship, LCT-804, which was sitting in the Pacific Ocean. Some ropes remained attached to my craft, and the LST pulled it along its side.

While it is on the deck of the LST, an LCT is technically a boat. Once removed from the vessel, it is referred to as a ship. My LCT was now in the harbor, and the time came for me to say goodbye to all the officers and crew on board the LST. It was an emotional experience; after all, we had been together on the same ship for two and a half months. There was not much we could say to one another except good luck on whatever the future holds. I shook hands with many of the crew members and prepared to board my LCT. The crew climbed down a rope ladder and once they were all on board, I likewise made my descent onto the deck.

I stood on the deck of the LCT, looked up at all the men standing along the side of the LST, and wondered what was in store for that ship and its men. What invasion would they be involved in? Would they ever come home to their loved ones?

From this day, and for the rest of my command, my nickname became Skipper. I climbed to the top of the wheelhouse and ordered the crew to man their stations and start the engines. This was quite an anxious moment for me because I had never started them before, but when I heard the hum of the engines, it was like music to my ears. My next order was to cast off the lines. It was a majestic feeling moving away from the LST under my own power. I proceeded out into the harbor and found a space that looked like it was suitable for us to anchor. Now I gave the orders to drop anchor, my ship came to a stop, and I secured the engines.

With the LCT now standing motionless in the harbor, I looked at the crew and they stared at me with a look suggesting they were thinking, "What now Skipper?" All of the men seemed to be in a trance; they looked forlorn and confused. The same feeling came over me. I know they were expecting me to say something. At this time, we were the only LCT in the harbor and several types of large ships surrounded us. This seemed to add to my confused state of mind, and I wondered if the captain of the LST had left me off at the correct location. I needed time to regroup, so I turned to the crew and said, "Everyone relax, and I will talk to you later."

I went into my quarters, sat down, and told myself to come up with some sort of speech to give my crew. I suddenly realized this was a very critical time in my command. If I did not come on strong and with the right attitude, I could lose their respect. After a few minutes, I went back to the deck. I gathered the men together to tell them how fortunate I felt to have them as my crew; however, there was no time for a speech. I looked up at the sky and saw a huge, black, ominous cloud lurking overhead. When I had gone into my quarters, the sun had been shining. What a change. Suddenly, strong gusting winds blew across the water and torrential rain fell upon us. At first, I could not believe it, but it was true—the ship was moving. I rushed to the bridge and there was no longer any doubt that we were dragging anchor.

What a predicament. I had no idea what to do. Adrenaline took over and I knew I had to find a solution; I could not just stand there looking at the anchor cable. If the anchor stayed down there would be no controlling her, but if I took the anchor up, the strong wind could take this flat bottom ship out of control. I had the sudden realization that I didn't know how to anchor an LCT. With all the instructions at Solomon's Island, I had never gotten any training as to the proper way to anchor. Was there some special way to do it other than just let this anchor out? There was no time to think about this now. With very little time for decisions, I decided to take the anchor up. This would be my best bet. I ordered the men to go to their stations in the wheelhouse and at the anchor winch. My first order was to start the engines, and they started immediately. I said "up anchor."

The engines were idling. Common sense dictated not to put them into gear until the anchor was up and out of the way, for the cable could twist around the propeller. The anchor winch was making its usual noise drawing the cable around the drum. Sixty seconds seemed like hours. Finally, the anchor was in place, and I could concentrate on what direction to steer the ship. Looking up, I suddenly saw I was about to crash into a destroyer. If I ran the engines at a slow RPM, I would have very little control; the wind was too intense, and it would be impossible to establish any direction. The destroyer seemed far enough away for me to avoid it if I turned away from it. I gave the order for engines ahead full speed and hard left rudder. "Oh my God," I thought, "this maneuver is not going to work! I am already too close to the destroyer to miss it and the LCT is moving at maximum speed." A collision would surely do massive damage to both the LCT and the destroyer. I had only one possibility to avoid a collision so I screamed to the bosin's mate, "Reverse engines, and set at maximum RPMs!"

The law of physics that states "a force in motion stays in motion" was proving itself. The 143 tons of steel beneath my feet continued on their way with the reverse engines appearing to have no effect on their movement. It seemed like an eternity before the LCT slowed down and came to a stop within ten yards of the destroyer. I can still see the expressions on the faces of the seamen looking over at us from the side of the destroyer.

I proceeded a safe distance from the other vessels in the harbor and found an extra large space to drop the anchor. Almost as quickly as the storm came up, the weather changed to bright sunshine with very little wind. I found this to be a very common weather condition in this part of the world. Manus Island is five degrees above the equator. The island's terrain forces the warm air from the ocean into the cooler air, causing flash storms. This weather condition, called mechanical convection, is a common occurrence. Now, not only was the weather calm, but so were my nerves. I did not need to make a speech since the men saw I reacted as a skipper was expected to respond under such adverse conditions. The crew would have to think that in the future I would handle adversity in a calm and reliable manner.

The next morning, after a restless sleep, I contemplated my next move. It seemed very strange that we were the only LCT in the harbor. This appeared very odd to me. Was there some mix-up as to us being here? Why had no one come over from the navy base to greet me? What a strange feeling, sitting there motionless in the bay. There was only one way to find out what was going on. I would have to go ashore and find Navy headquarters. Someone at the base would have to know the reason for my being there.

I sat in the harbor and realized I had no way to get ashore. The Navy did not provide me with a rowboat or any type of craft to go ashore, so I had two choices: swim ashore, or land the craft on the beach. Swimming ashore did not seem very professional for a captain of his own ship so I decided to beach the LCT.

All sorts of thoughts ran through my mind while I wondered what to do. I was not sure if I could just take up the anchor and go ashore or if I needed permission from some authority to do so. I figured the worst that could happen was that some naval authority— whoever that may be—would censure me.

After lunch—the first meal cooked aboard ship—I gathered the crew together to tell them I was going ashore. In my most professional manner, I ordered the men to man their stations. With them in position to get underway, it dawned on me that I had never, even in training, beached an LCT before. All my preparation had been around docks, and there were no beaches on which to practice. The maneuver never even came up in any training discussions, but since LCTs were designed to land on a shoreline, I decided to try it.

With much trepidation, I proceeded with my first beach landing. I gave the orders to start engines and said, "Up anchor." At a very slow speed, I approached the area I had picked to beach the craft. All I had to go on was logic, which dictated that I could land ashore if I dropped the anchor about twenty yards away and then let it out until I hit the beach. A bit of panic came over me, because I had no idea if there was some unknown object submerged in the water. Putting all fears behind me, I continued to head toward shore. I appeared to be 20 yards away from it when I ordered, "drop anchor." Seconds later, the craft stopped on the beach. Wiping the sweat off my forehead, I let out a big sigh of relief.

I told the anchorman to take up the slack on the cable. This was important, for I knew nothing about the height of the tide this time of day. I told the men to watch the tide while I was gone. If it went down, they were to activate the anchor winch so we would not be stuck on the beach; if the tide went up, they would start the engines and move the ship further onto the beach so we would not float free from the shoreline. Either scenario would be a great embarrassment. I ordered the ramp down and made my way to dry land for the first time in almost three months.

I told the men to stay on board until I returned. There was no sign of life, and I wondered if the captain of the LST had launched me at the correct location. It was not exactly a comforting feeling, but there was nothing for me to do but continue up the dirt road near where I beached to get some answers. There was no sign of any Navy personnel. I had a strange, lonely feeling on this path all by myself. About a quarter of a mile up the way, I saw a sign that read, "67th Battalion of the CBs." "My God," I thought, "my brother Maurice is a CB and that is his battalion number." I did not have time to look for him, and I proceeded up the road.

After walking for fifteen minutes, I finally saw a sign for the Navy Headquarters #2, Manus Island. Dense jungle lined each side of the path I walked along, adding to the suspense of not knowing what would come next. At last I found the building and went inside. A yeoman was typing at a desk. He stood up, we saluted each other, and he asked me why I was there. I told him the reason, and he disappeared into the next room. Finally, after what seemed like forever, he escorted me to the officer in charge. The officer was a robust man; it made me think the food at the base was high in calories. He made me feel very comfortable in his presence and said, "Welcome to Manus Island. I'm glad you had a safe trip." He told me other LCTs were arriving shortly and I should stay on the beach and wait for my orders.

Well, that was not much information, but at least I knew they had been expecting me. I was happy I could stay on the shoreline. I returned to the LCT and gave the information to my crew. It was late afternoon so I decided to stay aboard and look for my brother the following day. As badly as I wanted to see Maurice, I could not risk getting lost in the jungle after dark. "Thank God, I am staying here for now," I thought. "It would have been terrible if Maurice and I were so close and I missed seeing him because I was anchored in the harbor."

The next morning, around 9 am, I told my crew that one-half of them could go ashore in the morning to look around the island. After lunch, the other half could go ashore for no more than three hours. With this order in place, I went off to look for my brother Maurice. The dirt road was now familiar and did not look so ominous. I located the sign I had seen the day before and walked up the path to the CB encampment. Several men were milling around, and I asked if any of them knew Maurice Eiben. Sure enough, they pointed me to him. What a thrill to see his familiar face.

Maurice was completely shocked to see me. I never

thought a male hug would be so gratifying. We talked about old times back home and current happenings in our respective services. Is there any way to describe our feelings at this time? I do not believe so.

Maurice needs a little bit of explaining. His nickname was "Heckles." Rumor has it that at a very early age he rode his bicycle down a flight of steps and crashed at the bottom. He got bruises all over and said, "What the heck is the matter?" That is where the name Heckles came from. Any job he found in civilian life seldom lasted very long because he could not stand authority. The same thing happened in the service; he would advance in rank, and shortly after he would lose his rating for insubordination. Maurice had a heart of gold and was an expert mechanic and welder. His personality was such that he was always willing to help in any emergencies and expected nothing in return.

Maurice invited me up to the enlisted men's recreation center for some more old-time talk about our parents, our brother Paul, and our sister Lois. I had no contact with my wife or parents since leaving the United States. I was very curious about Paul; he was drafted into the service in 1941, before the United States officially entered World War II. Maurice knew Paul was in England but that was about all. We talked about our concern as to whether all three of us would ever enjoy the happy time of being with our parents and loved ones back home again. Maurice asked, "Can you imagine sitting down to one of those wonderful meals our mother makes?" That homecoming was a long way off, and we had to pray that joyous occasion would someday happen.

As we were talking, I could hear music. I told Maurice that I had a record player on my ship and a very limited selection of fine music. As only he would express it, he said, "You are a goddamn officer. You can do anything you want.

10

If you like those records, then pick up a pile and take them back to your ship."

It was getting late in the morning and I was concerned about my crew and our first day on the island. What if some high-ranking officer came looking for me, and I was nowhere to be found? I was sure that would leave an unfavorable impression of my ability to command an LCT. I said to Maurice, "As much as I hate to leave, I better get back on board my ship. I will do my best to come back tomorrow to visit."

He said, "Damn it, Mel, and don't forget the records." With a very guilty feeling, I picked up a pile and went on my way, afraid someone would yell, "Hey where are you going with those?" It did not happen, and the crew and I spent many hours enjoying the music.

Back on board, I met with my bosin's mate. He reported that nothing eventful had happened in my absence. It seemed very strange he would say that, for there had been a very eventful happening. While I was away visiting my brother, an LST had come into the harbor. I expected to see an LCT on top of the deck, but upon closer look, I saw five sections of an LCT on the deck. While I was contemplating the significance of this, one of my men interrupted me. He said a lieutenant (who outranked me) wanted to see me.

I met the Lieutenant and saluted him; he did the same in return. I invited him to my quarters for some coffee, and he informed me that in the morning I was to go to the other side of the island to Seadler Harbor. There I would find docks and supply depots. He supplied me with a map showing the location of the harbor. In a way, this was great news; we would dock in a more civilized environment. Suddenly, my heart sank. I would not be able to see my brother again. In fact, this is exactly what happened; we did not meet again until after the war. What a disappointment for me. I knew that he would wonder why I did not come back the next day. Would he think that I did not care enough to see him? I had to believe he knew better and pondered what luck it was to have met at all.

The lieutenant continued explaining my orders. I asked him why the LSTs had only sections of LCTs on board, and he told me that mine was the last one to come over as a complete ship. He explained that an efficiency expert in Washington, D.C. calculated that LSTs could transport more LCTs if they were in sections and assembled at their destination. By this method, more LCTs could be delivered to the war zone in a shorter time.

I was not there to witness the assembly of the ships; however, the lieutenant gave me the details. My first thought was the CBs on the island would assemble the crafts, but I was wrong. The captain and crew of the unassembled LCT had to do it themselves. The LCT that had only two of its sections delivered would have to wait until the third section arrived on another LST. I tried to imagine the captain and the crew of an LCT, waist deep in the water trying to connect the sections. Huge nuts and bolts had to be put in place to secure each part of it. Each wave had to make this a very difficult task. Luckily, mine had come over in one piece.

The next day I was anxious to disembark for the other side of the island. I ordered the night watch to observe the tide so we would have no difficulty removing the craft from the beach. At seven bells, I gave the order to start the engines and ordered the anchor up.

The LCT moved smoothly out into the bay. With the anchor in place, I ordered the engine ahead to cruising RPM and right 60-degree rudder. The craft was moving where I wanted it to, and I ordered rudder amid ship and steady as we go. I established direction by pointing the LCT to a distant landmark, and we were on our way.

I abruptly realized I was in control of the LCT, my own command, and it was my duty to proceed to Seadler Harbor,

25 miles away. This was my very first solo run with only a map and magnetic compass to guide me. Though the distance was only 25 miles, piloting a ship at sea is nothing like driving a car on a highway. While sailing close to shore, a map—often referred to as a chart—is imperative. It lists several types of information, such as buildings ashore, elevations of the terrain, and land projections out to sea. The most important thing though is the depth of the water, which cannot be seen. Running aground is always a threat and can do much damage to any type of ship, especially the thin steel hull of an LCT.

Manus Island is just a few degrees from the equator; it obviously has a very warm climate. It was a hot, windless, humid day. The sea was very calm; the screws of my ship caused the only ripples. A strange, relaxed feeling came over me once I was at sea. It was almost as if there was no war, just me and 12 men going down a shoreline in a landing craft with no other ship in sight.

I was about a mile from the dock at the harbor when an airplane flying a few hundred feet above me abruptly interrupted that calm relaxed feeling I had enjoyed. I did not hear him coming. His engine must have stopped and he slammed into the water about 200 yards in front of me. I was completely shocked but immediately went to his rescue.

It seemed that it took forever to arrive at the crash site on the cumbersome LCT. As I headed in that direction, I still wondered if I should even try. I was certain that faster rescue boats would be near the plane shortly, but much to my surprise, this did not happen. I was the first and only craft to arrive at the scene. I ordered all of the crew to look into the water for the downed pilot. Suddenly, Frank yelled out, "Skipper, I see the plane!"

The sea was very calm with no wind so we were able to remain nearly stationary over the plane. Frank Sloan immediately took off his clothes and dove into the water, but

I ordered him to come back on board. There was no way that he could hold his breath long enough and safely get to the pilot in time to save him, and I wasn't about to let one of my men kill himself in the process. It was tragic enough that we all had to witness this, and I could not let Frank put himself in danger although his motivation was valiant.

I looked down into the water; the plane was submerged at least 25 feet. The pilot was struggling to open the canopy above his seat but his efforts were to no avail. It would not open. His seat was almost engulfed by the water rushing into his cabin. The water continued to rise and the pilot stopped struggling and became motionless. What a horrible and frustrating experience for my crew and me, watching such a young man die right in front of us—knowing we were helpless.

I probably should have said a prayer, but I was in such a state of shock I said nothing. All of the crew appeared to be in a trance while they peered into the water. I am sure they were thinking that the pilot's unfortunate death was just one of the many we would witness before the end of the war. I broke the silence and ordered the coxswain to go to the docking area. I was very upset at what had just transpired. Surely, the Navy should have sent a more able craft than mine to rescue the pilot. Instead, we were all forced to watch this young aviator succumb and could do nothing about it. To this day, I can still see him struggling to free himself. This traumatic experience has stayed with me, and in all my life, I will never forget it.

I proceeded to the docking area. One of my men got a line over a piling, and I ran to an officer I saw on the dock and told him about the airplane crash. He said he knew nothing about it. Apparently, no one on shore had seen the accident. He immediately rushed off into a nearby building to report the crash. Shortly thereafter, an officer and four enlisted men dashed down to the dock and asked me where the downed plane was. They jumped into a speedboat and went to the area where the pilot crashed. Why they did not take me along, I will never know.

I often think about the crash. I try to analyze why no one immediately came to the crash site. As I recreate the scene in my mind, I remember there was no engine sound. All I heard was a swishing noise, which is what alerted me to his being overhead. I figure it was possible that no one from the shore saw or heard the crash. I would like to believe, as I look back on the incident, that there was no neglect on the part of the shore command.

Back on the LCT, I made sure all hawsers were in place that secured the ship to the dock. I placed bumpers over the side to make sure no damage would occur to my brand-new ship. As on the day of my launching, there was no one to greet me at the dock when I arrived. I went into my quarters and contemplated my next move. I was mentally and physically exhausted from the day's events. My first solo run on the LCT had begun with a feeling of accomplishment, which was quickly interrupted by the tragic plane crash.

The Navy operated in very strange ways out in the Pacific. In the States, documents directing me whom to see and what my orders were accompanied all my moves. I now felt like a tiny ink spot on a world map, and I had no idea what was in store for me next. I could have looked for the officer in charge at Seadler Harbor, but it was already late afternoon. I had had nothing to eat since breakfast, and with the combination of no food and 100-degree intense heat, I was too drained to concentrate.

The next morning I awoke and washed. I would have liked to shower, but there is no running water on an LCT. I finished eating breakfast and went to seek out the authorities on the island. Seadler Harbor was no small operation. It was a very important staging area for the fighting on New Guinea, which was 250 miles away. In addition to the harbor, there was an airport used to fly sorties. There were many merchant ships and some fighting ships in the harbor. At this time (9 a.m.), there was much activity. Important-looking people were going from building to building; I asked the officer on the dock which building I should go to for answers. He pointed it out to me and I was on my way.

I went inside and was directed to a large waiting room. There was an enlisted man at a desk. I thought perhaps he would hand me some typed orders, which would be a new experience. I gave him my name and the number of the LCT. Five other officers were in the room. I thought that maybe I could learn something from them regarding my purpose here. Some men were on ships and others were in other lines of duty on the island. None of them could come up with any logical reasons as to what I was doing here. I waited for more than an hour in the office.

Finally, I was escorted into an office, and I could tell by the officer's insignia that he was a captain. He had many ribbons on his uniform, indicating he had probably seen a lot of war action. The captain looked like he was a leader who commanded respect, and I was impressed with his demeanor and self-confidence. After asking how I was and welcoming me to the harbor, he immediately gave me my orders. He told me six LSTs would be in the harbor by March 2. Additional LCTs were being assembled and would be here that day as well. He went on to remind me how lucky I was to have an LCT that had come over in one piece. On March 11, the flotilla of LSTs would leave the harbor towing the LCTs—their destination, the island of Mindanao. On the south portion of the island is the Zamboanga peninsula, and the city proper is at the tip. I asked permission to remain at the dock until we disembarked for Zamboanga; my request was granted. I returned to the dock and introduced myself to the ensign in charge of the docks. His name was George Carver and despite it being a very warm day, he was very neatly dressed. I could immediately tell he was an affable man. George informed me that he was on duty here for six months and was very curious about the history of the islands. George told me Manus Island is part of the island group known as Admiralties. It was part of the Dutch empire until 1942, when the Japanese occupied the island. Manus Island is 50 miles long and has an excellent 20-mile long and 6-mile wide harbor. A harbor this size can hold a huge fleet of ships and as such, it can be used as a military staging area. The Japanese built an airstrip on the interior of the island a mere 250 miles from New Guinea. From this base, the Japanese could control the sea-lanes in this area.

On February 29, 1944, General Douglas MacArthur had made a surprise attack on the island, and in one week, there was no doubt as to its favorable outcome. Fighting continued for several more weeks before the United States totally secured the island. Now, the U.S. could use the base to their advantage in the battle for New Guinea. New Guinea is a huge island close to Australia. As such, it was very important for the Allies to secure it. Even in March 1945, battles were still going on in sections of New Guinea.

What luck to become friends with George; he also told me about the ongoing battle in the Philippines. Much to my surprise, I found out the invasion of the Philippines had begun. On October 20, 1944, General MacArthur had stepped ashore on the island of Leyte. This island became his headquarters where he staged the invasion of Luzon Island and eventually captured Manila, the capital of the Philippines.

On October 24, there was a huge naval battle in Leyte Gulf. The Japanese sent Kamikaze (suicide) pilots to attack our fleet.

Those pilots used their planes as "bombs" and slammed them into our naval fleet. The Japanese did not win the sea battle but delivered devastating damage to many of our ships. In January of 1945, another huge sea battle occurred in Lingayen Gulf while the Allies invaded Luzon Island.

I asked my friend if he knew anything about Mindanao. Had it been invaded yet? This he did not know. He did indicate, however, that all of the fighting he knew about was north of Mindanao Island. Zamboanga is located on the southern tip and the area below the city is called the Celebes Sea. This is the location of Borneo, a very large island—one of whose resources is oil—which was very important to the Japanese war effort.

I thought we were being prepared for the invasion of Zamboanga, seeing the importance of its location near Borneo. It was at least ten days before I would be towed to Zamboanga. Knowing that gave me a considerable time to just sit around and think about my past. I thought about the many "Forks in the Road" during my time in the service, and how they had brought me to be anchored at Seadler Harbor.

CHAPTER 2
DECISIONS

The time of year was early December; the date had no significance to me. It was just another typical Pittsburgh winter morning, cold and dreary as most. I climbed out of bed, went downstairs, and stood on top of a floor radiator. It was my favorite place to get dressed after coming from my chilly attic room. I was about to begin my daily routine; that is, until this day, December 8, 1941, suddenly became very important.

The radio was on, and I heard the devastating report about Japan's lethal assault on United States forces in Pearl Harbor the day before. Because of the unprovoked attack, the United States and Great Britain declared war on Japan. This day was no longer just another winter day; it was a major fork in the road of my life—and for millions of people around the world as well. A strange feeling came over me when I heard about the tragedy; the news was overwhelming. I immediately wondered how these events would affect my life. I knew that because of my age, I would inevitably be part of the military within a few weeks and my carefree life was certainly over. I would have to direct all my future endeavors to serving my country.

I was overcome with emotion. Although it shocked me at first, I was not oblivious to world affairs. History and current events interested me, and I had followed Hitler's rise to power beginning in 1938. That escalation began with his successful annexation of Austria, continued with his occupation of Czechoslovakia, and then culminated with his invasion of Poland in 1939. England and France had a treaty with Poland in which they agreed to defend her; therefore, they both declared war on Germany on September 3, 1939. By the end of 1940, the Germans occupied most of Europe and in June of 1941, Hitler invaded Russia.

The United States placed an oil embargo on Japan in an attempt to pressure them to pull their forces from China and French-Indochina (modern-day Vietnam). Without oil, the Japanese economy was greatly impacted, and it was nearly impossible for them to continue their war on China. Despite these events, the U.S. was reluctant to commit military power to conflicts around the globe. That all changed on December 7, 1941, when Japan savagely attacked Pearl Harbor.

I wondered what Japan could possibly gain by such a brutal and malicious attack on our powerful country. Three days after the United States and Great Britain declared war on Japan, Germany and Italy declared war on the United States. A major world war erupted.

When the United States entered World War II, I was in college and most of the draft-eligible men at school, including myself, were in the Reserve Officers Training Corps (ROTC). This program exempted me from being drafted, but I figured it was highly unlikely that I would continue with my college education. Although I was in the ROTC, being in the Army didn't appeal to me. I realized that I had to decide which branch I wanted to join before the military made the choice for me. The Army, Navy, and Marines all vied for enlistments, but I still didn't know which one I wanted to join.

The winter passed without my being called to active duty. Then one spring day, I went to a recruitment talk on campus with two of my friends from Duquesne University. A Naval Air Corps officer and a pilot with a chest full of medals gave a dynamic, energizing speech. We were convinced we wanted to be naval aviators, so George Lake, Bob Lawrence, and I went down to the Navy Recruiting Office in Pittsburgh to sign up.

After joining the Navy, we began arduous exams. We all passed the eye and depth perception tests and from there we took a timed written exam, divided into two parts, which included a general IQ test and a mechanical aptitude test. Following the test, the commander called George into his office and told him that he had failed the mechanical aptitude test but had scored the highest in the combined test. Since he failed the mechanical portion of the exam, it meant George would never be a Naval Aviator, but the commander asked him to join the Navy V-7 program for Navy deck officers. Bob and I passed both tests, enlisted in the Naval Air Corps, and a few days later, the three of us resigned from the Army ROTC. When George found out that Bob and I had passed both tests he commented, "How could you two guys be able to pass the IQ test? That, I will never understand!"

After the war, I had an opportunity to meet with George and talk about our Navy careers. It was hard for me to believe, but George—who according to the Navy had no mechanical aptitude—became the engineering officer on a Landing Craft Infantry (LCI).

With the mental part of the enlistment out of the way, I needed to pass a physical next. There is something peculiar about examinations to me. Regardless of how healthy I feel, I always worry that something may be wrong. During the physical, the doctor did the usual procedures; he checked my throat and asked me to take a deep breath in and let it out. He did not say anything so I assumed I had passed. I thought the exam was over, but then he did something odd. He asked me to inhale and he measured my chest, then exhale and he did the same. The doctor paused for a moment, looked at me, and told me that I had failed the physical. I immediately asked him why, and he said it was because my chest did not expand enough when I inhaled. Rather than accepting that I was not destined to be in the Naval Air Corps, I decided to seek a solution to my setback. I asked the doctor if there was any way I could correct the problem, and he recommended exercise. I decided to find out what types of calisthenics developed that part of my body, since I was quite determined to be a pilot. My predicament inspired me to go to the YMCA.

After just two weeks of weightlifting and doing other exercises, I returned for another physical. Much to my surprise, I passed. I was ecstatic because I met all the requirements to become an aviator. The doctor probably thought since I was strong-minded enough to want to be a pilot he would pass me as long as I was close to the physical requirements. With the mental and physical exams behind me, I enlisted as a Naval Aviator.

Before I could officially enter the program, I had to show my birth certificate along with another form of identification. I presented my driver's license that stated my name as Melvin Casper Eiben, along with my birth certificate--that stated my name as Casper Melvin Eiben—to the recruiting officer. What an embarrassment. I had never bothered to look at them. I had no idea at the time that they did not agree. He told me it was impossible to accept my signature for enlistment until they were certain I was M.C.E. or C.M.E. I asked him what he thought I should do, and he said he didn't know since he'd never seen anything like this before. He suggested I get a legal document indicating I was the same person. As it turned out, I had to hire an attorney to do just that.

In the 1920's when I was born, it was a Catholic tradition to name children after their uncles. As a result, my parents named me Casper Melvin Eiben. Apparently, they did not like the name Casper, so they never told me what my real name was, and since I didn't know any better, I had signed everything as Melvin C. Eiben. To avoid future problems, I now signed all legal documents C. Mel Eiben. That was the last glitch I ran into on the road to my enlistment. On June 30, 1942, I signed my enlistment papers, and I was officially part of the United States Naval Air Corps.

Once I was formally in the Navy, I expected to be sent to basic training, but months passed and my orders didn't arrive. My parents were only one generation removed from emigrating from Germany and I speculated that this might be a factor. I also remembered that when I was 12 years old, I had seen a group of teenagers doing gymnastics inside a recreation center. It looked like fun to me so I went inside. One of the instructors asked me if I wanted to join, and I asked him if it cost anything. He said no, and considering it was free, I decided to join. The organization had been called the Duetscher Tournaferon. I wondered if my membership in this club and my German heritage on both sides made the government think I was a Nazi sympathizer. However, I heard a rumor that the Navy had signed up too many qualified men and didn't have enough room for training everyone.

After almost a year, the Navy called me to active duty on June 13, 1943. This left me with just 11 days to put my affairs in order, which wasn't much time. I had to let Duquesne University know I would not be returning in the fall and I had to let both Kaufmann's Department Store and the City of Pittsburgh know I wouldn't be available for work. Perhaps the most pressing issue was breaking the news to Winnie Winner.

For the last two years, Winnie and I had grown very close. Meeting her at Duquesne was a very important fork in the road for me; we were madly in love. I knew from the first time I laid eyes on her that she was the one for me. I hated the thought of being separated from her, and I did not want to have to tell her that I had to go. Winnie and I were to meet on Friday. We were going to visit her Aunt Margaret together, which we did often. I decided to delay telling her the news until Friday evening.

To make the evening more special, I took my love to one of the better restaurants in Shadyside. This was unusual for me because of my limited funds, and it surprised Winnie too. I could tell she sensed that something important had happened. During dinner, I told her about my having to report to active duty in a few days. We both knew it was inevitable, but this did not ease the shock of knowing we would soon be parted.

After dinner, I suggested we take a walk in Frick Park, which was nearby. It was a warm night and dusk had set in. The sun reflected beautiful shades of blue, purple, and orange as it disappeared into the horizon and added a special dimension to the evening. Our walk was an anniversary of sorts because of a very special walk the year before on a night like this one. That evening in the park was still vivid in my mind and I wanted to relive that occasion. This we did, knowing that such a night might never occur again.

On Saturday, I stayed home all day with my parents. They were dreading sending their last son off to the service. The next three days, Winnie and I went to see her parents in New Salem. Those days were happy and enjoyable, intermingled with periods of sadness, at the thought of my departure.

On Wednesday, my parents invited us to spend the day with them. They were both very fond of Winnie, and we all had a good time. On our last day together, I decided to surprise her and take her to dinner at the Roosevelt Hotel that evening. We went there frequently for fraternity parties. I had no idea what her reaction would be to my plans for the rest of the night. I told her I had decided to rent a room at the hotel so that we could have our last evening together in total privacy. At first, she had no reply; then she said she wasn't so sure it was a good idea. At the time, we were alone on the porch of my house. I hugged her and kissed her without saying a word. Suddenly she said, "Why not? It sounds like fun." If it hadn't been for the war, I am sure she would have never agreed. Wartime circumstances can force difficult decisions.

Winnie and I met at her apartment on the morning of our last day together. She was waiting for me in the foyer when I arrived, and as usual, looked gorgeous. We intended to have a meeting with our mutual friends at school.

The cafeteria was filled with many of our friends, including some of the professors, which was a pleasant surprise. It was two hours before our last friends said goodbye. Winnie then turned to me and said she would meet me back at her apartment in an hour; she wanted to freshen up before our dinner date. I was back a bit early to be sure I would not miss a precious moment of our time together.

Ten minutes seemed like an hour, and then finally, Winnie appeared. I had never seen her look more beautiful. I gave her a gentle hug as I smelled the subtle fragrance on her neck. I was overwhelmed with love for her.

Around four o'clock, we were sitting in the lounge of the hotel having cocktails. We finished our drinks then moved to the dining room. From the time we sat down in the lounge and all through dinner, we recalled the splendid times we had had over the past two years. We both agreed that it had been a magical time in our lives. Though we knew the war might interfere with our love for each other, we made no mention of these concerns. We wanted this day to be an occasion we would long remember as a happy one.

After we ate, I excused myself, went to the lobby, and picked up the key to the room. We took the elevator to our floor and found the room. I turned the key in the lock and we entered the room without saying a word. My nervous anticipation of what was about to happen is indescribable. I was certain Winnie experienced the same emotions. I know that only because of the importance of our last night together—having no idea when we would meet again—did she agree to my renting the room.

Winnie and I walked inside. I called room service and ordered drinks. We sat on the couch, sipping our cocktails and talking about our overwhelming love for each other. I moved onto the bed, and Winnie joined me. Suddenly, we were in each other's arms. I found myself out of control and could sense Winnie felt the same way, but at the height of our passion, she suddenly broke from my embrace and said, "Please Mel, not now. We both should wait for this special moment until after we are married."

We continued to lie close, whispering our words of love. Winnie had made a wise decision, best for our future happiness. At two in the morning, we checked out of the hotel, and I drove her to her aunt's in Shadyside. We rang the doorbell, and Maggie let us in. She had not been expecting us because Winnie had told her how we were spending the evening. The three of us had a glass of wine, and Maggie wished us well for whatever the future held for us. In her usual understanding way, she left us alone in the living room. What we said in that last half-hour together, I do not remember. We had one final embrace and then we parted. My final words to her on that evening were, "Goodbye. I love you very much, Winnie."

Winnie stood in the doorway and watched me walk to my Chrysler Roadster. I hesitated before opening the door to my car and waved to her one last goodbye while blowing her a kiss. I drove off into the night, thinking about our last romantic day together and wondering if we would ever see each other again.

The following day, I had to leave. My parents and I were trying not to be depressed, but that was easier said than done.

I can still remember the morning I left home. It was a bright spring day; the temperature was about 70 degrees. As I walked out the front door, I stopped to look at the swing on the edge of the porch where I had spent many happy times with my family.

My Home and Birthplace

Across the street was an empty lot with a basketball hoop on it. I cannot tell you how many hours I spent playing ball with my friends on that space. I lived atop a steep cobblestone road. Up and down the lane were the many homes where my friends lived. Most of them were in the service now and it made me wonder if I would ever see this landscape again. I had never been away from home in my life for more than two weeks. It was very difficult to say goodbye to my parents, and I wondered how they really felt, as I was their third son to go into the service.

My father drove me into Pittsburgh and dropped me off at the train station. I said my last goodbye to my dad as he got out of the car and watched me disappear into the train station. I wasn't even out of town yet, and I already missed Winnie and my family a lot—though I was intrigued about what the future held for me. I had packed lightly and took only one bag with me, although I did need a belt around it to hold it together. I knew I would not need any civilian clothes for a long time. I boarded the train, took a window seat, and began to daydream about what it would be like at my destination, the University of Pennsylvania.

CHAPTER 3
THE AIR CADET

I took my seat on the train, and the locomotive slowly pulled out of the station and proceeded across Pennsylvania. Though the distance to Philadelphia was actually only 300 miles, the irregular terrain added to the travel time. We made many stops along the way, and it took nearly ten hours to get there. Once in Philadelphia, I hailed a cab and proceeded to the university.

The University of Pennsylvania is in the central part of the city and is surrounded by huge brick walls that make it look like a prison. I was surprised to find a beautiful campus inside those imposing walls. After registering in the main office, I received government-issue basic uniforms and got my room assignment. My room was in a section of campus called the quadrangle. As I looked out the window of my room, I saw well-kept lawns and flower gardens. There were many paths going in different directions to the other sections of the school.

I went to my room and introduced myself to my roommate, Dean Orenthop. We were total opposites. Dean came from Philadelphia's prestigious Main Line area, and there was no doubt that he came from a wealthy family. His affluent upbringing did not matter in the military; Dean and I were considered equals. We wore the same uniform, and we both had new beginnings. Dean and I immediately became good friends. My old college friend Bob Lawrence arrived at the University of Pennsylvania the same day. It was a help to know there was a familiar face in the school.

We all settled in on the weekend. First thing Monday morning, we went to class to learn the basics of flying airplanes. It is hard to describe what an overwhelming, emotional experience it was for me—being a mere twenty years old and beginning training in the US Naval Air Corps. I was excited yet nervous at the same time. I had no idea what training would entail, but I was surely interested in finding out.

We were not going to fly the planes until well after we mastered the classroom basics. I made sure to pay great attention to the instructors since it was imperative I knew what I was doing before I got airborne.

Not since my very first days in college did I concentrate on my studies as much as I was doing now. The subject that was the most difficult for me to learn was Morse code. In Morse code, a series of short and long beeps form words. It was enough to rattle one's brain. Somehow, I managed to master the basics and pass the course. The class on Navy regulations was boring, but it made me realize how important the chain of command was in the Navy.

Also included in our training was a physical education course that included long distance running. I had been on the track team in high school; distance running had been my specialty, and no one was able to beat me. I felt great about being the fastest person in our group until one day, a new battalion came in and a cadet from the South arrived. He ran the event barefoot and left me in his dust.

While at the university, I had a surprise visit from George Lake. He was at Villanova College for the initial stages of his training to become a Naval Deck Officer. He traveled the 20 miles to Philadelphia by commuter train to visit me, and I introduced him to my roommate, Dean. Bob Lawrence joined us as well, and the four of us walked to a tavern just outside the quad for dinner and a few drinks.

Time passed quickly as we talked about old times and new experiences. As the night wore on, Dean asked us if we would like to go to his girlfriend's house with him the following weekend, and we all agreed.

On the next Saturday, Dean's girlfriend Jennifer picked us up in a late model Lincoln Town car and drove us to her home in Northwest Philadelphia. It was obvious that Jennifer came from a wealthy family like Dean. When we arrived at her house, I was overwhelmed by its size and beauty. It was a two-story stone house with at least 12 rooms. After we passed through the front door, we entered a spacious foyer, and Jennifer escorted us to a large back yard with a huge in-ground swimming pool. Much to our surprise, three beautiful girls were there waiting for us.

The ladies were in their bathing suits. Their well-shaped figures in skintight suits captured our attention. They invited us to change into our trunks, and we all sat in chairs around the pool. The conversation centered on our training at the University. All the girls had boyfriends in the service, which added an extra dimension to the conversation. After some friendly conversation, Dean suggested we all go for a dip.

After we swam for a while, Jennifer's parents served us a wonderful grilled steak dinner. We definitely enjoyed Jennifer's hospitality, and mingling with the girls was a treat since we had not been in the company of women for some time. Dean drove us back to the university at 1 a.m. George, Bob, and I could not thank him enough for the enjoyable evening.

Since it was late and Dean had returned to Jennifer's house, George spent the night in my room. That is where he came up with the idea of our traveling to Atlantic City the next weekend. The idea intrigued him since he had never seen the ocean before. Atlantic City was a mere 80 miles away from us, so it seemed like a good idea to go.

The following Saturday, George arrived from Villanova around 10 a.m. We went to the station and purchased two seats on the 11:30 bus to Atlantic City, New Jersey. We arrived there around 2 p.m. and decided to splurge on a cab ride to the Boardwalk.

George and I walked up the steps to the pier. The first thing he said when he saw the ocean was "Wow! There is nothing but an endless beach with water stretching out as far as I can see." I was excited to be at the ocean too, but not nearly as much as George was. After all, he was experiencing it for the first time. The water breaking against the shoreline created a mist, and we could smell the salt in the air. The sky was bright blue and cloudless and George commented that our trip was already well worth it, even if nothing eventful happened the rest of the day.

Near the water's edge, we took off our shoes, rolled up our pants, and walked into the cool refreshing water. From there we walked a half-mile down the beach along the edge of the water.

Late in the day, we decided to look for a second-rate motel away from the beach since we did not have much money. Once we checked in, we headed back to the beach, and the lack of lights at the shore astounded us. For most of the day, the war was not on our minds—until we noticed the darkness. Except for some very dim blue lights, almost all lights were prohibited this close to shore. Yet despite the distressful thoughts of war, looking out over the ocean and hearing the waves break on the beach relaxed us.

Early in the war, the U.S. coastline was anything but peaceful. German submarines were sinking our Merchant Marines ships at an alarming rate. The percentage of casualties in the Merchant Marines was far greater than in any other branch of the service. Obviously, when a torpedo struck a ship, death came instantly to a lot of them; some died from severe burns while others drowned in the ocean. The men lucky enough to be in lifeboats did survive. Since George and I were in the service during the middle of a war, these were not happy thoughts for us.

We located a bar on the boardwalk and went inside. We could barely tell the place was open. The windows were covered by heavy black drapes, and the lighting inside was dim. A couple of women joined us in the small booth. We all enjoyed the evening, drinking more than we should have. George and I stumbled back to the motel, two drunken sailors, and collapsed into bed.

The next morning we awoke with severe headaches and found our way to the boardwalk one last time. We ate breakfast and took a short walk on the beach to say goodbye to the ocean. From there we were on our way back to Philadelphia and reality, but we will remember those two days the rest of our lives. That was the last time I saw George until many months later.

Things continued as usual at school. We had two more months of classroom instruction that ended in early October. On the last day of class, we were ordered to pack all of our gear because we were moving to Westminster College, where we would begin flying planes.

Monday morning we boarded a train to make the long trip to Pittsburgh. From there, we had a 45-minute bus ride to the college. Much to my surprise, I found myself rooming with Bob Lawrence.

Even in college, Bob had always managed to accomplish the impossible. Dean had been a great companion, but he was nowhere near as much fun or as spontaneous as Bob. I was excited to be lodging with my old friend; I knew I was in for some fun times.

We had one day of classroom instruction before the Navy transported us to New Castle Airport for our flying lessons. The night before our first flying lesson, I had difficulty sleeping. The anticipation of actually flying an airplane made me restless. The morning could not come soon enough for me, since it was a day I had thought about for many months. At 8 a.m., we boarded a bus and left for the airport.

After a 20-minute ride, we saw a flat expanse of land. At first, it looked like a huge grass field, but upon closer inspection, I noticed two asphalt runways going in slightly different directions. There was a small building near the edge of both runways with a windsock indicating the wind's direction. The runways appeared to be 75 yards long. To a man who had never flown before, that seemed a very short distance.

Parked near the end of a runway, were at least a dozen airplanes. As we drove closer to them, I could not believe my eyes. The planes seemed incredibly small to me and looked like they were almost all made from canvas. It certainly was not what I expected after seeing the pictures of training airplanes at school. World War II fighter planes looked much more advanced than these crafts.

J-3 Pipercub, known as "Grasshoppers" in World War II

I was assigned an instructor named Paul. The two of us boarded the plane, with me in the front seat. There were dual controls in the plane—one set for me and one set for him. Since I had never been in an airplane before, this was a traumatic experience. One of the other instructors walked over near the front of the plane. Much to my surprise, he turned the propeller to start the engine. This seemed odd and very dangerous, and I wondered if he had ever been struck by the propeller.

Once we were airborne, it took a long time to get to the elevation needed to seek out a destination. The engine made a very loud noise. It almost sounded like a lawn mower. That sound, in combination with the noise made by the wind hitting the canvas wings of the plane, created quite a racket. It was difficult to hear the instructor's voice. A stick controlled the airplane, but I got the sensation it was not a plane at all—just some strange contraption that happened to get airborne. If you pushed the stick forward, the plane would go down; backward, you would increase the elevation. If you moved it sideways, the airplane would go to the right or left.

What an exhilarating feeling to be flying in an aircraft at an elevation of 1000 feet above the ground. You cannot imagine the sensation of flying this low. I saw the farmland below, shades of green and brown, all divided into geometric shapes with streams and rivers going all different directions influenced by the terrain of Pennsylvania. The cruising speed of the plane was 87 miles per hour, and it had a range of 220 miles.

When you fly, all of a sudden you are aware of the railroads. Most of them follow the rivers because that is where land elevation is the lowest, and it was the easiest place for rail to be laid. Next, you become aware of the ribbons of roads and highways connecting the cities and towns.

Suddenly, Paul broke his silence and told me he wanted me to control the plane. The stick protruding between my legs did not seem like it could control anything—much less an airplane. It did not take long to figure out the slightest movement changed the direction of the plane. After about an hour of flying, Paul took over the controls and headed back to the airport.

We went in for a landing. Those 75-yard runways looked like tiny ribbons on the ground below. Paul set the plane down gently, and it ran for what seemed like quite a ways before stopping. Paul said, "By the way, there are no brakes on this thing. When you land, you have to be sure a lot of runway is available so you can come to a stop." I have to say my first time in the air was quite a stimulating experience.

I got out of the plane and commented to Paul that the engine did not seem too powerful. He replied, "You are right about that one, Mel. It only has a 60 horsepower engine." Paul seemed to be very proud of the plane and told me it had been manufactured in Lock Haven, which was only a short distance from where we were. The name of the plane was the J-3 Piper Cub, and it sold for $1500, making it possible for a person with a moderate income to own one.

In December 1941, one third of all the airplanes in America and two thirds of all the light planes in the world were Piper Cubs. Not only were hundreds of these planes used for basic training in the military, they also played an important role in actual fighting in World War II. The army bought nearly 6000 of these planes during their involvement in the war. The J-3 Piper Cubs were nicknamed "Grasshoppers" due to their ability to land on beaches, back roads and pastures. In certain operations, they transported such high-ranking officials as General Eisenhower, General Patton and General Bradley.

At Westminster, we had physical training, which included swimming. To increase our competitive spirit, we had swimming races. Again, as in running, I had an edge in the swimming race. Not for too long though, because Hobbie Moore came in with the next class. He had been in high school with me and was one of the best swimmers in school. I was no match for him; he was the best swimmer at Westminster.

One weekend we went into the local town of New Castle for some fun. We visited a typical bar with miniature bowling machines, darts and a pool table. It also had slot machines, which were our undoing. Quarter after quarter went into the machines with no results. We got down to our last quarter and had no bus money to get back to school. We all had to beg for money from the locals for the bus back to the college. Outside the bar, we counted our money and realized we were still short. All of a sudden, Bob came running out of the bar with additional cash. We asked him where he had gotten it, and he replied that it was tip money lying on the tables. We were not too proud about this caper, but we did get back to school on time.

I continued my training as a flyer over a period of many weeks, becoming more and more at ease flying the airplane.

Landing an aircraft is the most difficult part of flying. I made many landings without any problem until a cold day in the middle of December. The temperature was about 35 degrees; there was a cold mist in the air. Massive cumulus clouds filled the sky. The wind was very strong and gusty. I was up with my instructor doing the usual training exercises until it came time to land. The procedure for landing an airplane is to follow the airstrip on a downwind run. The next move is to head into the wind for more control, then level off and gently set the craft on the runway. This is all very easy on a calm summer day, but this was no such day. I made my downwind run. It felt like we were going 200 miles an hour. I tried to turn the plane, and the craft started doing some intense crabbing.Then I headed into the wind, which was so intense I thought the canvas wings would blow off. I went in for the landing, leveled off too high, and cut the power. The plane dropped like a stone, only to bounce up in the air again, then down again. Finally, I came to a stop. I turned around and saw the instructor looking a bit pale. He said, "I don't believe you are destined to be a pilot."

I hoped the instructor's statement was just that. I hoped he was not the man making the decision about whether I stayed in or left the Naval Air Training Corps. The next day I was called into the office of the officer in charge. He was a very quiet-mannered man, and in a nice way, he gave me the bad news. On the strength of the instructor's recommendations, he felt I should leave the program. On November 15, 1943, I left his office a very depressed individual.

I went back to my room and told Bob about being a "washed out" air cadet. We spent the next several hours talking over old times. We had been friends since 1940, our first year in college. I was very sad knowing that on the next day we would go our separate ways.

In the morning, I went back to meet with the officer in charge. He gave me a train ticket. I was to proceed to the Bainbridge Naval Base in Maryland. Sitting in a passenger seat on the train, hearing the steel wheels against the train rails did not help my state of mind.

As would often occur when I finally had a chance to relax alone, my mind wandered to my romance with Winnie. I wondered how my washing out of the Naval Air Corps would influence our lives and if she would even still be in love with me despite my failure. I also worried about what the Navy had in store for my future. It seemed apparent to me that I was being sent to boot camp for basic training in the United States Navy. The next fork in the road for me was once again out of my control.

CHAPTER 4
MY NEW NAVY CAREER

I arrived at Bainbridge Naval Base in Maryland on December 20, 1943. I will never forget that afternoon. My mind was filled with nothing but negative thoughts. I was given no indication at Westminster what might be in store for me at this base. Is this the location of basic training that I was about to be assigned to? If I hadn't resigned from ROTC at Duquesne I would be an officer in the Army by now.

I was depressed about my failure as a naval pilot, and the weather added to my miserable mood. It was a chilly 40 degrees. Low stratus clouds hung over the base. There was no wind, indicating that light rain would continue all day. There was nothing I could do but resign myself to the worst possible scenario.

The base was obviously a huge military operation. Up to this point, my training had been on college campuses, so being at Bainbridge was an entirely new experience for me. Countless military personnel of various ranks and branches of the service walked from building to building. This was the first time I had actually seen such high-ranking military officials since I joined the Navy. The whole atmosphere was overwhelming to me.

After walking past many buildings, I finally found the office where I needed to report. I handed my papers to a yeoman behind the desk. He looked them over and told me to have a seat; he would present them to the lieutenant. After 20 restless minutes, I received my room assignment where I was to go, unpack, and await my orders.

Much to my surprise the room looked like a hospital space. I had expected to stay in the barracks since I was a washed-out cadet. I really had thought I would be assigned to basic training as an enlisted man. In my dismal state of mind, and exhausted from the day's events, I fell asleep.

I woke up the next morning at the crack of dawn, showered, shaved, and prepared for the day's events, whatever they may be. I was definitely at another fork in the road of my life and I had no control over where my military career was headed. All I could do was wait for my orders.

About an hour or so later, an enlisted man came to my room and told me when meal times were and that I should relax for the rest of the day because I would be getting my assignment the following morning. He also said there would be a truck waiting outside at 8 a.m. to pick me up.

The mess hall I was assigned to was for officers only, which surprised me. I wondered why the Navy had sent me there since I was not an officer. I noticed another man without an insignia indicating rank on his uniform, and I asked him why we were eating with the officers. It turned out that like me, he had also washed out of the Naval Air Corps. He explained to me that because we were both in the Naval V-5 program, the Navy considered us officers until they decided what to do with us. It was hard to believe, but we actually outranked a warrant officer, which is the highest enlisted man's rank. After breakfast, it seemed strange not to be marching to a class, and it was the first day I could remember where I was able to relax.

The following morning, I waited for the truck to pick me up. I jumped into the passenger side and was surprised to see a civilian driver. His name was Jim, and we exchanged the usual pleasantries. It seemed strange to be next to non-military personnel after viewing only uniforms for two days. He looked disheveled. His hair was messy, and it had to have been at least three days since he had last shaved. Jim and I didn't go far in the truck; we only traveled a few miles to a ball field, where there were five other trucks and enlisted men waiting.

When we got to the field, a warrant officer in charge was assigning men to the six different trucks. Everyone seemed reluctant to climb on board my vehicle, and I wondered why. I guessed that it was because I was the new kid on the block, and I was probably about to be assigned to the least desirable job. Besides, perhaps they thought I was some young punk and didn't want to take orders from me. After all but four men were assigned to other details, these were assigned to mine. They all seemed to know something about our job that I certainly was not aware of. They didn't hop in our truck; instead, they got into yet another truck to follow us. Finally, the last one told Jim our destination. It was the mushroom farm. I knew nothing about mushroom farms, and Jim told me mushrooms were grown in enclosures fertilized with cow manure.

We arrived at the farm. There was no question that this type of fertilizer left off a most unpleasant odor. The men went to work loading the truck, but the detail seemed to be making little progress. I had always prided myself on being a good judge of personality, so I decided to motivate the men. I felt that Jim could be trusted to go along with my plan, so I asked him if there was a bar nearby and if he minded if we stopped for a few beers when the guys were done with the shoveling. Jim instantaneously perked up and said it was a great idea. I then sprung my idea on the men and told them that if they hurried up and filled our truck, we would go to the bar. Wow, you should have seen the shovels move and the manure fly onto the truck.

Once the truck was full, we stopped at the bar as promised and had a great time getting to know one another. After that, the men were friendly towards me and no longer seemed to think of me as a young punk giving them orders. The next day, no one could understand why the men were so anxious to be on my truck detail.

I kept up with my usual assignment, and one day went into the next. With each passing day, I became more despondent. Finally, a naval captain called me into his office. I became paranoid that somehow he had found out about our ritual of stopping at the tavern once the truck was loaded.

To my relief, he didn't mention the tavern at all. Instead, he asked me several questions about different things. All my responses came with ease, probably because of my Air Corps training. It turned out that I wasn't in there to be reprimanded; unbeknownst to me, I was actually a candidate for the officers' training program at the University of Notre Dame. Apparently the interview went well because he told me I was going into the program and I needed to get a physical before I could leave. I figured it would not be a problem since I had already passed a tough physical to get into the Air Corps.

On the way to the doctor's office, I was walking on air. What a relief knowing that I had a meaningful future. I walked inside and was greeted by a captain who was immaculately dressed. Many doctors were automatically given a captain's rank when they enlisted. He ran the usual tests, and I had to give both urine and blood samples. I thought the physical went well and was still elated about the fact that I was going to Notre Dame.

The following morning I was called into the doctor's office. He had a very peculiar look on his face, as if he was about to give me bad news. Sure enough, he told me I had failed the physical, and my world suddenly crumbled beneath me. He told me he couldn't pass me because I had flat feet. With that, I lost my temper and in a fit of anger yelled, "For Christ sake, I passed the toughest physical in the Navy for the Air Corps." He looked at me oddly, and I was in an obvious state of panic as to what his response would be. The thought flashed in my mind that my next stop would be the brig. Then he said the most unexpected thing: "I guess you are right son; I've reconsidered and decided to pass you."

He signed my papers; we shook hands, and he wished me good luck. As I walked away from his office, I felt like I had just won a high-stakes poker game. Although my outburst could have landed me in hot water, it saved my military career. Thank God I had an understanding doctor, or my next stop surely would have been the lowest enlisted man's rank. Life certainly takes many twists and turns, and this one happened to be a fortunate one for me.

On February 5, 1944, I was on my way to Notre Dame. It was another long train ride, and 20 hours later, I arrived in Chicago. After that, I took a 65-mile bus ride to South Bend, Indiana, and on to the university from there. While on the bus to Notre Dame, I imagined what it would be like. Notre Dame was a place where many gifted athletes, especially Catholic ones, aspired to attend and I had always been intrigued by the school. Growing up, I listened to their football games on the radio with my dad. We even wagered 25 cents on the games, and my dad always let me pick Notre Dame. I was thrilled to be heading to the place I had envisioned.

I had some idea of how the campus looked, but I was not prepared for how impressive it truly was especially in comparison to Duquesne University, which merely consisted of Canevin Hall and an administration building. The rest of Duquesne's campus was office space in downtown Pittsburgh. Merely walking past Notre Dame's football stadium sent chills down my spine, and I remembered all the times I listened to the games on the radio. What a strange twist of fate that I should be here now; being here was like a dream come true.

I found the administrative building. The Navy occupied one of the floors. I registered in the training program and got my room assignment. My roommate was John Mayer, a college graduate from the University of Illinois. It seemed strange to me when I realized most of the students were two to four years older than I was. I suddenly realized how lucky I was to be there at all.

Just like in the Naval Air Corps, we had to do the usual marching, which I had learned to hate back at Westminster. In class, we had intense study with emphasis on navy regulations, far more than in the Air Corps. We studied aircraft carriers, battleships, and all types of assult ships. It was as if amphibious ships did not exist. We did not know it at the time, but most of us were destined to serve on amphibious ships used as landing crafts.

One weekend in the middle of March, my roommate suggested we visit Chicago. What a great idea. I had never been there. John was a great companion to live with, and an overnight stay in Chicago would surely be fun. He was very familiar with the town; he had been there many times since he graduated from the nearby college.

He said, "Why not go to one of the fine hotels? When I wanted to impress my girlfriend, I would go to the Drake Hotel." He said, "Who knows, Mel; it may not be too long before we will be out of the country." Chicago is about 90 miles from South Bend. It was about an hour and a half trip by bus. We arrived at the hotel around one in the afternoon, checked in, took a walk around the city, and stopped for a few beers. I was in awe seeing so many massive buildings.

After exploring the city, we went back to the hotel and had a marvelous steak dinner, the likes of which I had not seen in many months. Once we finished our dinner, we moved over to the bar and experimented with various mixed drinks. By this time, it was one in the morning, and the bar was empty except for a middle-aged couple.

I looked over at them, and in my inebriated condition, I asked them why they were still there. I think they enjoyed our muddled conversation. The man said we might need help getting off the floor after we passed out from all the alcohol we were consuming. Despite his remark, we managed to leave on our own two feet.

Getting up the next morning with hangovers was difficult, but we sat down to a hearty breakfast. We ate nothing like this at Notre Dame; we abandoned any thought about how much all of it cost and indulged ourselves. We wanted it to be a weekend we would remember for a long time. John and I boarded the bus after breakfast and went back to the reality of completing our officer's training.

The meals at the university were as good as could be expected for cafeteria-style, but there was always a long line outside the building. Notre Dame was very cold that time of year, and the constant strong wind made the wait outside very miserable. For some reason, the nutritionist must have thought pork was an excellent food for us servicemen. Many a day, the word "oink" would be passed down the chow line, indicating it was a pork meal again.

About a week before graduation, our class of trainees assembled in the gymnasium, where we saw a strange contraption sitting on the floor. About 15 feet off the floor was a pipe two inches in diameter and 20 feet long. Six feet above the pipe was a rope parallel to it. At one end of the apparatus was a ladder; on the other end was a rope dangling to the floor. Climbing up the ladder, we had to move across the bar with the rope supporting us, then drop down the rope to the floor. Six of us carried out this procedure with no trouble. The seventh individual got to the end of the bar and froze. He could not get himself to drop down to the floor. We found out later in the day that he had been eliminated from the officer's training program for failing the test. In our room, John and I discussed his misfortune. We felt bad for him. Although it may seem trivial that the simplest test could end his career, the officers made the correct decision. If he could not accomplish this easy maneuver, he could cause disaster on a ship.

As we neared the end of our training, time passed very slowly. My desire to find a way to bring some laughter into our humdrum routine gave me idea. I decided to make a large poster counting down the last ten days of our training, I posted it at the end of the hall. Each day, all of the men on the floor would gather near the sign, and as they cheered, I would mark off a number. As the days went by, many men from the other two floors heard about our project. Finally, number one appeared on the sign. Almost all of the trainees were on our floor for the final day. I yelled out at the crowd and said, "This is the last day." With my dry mark, I struck out the number one. A massive cheer resounded in the hall. After breakfast, we assembled on the parade grounds, and a lieutenant commander presented us with our gold ensign bars. I officially became an ensign in the United States Navy.

There was no throwing of our hats into the air as they do at Annapolis. We just wished one another good fortune in whatever the future may hold. They referred to us as ninety-day wonders, for in the short period of three months, we had become officers. It came as a shock to me when I realized I had the same rank as a four-year graduate from Annapolis. I wondered what my next fork in the road would be.

As I have mentioned before, in the service all decisions are made by the military. There was no way I could go up to the officer in charge and request to be on an aircraft carrier or destroyer. All I could do was wait for the decision. I resigned myself to the obvious—that I would be part of the amphibious navy. I wondered what type of craft I would be on and whether I would be serving in the Atlantic or Pacific theater of operation.

On the third day, I was told to report to the headquarters office. A lieutenant junior grade gave me printed orders to report to Fort Pierce, Florida. There I would be trained to operate a group of LCVPs, small craft holding about a dozen men. These boats had many uses, including landing troops on enemy beaches. I wondered why me. Of all the possible duties, this was the last one I wanted. I was given train tickets to proceed to my home in Pittsburgh and then on to Fort Pierce. I had two weeks' leave, which included travel time. I called Winnie and told her to expect me in Brownsville on the 13th or 14th of May. Mel Eiben was now about to embark on a new fork in the road that I was sure would have many twists, turns, and bumps as each day went by.

CHAPTER 5
FORT PIERCE

On the morning of May 12, 1944, I was on my way to South Bend to catch a bus to Chicago. From there, I would head to Pittsburgh and then on to Fort Pierce, Florida. I boarded the train and settled into a window seat so I could have an unobstructed view of the city and scenery outside the window.

Air conditioning did not exist on trains of this era, and it happened to be a very warm spring day. Steam locomotives spewed an excessive amount of soot that easily found its way into the passenger cars, especially the window seats. Although the train ride was miserable, it did not dampen my spirit and my excitement about going home. The long ride gave me a chance to think about my love for Winnie. To imagine we would soon be in each other's arms thrilled me. I thought a lot about what a wonderful, loving sensation it would be.

Washing out of the Air Corps had convinced me that an engagement to Winnie was out of the question; however, now that I was an officer, I had new hope about that prospect. Although I wanted to marry her, I worried about

51

worst-case scenarios like suffering a serious injury that would make me a burden to Winnie for the rest of her life. Despite these negative thoughts, I wanted to marry her anyway. Winnie was an incredibly beautiful woman with a great personality. Would she still be in love with me if I were away for a long time? If I didn't place a ring on her finger before going overseas, she might think I didn't really love her. Moreover, I am not so sure the adage "absence makes the heart grow fonder" is reliable. So, I decided to buy an engagement ring and propose to Winnie while I was home.

By the time the train pulled into Pittsburgh it was Sunday evening. Before I left the city, I called my parents and told them to expect me in about half an hour. It felt wonderful to stand in the beautiful rotunda of Pennsylvania Station. I was home at last. I quickly flagged a cab and was on my way to Mount Oliver to see my parents.

Winnie did not know the exact day that I would be back in Pittsburgh so I did not call her right away. My father was a close friend of Frank Becker, who owned a jewelry store in the Clark building in the center of Pittsburgh. Since it was Sunday evening, the purchase would have to wait until first thing Monday morning.

I finally arrived at home. What a cherished moment it was to ring the doorbell and see the smiling faces of my mother and father running toward me. I shook hands with my dad and hugged my mom. We walked inside, and I could not believe the smell of the food emanating from the kitchen. I turned to my mother and said, "Are you kidding me... you cooked my favorite meal of ground meat and potatoes?" My dad then went into the kitchen for two bottles of beer, and we sat down in the living room together and began to talk. I told him that I was now Ensign C. Mel Eiben, and my father said he was proud to have a United States Naval officer in his family.

After a while, my mother came into the room and called us to dinner. We all sat down together and talked non-stop for a couple of hours about my experiences in the Navy. Dad also filled me in about my brother Paul, who was stationed in England, and my other brother Maurice, who was serving somewhere in the Pacific.

We continued to talk, and my parents asked me why I had not called Winnie yet, so I told them of my plans to propose to her. They were both very fond of Winnie and naturally thrilled about my decision. I said to my mom, "I hate to ask you to do this so late in the evening, but would you please iron my officer's uniform? I want to look my best when I ask Winnie to marry me." Without hesitation, my mom put up the ironing board and pressed my uniform while we continued to talk. It was 2 a.m. before we all decided to go to bed.

The next morning, after breakfast, I called the downtown station to find out what time I could catch the bus to Brownsville to see Winnie. There was one leaving from Pittsburgh at 1 p.m. That should give me plenty of time to buy a diamond ring. Just like old times, my dad and I walked a half a mile to the streetcar line together and boarded it for our trip into Pittsburgh.

Once we were in the city, my father and I went to Frank Becker's office. Mr. Becker made several suggestions as to what size and quality of diamond I should purchase. I decided on a .60-carat diamond with a couple of smaller diamonds on each side. The price was $125, and it seemed like a fortune to spend on such a small piece of jewelry. Little did I know at the time what an important part of my life would be spent in the same building that housed Frank Becker's store.

My father and I said our goodbyes, and I boarded the bus to Brownsville. I was decked out in my officer's uniform and very excited to see Winnie again. It was standing-room only on the bus, and the hour and a half trip seemed to take forever. I had never been in Brownsville before. The Winners had recently moved there from New Salem. It took a long time, but I finally made it to her town. My nervous anticipation was at an all-time high. After twenty minutes, I finally located her house.

I walked up to the porch and rang the bell. Through the window, I saw Winnie walking forward to answer the door. After all these months of not seeing her, she looked unbelievably gorgeous. Her body against mine and a kiss like none I had experienced gave me an overwhelming feeling of love for her. I said to Winnie, "I cannot begin to express how much I love you." Winnie replied, "I love you Mel."

Joe and Cecilia came to the door, and we moved into the living room. Joe broke out a bottle of Jack Daniels whiskey and mixed drinks for the four of us. We all raised our glasses and Joe said, "Welcome home Mel."

Winnie's engagement ring was burning a hole in my pocket, and I could not resist using this joyous time to propose to Winnie. I took the ring box out and handed it to Winnie. She slowly opened it, and a look of disbelief came upon her face. I said, "Winnie, will you marry me?"

There was a moment of silence that seemed like an hour when she just stared at the ring. Finally, she allowed me to put it on her finger and said, "Yes Mel, I would very much like to be your bride."

Obviously, the Winners had no idea I was going to propose, and neither said anything until they regained their composure. Once they did, they congratulated us on our engagement. Mrs. Winner was a wonderful cook, and she prepared beef stew for dinner. It was another one of my favorite dishes. After dinner, Joe pulled out his saxophone. He used to play the sax in a major ballroom dance band when he was younger. Mrs. Winner had been a music teacher, and she accompanied him on the piano. They played the song "This Is a Lovely Way to Spend an Evening," and it was.

What a remarkable setting; we were listening to the wonderful music, Winnie was wearing the diamond ring, and the Winners had welcomed me into their family.

Joe and Cecilia, knowing how much Winnie and I would like to be alone, retired for the evening, and I was finally alone with Winnie. We had had some wonderful, passionate moments before, but our engagement gave new meaning to our embraces. There is no way to describe with words the wonderful feeling of having her body next to mine after so many months of separation. Unfortunately, all wonderful moments must end. Winnie escorted me to the guest room, and we shared one last kiss before we retired for the evening.

Winnie and Mel - Time of our Engagement

Winnie and I spent the next day and night at my parents' house in Pittsburgh and the rest of my leave in Brownsville visiting her friends and relatives. The possibility existed that I might not see Winnie until after the war was over—that is, if I survived. This was a World War, so large and intense that there was no way of knowing how long we would be separated. The night of our engagement had been filled only with happiness and love for each other. The last evening together was different. Our embraces were long and intense, with very few words spoken; indeed, it was a heart-wrenching experience.

The following morning, Joe drove the two of us to the train station in downtown Pittsburgh where Winnie and I shared one last embrace and passionate kiss before I boarded the train for the long trip to Florida.

After spending 36 hours on the train, I arrived in Fort Pierce, Florida. I had the address of the naval base in my wallet and the number of the bus that would take me to that section of town.

I made my way to the base, but I was not prepared for what I saw once I arrived there. Fort Pierce consisted of two small two-story buildings and about twenty tents in a field a short distance from the shoreline. I went inside what looked like the main building and presented my papers to a yeoman sitting at a desk. He welcomed me to the base and escorted me into an inner office to meet with the lieutenant commander in charge. We saluted each other, and he simply said, "Welcome aboard. Ensign Paul Evans is outside, and he is the officer you are going to share a tent with." This was the coldest reception I had ever received on a new assignment.

I left his office and saw my new roommate standing outside. I introduced myself, and we were on our way to our tent. Inside the tent was nothing but a dirt floor with two beds and a locker for us to store our gear. I sat on the edge of the bunk, and Paul told me about his hometown near San Francisco. The service was the first time he had been away from home. Like all the other total strangers I have roomed with in the service, he seemed like a very likeable companion.

I desperately needed to clean up after such a long trip, and I asked Paul where I could shower. He took me to a building that housed the showers, bathrooms, and cafeteria. Paul said he would wait for me to clean up; then we could walk down to the shore so I could inspect the LCVPs we would use for training. I still could not believe my surroundings, and on our way down to the beach, I commented to Paul that as a boy scout, I had stayed at a camp that was far superior to this place.

Landing Craft Vehicle Personal (LCVP)
Attack Transport in Background

I looked at the LCVPs docked in the ocean and realized they were probably used during the first wave of invasions. In this type of craft, the chance of survival would be limited. After a while, Paul and I walked back to the cafeteria and ate dinner. If my first meal at Fort Pierce was a sample of the food at the base, it left a lot to be desired.

Posted on the wall in the cafeteria was a schedule of our training for the week. The first week did not include actual running of the LCVP, and it was hard for me to imagine what a week of classroom instruction could entail. Paul and I went outside the building and relaxed on a bench where we talked about family and friends back home. After about an hour, he said he was going back to our tent to write a letter to his family. I decided to walk down to where the boats were lying on the shoreline.

Looking at these little crafts made me wonder about what I might be doing if I had not washed out of the Naval Air Corps. This certainly was not what I envisioned my Navy career to be. I was going to be a hotshot pilot flying in a fighter plane or some kind of attack bomber soaring off the deck of an aircraft carrier. All the men in the service had to be somewhere doing their part to win this war. Most of us had no choice as to where the Navy stationed us, and I was a prime example. This was not the type of duty I wanted.

Around 8 p.m., I made my way back to my sleeping quarters. As I walked back, I became aware of a few insects flying around me. Suddenly, a swarm of mosquitoes surrounded me. My walk quickly turned into a run, and I was glad to get inside the tent. I said to Paul, "You will not believe the mosquitoes outside." He told me that I should get used to them because they were like this every night.

I decided to lie down on my bunk and relax; I could not help being depressed. This seemed to be the bottom of the barrel of the amphibious crafts I could train for. It was hard for me to imagine that eleven short months ago, I had been a college student at Duquesne University. Since being called to active duty, I had been at the University of Pennsylvania, Westminster College, Bainbridge, Notre Dame, and now Fort Pierce, Florida.

At Force Pierce, I was about to learn how to operate a small craft used to invade enemy-occupied beaches, with men under my command. I was disinterested in the training. My mind often drifted to other thoughts, and I contemplated the meaning of war. Why would civilized people want to kill one another? It did not make any sense to me. I certainly did not have any control over major decisions concerning this war, so I would have to get on with my own little piece of the picture.

On the first day of class, the instructor highlighted the basic concepts of LCVP use during invasions. As the week progressed and more details emerged as to the exact execution of an invasion, it was obvious that operating such a craft was extremely dangerous.

One night while walking along the beach, I noticed a large craft anchored in the bay. I had no idea what it was doing there. It was an attack transport. The purpose of an attack transport is to approach shorelines as close as its keel would allow, then lower the LCVPs into the water next to its side. The ship displaces ten thousand tons and is twice the size of an LST. A coxswain operates the boats, and during an invasion, squads of 20 infantrymen climb down large rope nets from the deck of the transporter onto the boats waiting in the water. From there, the LCVPs maneuver into a circle where a group of 12 boats is under the command of one ensign.

After all the LCVPs are loaded with men, a signal is given and they all approach the beach. Once the LCVPs are ashore, the officers organize the unloading of the landing craft. When finished, the boats head back to the transport for more soldiers. The officers in command of these boats were called Landing Control Officers. I realize now why officers' training was only three months long. Being in command of the boats that carried the men who were fighting during the first wave of combat, we had a very limited chance of survival.

That week at Fort Pierce went by slowly. Friday morning while I was eating breakfast, an enlisted man sat down next to me and told me to report to Navy Headquarters. There was no point in asking him why I was to go there because I was sure if he knew he was not about to tell me.

The short walk up to the Lieutenant Commander's office seemed like it took forever, and I was anxious the whole way since I did not know what to expect. Could it be that my instructor had noticed some weakness in my character that made him question my qualifications for this type of duty?

Sitting on a chair on the other side of the Lieutenant Commander's desk, I felt very intimidated as he stared at me. He broke the silence and said, "You will no longer be training at Fort Pierce." I had a sudden flashback to being told I was not qualified to be a pilot. Was he about to say I was not a fit candidate for this type of duty? He then told me that I had been picked to be sent to Solomon's Island, Maryland, to be in command of a Landing Craft Tank. He then picked up a picture of the craft and showed it to me. I quickly glanced at the specifications of the ship and was amazed at its size. He went on to tell me that the LCT's crew consisted of one officer and twelve enlisted men.

The thought flashed into my mind, "Why me?" Did I appear to have some leadership qualities for him to make this decision? Or was it just the luck of the draw? I will never know why I was chosen, but I was glad to get out of that hellhole.

That evening I gave the news to Paul, and he said he wished he were going with me. The next morning the base van drove me to the train station. I stepped aboard the Pullman car and was on my way to Solomon's Island, Maryland.

The long train ride was anything but pleasant. It would take a minimum of 30 hours to arrive at my new destination. I was very happy to be heading north and out of this miserable bug-infested climate even though I didn't know what would be in store for me as captain of this huge craft.

CHAPTER 6
SOLOMON'S ISLAND

I arrived in Washington, D.C., around 10 in the evening. The long train ride was at last over, and I had to find my way to Solomon's Island, Maryland. Inside the train station, the man behind the information desk directed me to a bus stop a block down the street. Exhausted, I climbed on board the bus; I still had an hour and a half ride ahead of me to Solomon's Island.

I finally arrived at the base around two in the morning. I dragged my luggage down the street looking for someone to ask where I could shower and sleep. I found an officer inside a building who was on night watch. He was of no help and merely suggested I stretch out on the couch until morning. It was definitely an undesirable place to try to rest after the grueling travel experience I had just been through, but I was desperate to get off my feet.

I lay down on the hard, uncomfortable couch and was so drained it was hard for me to fall asleep. I kept thinking of all the times I had moved from base to base by myself. I had expected the navy to transport me with a group of other men. Little did I know that moving alone from place to place, never knowing what to expect next, would dominate my time in the service.

After succumbing to exhaustion, I slept until dawn. There were military personnel around so I asked the first yeoman I could find where I should go. I explained why I was at Solomon's Island, and he told me he would let the lieutenant commander know I was there. I was invited to meet with the officer in charge of the base. After the usual saluting and introductions, he gave me a warm welcome that was completely different than my reception at Fort Pierce. He appeared to be in his early sixties and in excellent shape for his age. I felt very comfortable in his presence, and he gave me a positive feeling about my new training. He assigned me to a room and told me to report back in the early afternoon.

I found my sleeping quarters and discovered there were two beds in the room, which in all probability meant I would have a roommate. I settled in and then took a nice long, hot shower and shaved. It is amazing how delighted I was by doing the basics in life. I dressed in a fresh uniform and ate a wholesome lunch before making my way back to the lieutenant commander's office. He told me to wait outside for Lieutenant JG Edward Higgins; he would give me a tour of the base. Ed arrived shortly thereafter. He appeared friendly but standoffish, and impressed with his own "importance" to the navy. As we walked down to the dock, Ed told me he would be my LCT instructor.

About 50 yards away from the pier, I noticed a huge landing craft in the water. We walked up to the ship, and Ed told me it was a Landing Craft Tank—in fact, the same one I would train on. Ed surely noticed the shocked look on my face when I saw its immense size. I tried to pretend it was just another landing craft, similar to others I had seen before.

Landing Craft Tank (LCT)

We boarded the LCT. An LCT is not exactly a sleek-looking craft; it looked a lot like a river barge and was the equivalent to almost half the length of a football field. Measuring 120 feet long and 32 feet wide, most of the LCT consisted of open space. Twenty percent of the LCT housed the living quarters where the captain lived with a crew of 12. It appeared much too small to accommodate all these men. After the tour, Ed told me to report to the LCT at 8 a.m. the following morning, which surprised me. Instead of beginning with classroom instruction as I had at all the other bases, actual training on how to operate the ship would start immediately.

Back in my quarters, my roommate greeted me. He was an impressive looking individual who appeared to be about 6' 2" and weighed nearly 200 pounds. After I introduced myself, he told me his name was Jerome Markillitis. I could tell immediately that I had lucked out again by having a pleasant companion to share a room with. I had dinner with Jerome at the base cafeteria, and we discussed the usual details: hometowns and careers. Jerome was from Sheffield, a small town in Northeast Pennsylvania.

The rest of our dinner conversation was dominated by our amazement at the size of the LCT we were about to command and the responsibility that would be involved. We agreed that our first day as future captains of a new LCT would indeed be very interesting.

The following day we were both up at dawn eagerly anticipating our first day of training. I arrived at the LCT about thirty minutes early, and there was not a person in sight. As the minutes passed, one sailor after another arrived and boarded the LCT. I did not bother with the formality of saluting each arrival. I shook their hands, and we exchanged names, and I said welcome aboard. It was somewhat intimidating to realize that most of the sailors were older than I, and a few much older.

I found out after Ed arrived that these 12 men were my crew and that they would serve under me for the duration of my command. Ed began by briefing me on what I would learn the first day. He mustered the men and assigned each one a station they would man while I was running the ship. Ed told me I would be on the bridge with the signalman, Pete Romabaker. Clarence Whitehead, the bosin's mate, was in the wheelhouse along with Randy Nyack the motormack. Walt Houseman, the gunner's mate, was stationed at the anchor winch, near the 20-millimeter cannon. Ed continued to position the rest of the men on the LCT. Once all the men were in place, he gave the order to start the engines. His next order was to cast off the lines, and we moved slowly into the bay. It seemed odd to me that the instructor and I were on the bridge, and all orders regarding engine speed and direction were verbally given to the men in the wheelhouse. We cruised around the bay performing different maneuvers and then came the difficult part, docking the craft.

The only man experienced in handling the craft was the instructor. The bosin's mate had experience docking various small boats, but he had never docked one this size. Ed was on the bridge with me; he had no control of the ship other than giving verbal orders to the bosin's mate. It was hard to rely on Clarence to do exactly as instructed. Ed gave various orders as to the revolutions of the engine and the degree of the rudder, and we moved into the dock. It wasn't exactly a smooth docking. We bounced a bit off the dock, and the stern of the LCT was well away from the pier. Ed didn't seem disturbed, as if expecting this to occur on our first docking.

My Crew

As the week went by, I became more familiar with my crew. The most interesting man aboard was definitely Clint; he was an enlisted man with no rating. His record showed he had below-average intelligence, but his skills on the LCT indicated quite the opposite. I took him aside and asked him about his military file. Clint told me that after he was drafted at age 38, he had been given a test and had purposely put down wrong answers in hopes that his poor results would declare him unfit for service. Apparently, the test results did not matter to the Navy because they assigned him to the LCT.

Another crew member was Larry McCormick, the radio man. He was 18 years old and had a pleasant way about him. Petty Officer, Frank Sloan, was 22; he had a great sense of humor and was always able to lift our spirits when times were depressing. Randy, the motormack, was in his early thirties. He was a quiet man who went about his duties in a professional manner. Bill Stephens was a very important man aboard for he was the electrician's mate. The crew was rounded out by two deck hands, seamen Frank Forest and Wilber Miller.

Perhaps the most important man aboard was the cook, Bill Miller, better known as Cookie. The crew and I were very fortunate to have Bill as our chef. He deserved to be called chef, because he had to be a miracle man to prepare three meals a day for fourteen men. Most of the food had to come out of cans for we rarely had access to fresh food. On occasion, we would have a treat for he would barter with the natives for some fresh food. How he managed to keep his sense of humor having to feed fourteen men three meals a day I will never understand. Given these circumstances, the cook did a good job, and we all stayed healthy and well-nourished. All of the men on board had personalities that blended in with the other sailors. They all had various skills necessary to run the ship efficiently.

In my letters to Winnie, I tried to explain the nature of my command. In her return letters, she said she couldn't believe the responsibilities that had been thrust on me and wondered how they could expect me to run this massive ship. Despite her concerns, many encouraging words were written to boost my morale. Her endearing words of her love for me made me feel good about myself.

As the weeks went by, I began to feel confident that the men had accepted me as their commanding officer. I was very fortunate to have 12 men who got along so well with one another. Although I felt accepted as their captain, I still wondered how they felt about my leading them. Only three of the twelve were younger than I was. What did they think as I gave them orders? Did they say to themselves, how would our captain react if we were in a life or death situation? There was no point for me to dwell on this issue;

the officer in charge at Fort Pierce must have felt I was mature enough to be commanding officer on an LCT. Imagine my situation. I had never been on an oceangoing ship before in my life. Now, not only was I on one, I had to command it. At the end of my training, I would be responsible for making all of the decisions and had no one to turn to for advice.

It is hard to comprehend how difficult it was to control the LCT. It was a flat-bottomed boat drawing only two feet of water. Most oceangoing ships have keels to help stabilize them in the water; however, on an LCT, you are at the mercy of the wind since there is no keel to keep it from going sideways. Once you add that to all the unknown factors and the direction of the water's current, which is not visible, the direction of the LCT can change in an instant. In addition to all these obstacles, LCTs do not have powerful engines. Although the craft had three engines, it had very low horsepower. The cruising speed was a mere seven knots, and the top speed was eight knots, which is equivalent to about 10 miles an hour. The lack of power made it cumbersome to change direction in a hurry. When trying to control a 120-ton LCT during docking, your slightest miscalculation could knock over pilings and do great damage to a pier. Docking an LCT is not like parking a car where, if you make a mistake, you can stop and start over again. There were no brakes on an LCT.

The nerve-wracking part of docking the LCT was that it seems to take forever for the craft to respond to a change in direction. In addition, since I stood on the bridge, I had to depend on the coxswain to follow my commands. Typical orders for docking may sound like this, "Reduce engine revolutions for docking, right 20 degrees rudder, stop starboard engine, reverse starboard engine." Once the ship was next to the pier, I would order lines over the pilings and in the final order, secure the engines.

If the craft did not respond as I expected, I was never sure if I had given the wrong orders or if the sailor controlling the wheel and the engines had not carried out my orders as directed. Docking this large bulk of steel with little engine power was no easy task.

Another part of training was firing the 20-millimeter cannon. There were two on the LCT, one at each side of the ship. We were instructed to go a considerable distance out into the bay. Looking up at the sound of the engine, we observed an airplane towing a cloth sleeve, which was our target. About 100 feet of rope extended from the airplane to the sleeve. Frank and Clarence both had prior training on these guns and were instructed to operate the cannon on the first pass of the sleeve. Thanks to tracer bullets, it was possible to see the flight of the missiles that were fired. These two men, on occasion, hit the sleeve. When it was my turn to fire the cannon, I had to sit down in a chair attached to the gun and pull the trigger while aiming at the sleeve. I was nowhere near the target, and the pilot was lucky he had 100 feet of rope because he needed it for his safety. A 20-millimeter cannon is not a very large gun, but when I fired, it seemed as large as a gun on a Sherman tank. The noise and vibrations were overwhelming. After several days of practice, we all became much better at operating the cannon. Who knew, out in the Pacific maybe we would get lucky and shoot down a Japanese Zero?

On weekends, my mind was consumed with thoughts of Winnie. I sent many letters to her expressing how much I missed and loved her. In return, I would receive letters telling me the same. One day, I opened a letter from her saying she wanted to be married before I was shipped overseas. Looking at the words she had written, I could not believe my eyes. Flashes of heat came over me and my heart was racing. This indeed was a major fork in the road for me.

What could be a more important occasion than marriage

to the one you expect to spend the rest of your life with? But the logistics of a marriage were nearly impossible. Saturday and Sunday were my only days off and I had no hope of getting leave. Well, maybe there is some merit in the old saying, "Love will find a way."

CHAPTER 7

THE WEDDING

I never doubted my desire to marry Winnie, but I was concerned about the predicament this might put her in. I still worried that she could end up a war widow or possibly spend the rest of her life with a cripple. I seriously considered writing my thoughts down to make sure she knew the potential future she could have. I wanted to, but there was a chance she would take such a discussion as my not having the same passionate love for her that she had for me. I decided to proceed with the marriage. Any hesitation on my part could have a negative impact on us for the rest of our lives.

To answer her by phone would not do justice to my reply. My response needed to express the loving emotion that only the written word could convey. It is a shame that our love letters no longer exist. Winnie and I wrote to each other frequently during my time in the service, and it would give me great pleasure to read some of those letters today.

In part of the letter, I told her I had no idea how long my training would last. One thing I was certain of, it would be at least a month long, which meant all the details regarding our wedding would have to be in place as soon as possible.

All week long, my thoughts were on how Winnie and I could possibly arrange our wedding with so much distance between us. We rejected one plan after another because they did not seem to work. The following weekend, I called Winnie, and we discussed the wedding. It was a lengthy call, and I was glad I had reversed the charges because there was no way I could have carried enough change in my pockets to pay for it.

As usual, two minds were better than one. Winnie and I discussed several possibilities that could work. I told her my only days off were Saturdays and Sundays. Marrying in Pittsburgh would be nearly impossible due to the time it took to travel. I thought that maybe a priest on the base could perform the ceremony, and then I thought of an even better solution. I suggested that because of my time constraints, we could meet in Baltimore and have someone local perform the ceremony. I thought it could be a wonderful solution to our scheduling concerns. It turned out that my uncle, Father Conrad, was the priest at St. Joseph's in Baltimore. I could not think of anything that would make our wedding more special than having a relative conduct the ceremony.

I phoned my dad and asked him to call Father Conrad to see if it was possible for him to say our Mass. Time was of the essence, and I told my father that the rest of our wedding details would be in place within a week. Two days later, I talked to my dad again, and he gave me the good news. Father Conrad was more than happy to perform our ceremony; in fact, he said it would be an honor to preside over my marriage. Marrying in Baltimore had another advantage: there was a direct train route from Pittsburgh to Baltimore with no need for Winnie to take a miserable bus ride to Solomon's Island.

The following weekend, I called Winnie, and she told me

her cousin Peggy Spates would be her maid of honor. She also checked the train schedule and found out it was about nine hours by rail to Baltimore. As far as the marriage license was concerned, she could get the forms in Pittsburgh and complete them except for my signature. I told Winnie the good news about Father Conrad performing the ceremony, and I suggested that we marry two weeks later, on July 15, 1944. The time went by quickly as all the plans fell into place. We would be getting married a mere three weeks after our engagement.

My good friend Jerome agreed to be my best man. I liked Jerome very much; he was a good person and a lot of fun to be around. Unfortunately, after being shuffled from base to base during my military career, I had close friends only on a very temporary basis because when it was time to move on, they were out of my life forever. Jerome was a typical example of this, and it is sad not to know whether he even survived the war. You may wonder how I could have been so careless as to not have a home address for him, but it is amazing how easy it was to let these details slip through the cracks. After the war, I tried looking him up, but I wasn't successful. His absence has left a void in my life.

Jerome was one of those exceptional friends who was a cut above the other many acquaintances in my lifetime. Jerome's great sense of humor put me in a good mood whenever I was in his company. He had some unusual ways about him, like the day he could not get his cigar lit, and I had to remind him to cut the end off. Then one day, when all the captains were supposed to be off, I saw him cleaning some debris off his ship. I asked him why he was the one doing the dirty work, and he told me that he had given his crew liberty instead.

The two of us talked frequently about my upcoming marriage. He thought it was a bad idea for obvious reasons. We knew we would be deployed into the war zone soon, but

I did not need to be reminded of the negatives. I was determined to continue with the ceremony.

Even the day of the wedding, Jerome took me to a bar for a drink so we could discuss my decision one more time. The cocktail lounge was close to the hotel where the Winners were staying, and although it may be hard to believe, Mrs. Winner was looking out the window when we walked inside. A few minutes after we sat down on our stools, she called the cocktail lounge and asked the bartender to tell us to get over to the hotel so we weren't late for the wedding. When I arrived at the room, I thought for sure Mrs. Winner would severely criticize me for drinking before the ceremony. Instead, she acted as if the incident had never occurred.

Arriving at the suite, I was nervous and anxious to see Winnie, and there she was. There is no way to describe how I felt when I first saw her in her wedding dress. She looked beautiful. Knowing that this was the day the two of us would be joined in marriage elated me. I introduced Jerome to Winnie, her parents, and Peggy. Joe mixed drinks for us, and everyone toasted Winnie and me, wishing us much happiness for the rest of our lives together.

It was early afternoon, and we still had plenty of time before the ceremony to relax, but there was one serious glitch. Our Pennsylvania license was not valid in Maryland. Winnie and her mother had called the local licensing bureau in the morning to make sure that our document was official and found out we needed a Maryland license. The Winners went over to the bureau to complete the new paperwork, but Winnie and I needed to go to the office and sign the license to make it official.

Winnie and I arrived back in the room about 3 p.m. to find Jerome and Cecilia singing. As a music teacher in a small mining town, Cecilia knew many Polish songs. Jerome happened to have a great voice, so the two of them were having a ball harmonizing. They were singing polkas together—Jerome was Polish and definitely liked having someone to sing his favorite songs with. We enjoyed hearing them sing together, but Winnie finally cut in and said if they kept this up, we would be late for our wedding.

We arrived at St. Joseph's Monastery at the designated time, which was a miracle considering our close call with the license. As we entered the vestibule, Father Conrad was waiting. It had been five years since we had last met, and everything about him was exactly as I remembered. He had the same pious look. After I introduced him to everyone, he opened the church door. The interior of the massive church was beautiful. Much to my surprise, about 30 people were in the pews, they were all strangers to us. I asked Father Conrad who they were, and he told me he thought it would be nice for us to be married with some people in attendance. It was incredibly thoughtful of him to do this for us, and Winnie and I truly appreciated it.

An usher escorted us all to our places. We didn't have a formal wedding rehearsal, and I wasn't sure what to expect. Father Conrad was not yet at the altar. It was ten minutes before he appeared, and the time seemed like an hour. I was disappointed that my parents couldn't make the trip to Baltimore to see me marry. It would have been special for my dad to be there since his brother was performing the ceremony.

Father Conrad suddenly walked out of the sanctuary dressed in a special robe. As the ceremony began, I was nervous but focused on the vows we were about to take before God that would join us for life. Father Conrad motioned for the four of us to approach the altar and stand in front of him. He began to speak, and I can honestly say I don't remember a word he said until he asked me, "Do you Melvin take Esther to be your lawfully wedded wife?"

With deep sincerity I replied, "I do."

He then turned to Winnie and said, "Do you Esther take Melvin to be your lawfully wedded husband?"

There seemed to be a hesitation that gave me a few seconds of panic, but then sounding very sincere, she replied, "I do."

After we exchanged vows and wedding bands, Father Conrad turned to the congregation and joyfully said, "I now pronounce you husband and wife."

For a split-second after that, I felt a strange sensation as the significance of being married overwhelmed me. The day, July 15, 1944, was definitely a major fork in the road in my life. Father Conrad asked for the marriage license. I panicked when I realized I did not have it; we had left it at the license bureau. There was dead silence as we all looked at one another. I was ready to crawl under the altar. All of a sudden, the clerk from the marriage license bureau came running down the aisle yelling, "I have the license!" This had to be one of God's miracles.

Best Man; Jerome Markillitis, Bridesmaid; Peggy Spates, Groom; Mel Eiben, Bride; Winnie Winner

After the wedding, we all had dinner together at a restaurant near the church. Father Conrad joined us, and his prayer before the meal made the whole experience a more endearing memory. There was an exchange of much happy conversation, making it a very delightful evening. We all became melancholy knowing that soon we would have to go our separate ways. Throughout the day, I couldn't help noticing that Jerome and Peggy spent a lot of time conversing with each other, and I was not surprised when they left the dining room together.

My father-in-law went to the desk clerk and had him arrange for a cab for the four of us. Unbeknownst to me, the Winners had reserved a gorgeous room for us that was normally rented to upscale clients. As we said goodnight to her parents and walked down the hall to our room, my whole body was a bundle of nerves, tingling with anticipation.

The thought never entered my mind to sit down and order us a drink. My thoughts and emotions were centered on what was about to occur. I embraced Winnie with intense emotion, knowing that we were released from all pre-marriage conventions. This was by far the most exhilarating experience I ever had in my life. It was my sincere hope that she felt the same way. We fell asleep in each other's arms.

In the morning, we all had breakfast together at the hotel. Jerome and Peggy, looking very tired, told us about the wonderful time they had had together in downtown Baltimore. Then came the sad time of saying goodbye to Cecilia and Joe. This was especially difficult for Winnie, realizing her future was to be with her husband.

Peggy and Jerome could sense this was an emotional moment for her, so they excused themselves and waited in the lobby. As she hugged first her mother, then her father Winnie's eyes filled with tears because she realized that she would soon be far away from them.

All six of us were now in the lobby. Jerome gave Peggy a hug and kiss goodbye, shook hands with Joe and hugged Cecelia. He told them what a pleasure it was to be in their company for the last two days. He then turned to me saying he would see me back at the base on Monday, and he was on his way.

Winnie then gave her mother and father one last hug. She said, "Goodbye and I love you both very much." She then hugged Peggy and thanked her for coming all the way to Baltimore to participate in the wedding.

Finally, Winnie and I sat alone in the lobby. Not a word was said; my wife looked very forlorn, and I was having somewhat the same sensation. I broke the silence, knowing that the reality was we were husband and wife, and we needed to board the bus for Solomon's Island.

We went back to our hotel room, packed our bags, and went to the bus station. The ride to Solomon's Island was at least 90 minutes. I hoped that she would cheer up along the way.

Winnie had made prior arrangements for a room at a hotel near the base. It was a good thing she had, for space was at a premium on the island. The difference in the quality of the hotel from the one we just left was a bit of a shock. I looked at our surroundings, turned to my wife and said, "Welcome to my life in the service."

It was early evening, and I helped Winnie unpack and settle in. I said, "I better go down to the dock and see when the next liberty boat goes to the training base."

I went back to the hotel after checking the schedule, and we had time for dinner since it was only 5 p.m. We went over what our new life would be like for the next month. On Monday, Winnie would look for an apartment to rent. I would be able to come visit on Friday night.

It was hard to say goodbye, knowing it would be five days before I would see her again.

On the way back to the base with reality setting in, I could not help wondering if Jerome was right. Marriage may not have been the thing to do.

The next weekend I stopped at the hotel, and the desk clerk gave me a note from Winnie with the address where she was staying. All that had been available was a large summer home converted for servicemen. The accommodations consisted of a bedroom with kitchen and bathroom rights to be shared with two other couples.

Back on the base during the week, I had no time to miss Winnie during the day, but after dinner, the evenings were very lonely. Friday evening, as soon as the ship hit the pier and I ordered secure the engines, I jumped out onto the dock and ran down to catch the next liberty boat. It was a mad dash to be one of the first in line. Officers had no priority over enlisted men, and if the boat was filled, one had to wait for the next trip. Winnie would be at the dock anxiously awaiting my arrival. The weekends were cherished times together as we knew full well that each one may be the last before I was shipped out.

There was one down side to the weekends: we were never alone in our room; we had to share it with a colony of red ants. All complaints were to no avail, even though the landlord said he was doing everything possible. As I look back, "everything possible" was just lip service.

Monday morning I had to be back at the base at 9 a.m. However, one Monday morning I missed the boat and arrived back on base an hour late. All the other LCTs were already out training. My instructor was livid, and when he left I told my crew that we had better have a good day if they wanted me to remain their skipper. The rest of the day went well, and the instructor didn't say anything to me.

As training progressed, the captains of the LCTs would carry out maneuvers without the instructor on board. The lead ship would carry the commanding officer in charge of the group of LCTs. We communicated via flags. The flag on his ship indicated the six LCTs should be in line behind his craft; the next set of flags indicated that we should scatter. After several different maneuvers at the end of the day, a flag went up on the lead ship. I said to myself, "The flag must mean go back to the base." I set my ship on a course that would take me back to the base.

All of a sudden, I was on a collision course with the lieutenant commander's craft. According to the rules of navigation, I had the right of way. I thought to myself, "he is testing me," so I stayed on course. We came very close; in fact, we almost collided. When I arrived back on the dock the ensign on board the lead LCT informed me that the lieutenant commander wanted to see me in his office at once.

On the way to his office, I was thinking he wanted to congratulate me on my knowledge of seamanship. I was barely through the door when he started shouting at me, why did I steer my ship directly at his? I said I had the right of way according to laws of navigation. He then informed me that the flag meant to go back to the base in the order you came out. My mind had a quick flashback to my flying days when the flight instructor said, "Sorry son, I don't believe you are suited to be a flyer." I thought for sure he was about to inform me I was not qualified to be a captain of an LCT. Much to my relief this did not occur.

In late November 1944, on Monday morning, we were all assembled in the cafeteria when the lieutenant commander told us we were finished training. The LCTs we were assigned to were placed on top of LSTs manufactured at the Dravo shipyards in Pittsburgh. These amphibious ships were in New Orleans awaiting the crews for the LCT. Next Monday at 8 a.m., we would take a bus to Baltimore for the train ride to New Orleans. We were told only that our ultimate destination was somewhere in the Pacific. That evening, I phoned Winnie and told her the news.

Immediately following the news of our imminent deployment, we were to report to sickbay for various shots to protect us against tropical diseases. These shots would be spread out over a few days. Jerome and I went for our shots together. We had our last injection on Thursday afternoon. As we left the building, I asked him to hold my records, but somehow, he dropped my file. The verification that I had my inoculations was lost. I didn't panic about the lost paperwork; I thought it was just an inconvenience. I went back to sickbay and asked the doctor if he could issue new forms and sign them for me. He said he was sorry, he couldn't help me since the only evidence I was given the shots was in my file. Because of this debacle, I had to go back to sickbay on Friday and have all the injections again and all at once. I could not help but be concerned how this would affect me since it was the last time Winnie and I would be together for a long time.

Friday evening, Winnie waited at the pier as usual for my arrival. I informed her about my episode at sickbay with Jerome losing my records. I was still groggy from all the shots, and on the way back to our apartment, I started to feel nauseated. This miserable sensation did not disappear until Sunday afternoon. Feeling comatose from the shots, I hardly remember anything about our last two days together.

At 10 p.m. Sunday night, I kissed my wife goodbye and boarded the liberty boat. Little did I know on that day that I would not see her again for a year and five months. As the boat pulled away from the dock, I kept Winnie in my sight for as long as I could. My heart ached, and I was depressed about having to leave her. Sunday evening was a hard time for Jerome and me, knowing that our LCT training was over and his destination was not the same as mine.

The last evening on the base I had difficulty sleeping knowing this was not the same as all my other moves in the

Navy. The next day I would be on my way to New Orleans to board my ship and proceed out of the country, destination unknown. My last training was over and I now would have total responsibility of commanding a ship in a war zone. My fate as to my future and my chances of survival was now in the hands of God.

CHAPTER 8
DESTINATION

On Monday morning, December 2, 1944, my crew and I boarded a bus destined for the Baltimore train station. From there, we embarked on the 1100-mile, 28-hour trip to New Orleans. I wasn't particularly thrilled about the long ride on a train. It ran on steam power, so dust, dirt, and grime constantly bellowed into the passenger cars, making the journey uncomfortable at best. There was no place for us to stretch out and sleep so the only rest we got was from dozing off in our seat. We also ate all of our meals, served cafeteria style, in those same seats.

I did manage to get a little bit of sleep the following afternoon, but I am certain that was only because I passed out from exhaustion. I finally woke up when the train made a loud screeching noise and came to a stop around 3 p.m. We all gathered our gear and stepped off the train and onto the platform in New Orleans where a bus was waiting to take us to the base.

We reported for duty, and I was assigned to a room in officers' quarters while the crew was sent to the enlisted men's barracks. The first thing on my list was to shower and remove the soot from the long train ride. After that, I went to the officers' mess hall for a nice relaxing meal. The food may not have been gourmet here, but it definitely tasted like it after the meals I had eaten on the train. I walked around the base after dinner and then retired to my quarters for a much-needed rest in a real bed.

On December 6, I was ordered to find my crew, and we were escorted down to the docks. It was a bright sunny day; the temperature was well into the 80s. All of us were excited about the prospect of seeing our LCT. No wonder, for we all knew it would be our home for some time to come.

As we walked along the dock, we saw our first LST. It was a 5,000 ton vessel, 430 feet long, with a complement of 14 officers and 90 enlisted men.

At the time, the LST was docking, and we hardly noticed it moving forward. I thought either the captain had given the wrong command, or the reverse mechanism had failed to work. The pier was made of heavy pilings supporting a wooden deck, and the LST made a large crashing sound as it knifed through the dock like the dock was a piece of cheese. It was an amazing first view of such a large amphibious landing craft.

We proceeded along the dock, sidestepping the damage, and our escort said, "There is your ship." Imagine my surprise to see the shining dark green LCT sitting on top of the LST. It made me feel very proud that I was in command of it. There was only one thing odd about the LCT—it looked entirely different from the craft I had trained on. I asked the escort officer about this, and he said my ship was a newer model.

I went aboard and met the captain of the LST. His name was Peter Baxter, and he couldn't have been more than 35 at the most. He was certainly very young to be in charge of this huge ship and was probably a 90-day wonder like me.

Prior to World War II, the United States had no existing

amphibious Navy. Hundreds of LSTs and LCTs were built and were manned by men yanked out of civilian life. This captain may have been the owner of a small accounting firm. The Navy looked at his ability to run a small company and surmised that he could learn to operate and command an LST. Almost all Naval Academy graduates were assigned to conventional ships during WWII.

The captain asked me to join him in his quarters. Over a cup of coffee, we talked about various subjects, such as our hometowns and where we had received our training. Waiting for a break in the conversation, I asked what was foremost in my mind. How did the huge ship and my LCT arrive in New Orleans? One thing I did know—LSTs were built at the Dravo Shipyard in Pittsburgh. He told me that after training, he and his crew had been sent to the Dravo Shipyard. Boarding the completed ship, they sailed down the Ohio River and docked at Mt. Vernon, Ohio. At this location, the LCT was placed on top of the LST. They then proceeded down to the Mississippi River and on to New Orleans. The trip was a lot more difficult than sailing in open water. Navigating the large LST for the 1600 miles of twisting river at a cruising speed of 11 knots had taken 14 days.

The following day we picked up our gear and moved aboard the LST. We stayed on the ship for 15 days before we finally heard the captain shout, "Cast off lines." The engines pounded loudly in reverse, and the ship gently moved away from the dock. Once we were safely in the open water, the engines were put into forward motion and we were on our way. I would hear the steady hum of the engines for many days on the almost 6000-mile trip to Hawaii.

The day we left New Orleans was a beautiful day. The LST proceeded out into the Gulf of Mexico at a cruising speed of 11 knots. I remember looking out over the water and watching the shoreline disappear while a soft breeze brushed against my face. I had never seen dolphins before in my life; they gracefully swam up and down in the water, keeping pace with the LST.

A relaxing feeling came over me which I had not experienced in many months. Leaving home, washing out of the Air Corps, being sent to Bainbridge, Notre Dame, Fort Pierce, LCT training at Soloman's Island, and the marriage all within 18 months were a lot to digest. Obviously, these happenings had left me little time to relax.

All my life, my tight little world had been Pittsburgh, Pennsylvania, and some vacations to the East Coast. I never knew the Panama Canal was about 1600 miles south of New Orleans, and now I was sailing to it. With the shoreline out of sight and the dolphins no longer beside the ship, only a cloudless sky and open water remained. Looking into the vast blue horizon, I quickly realized the massive amount of water on the Earth, and it overwhelmed me.

Sea travel is of course much different from any form of land travel. The ship never stopped; it was in continuous motion. Even at the LST's slow speed, we managed to travel a great distance in what seemed like a short period of time. The LST is a large ship, and it was refreshing to walk around the deck. I often talked with the other seamen aboard. Some people may think such a long trip is very boring. It is boring only if you do not take advantage of socializing with the many different people on board.

Since I hadn't traveled the country much, I thought all American citizens sounded the same, but being on the LST exposed me to people with different dialects. The personnel aboard the ship were from all sections of the United States, and much to my surprise, many of the sailors thought that I sounded funny. Each person I met had some story to tell so the days went by very fast with few boring moments.

Spotting the islands also helped the time pass. By

following the sea-lanes, I saw Cuba and soon the island of Jamaica was left behind. After six days of travel, we arrived at Colon Harbor, the entrance to the Panama Canal. We entered it without delay. The huge locks staggered my imagination. The LST was actually towed through the locks by an electric train. After passing through the last lock on the Atlantic side, we entered a huge freshwater lake. Under the LST's own power, we traveled across that lake. On the other side, we entered another set of locks that lowered the ship into the Pacific Ocean. On this side of the canal is the city of Panama. It took about 12 hours to travel the 50-mile distance across the isthmus from the Atlantic to the Pacific.

Once we disembarked from Panama, we sailed toward Hawaii. I had said earlier that a long voyage on a ship is not boring. That good theory was put to the test since we had 4300 miles to go from Panama City to Hawaii. It is only 2300 miles from San Francisco to Hawaii but we were traveling from a different angle. From San Francisco, we would pass through 40 degrees of longitude. Coming from Panama, we passed through 75 degrees of longitude, a big difference. At best, we would travel 320 miles per day. The trip would take about 16 days counting refueling at Panama.

The Pacific Ocean is vast beyond comprehension. For the whole trip, the sky was almost cloudless and the temperature very warm. In Panama, you are very close to the equator, and even the latitude at Hawaii is only 20 degrees above it. Both places are indeed hot.

While on board the LST, I learned how to use the sextant. This consumed a lot of my time. The navigation officer allowed me to assist him. With this instrument, you can measure the height of stars above the horizon, then use charts that tell the star's height at certain times and dates. By calculating the information, you can identify your position within a few miles of where you are in the world. It is hard to believe some of this knowledge is hundreds of years old. The sextant can also be used to gauge the sun's height during the day, but it is much more difficult to navigate this way. Obviously, this method is antiquated in today's day and age since the advent of satellite positioning. Unfortunately, we did not have that type of technology at our disposal in the 1940's, and although the sextant seemed primitive, it got the job done with remarkable accuracy.

I continued to pass my time aboard the LST by talking to the other seamen and honing my sextant skills. Then, one day the anchor of my LCT began banging against its housing, making very loud noises. The executive officer of the LST gave my crew a hard time about it. I heard his dissertation and clearly told him to come to me in the future and I would do whatever was necessary to correct the problem. He outranked me, but the captain of one naval vessel has the right to question any orders from an officer of another ship. I know my men felt good about the way I handled this situation.

After looking at cloudless sky and calm water for most of the trip, I anxiously waited to see land. We had been at sea for more than two weeks. The navigation officer told me when to expect to see the coast of Hawaii, and I stood on the deck with my binoculars, straining my eyes to see it. I thought I saw land, but my eyes were playing tricks on me. Sure enough, the coastline finally appeared. Although it was very faint at first, Hawaii finally came into view. I could not wait to put my feet on solid ground. I had heard the humming of the engines and felt the rocking of the ship under me for long enough.

Maybe I was just too anxious, but it seemed like a long time before we arrived at the entrance of Pearl Harbor on January 2, 1945. Being inside the harbor was surreal, especially considering the magnitude of devastation a mere three years before. I looked to the sky and wondered how the men on the ships the day of Japan's attack felt when they saw all the warplanes. I tried to imagine what my thoughts would have been at this time.

As we continued into the harbor, we passed the sunken hull of the battleship Arizona, and that's when it hit me—I was catching up with the war zone. It was hard to get out of my mind those 1100 sailors entombed forever inside that ship.

After the war, as veterans of World War II will often do, I talked about the bombing of Pearl Harbor with some of my friends. It turns out that a friend of mine, Jim Fowler, was actually there that day. He was a private in the Army, stationed in Schofield Barracks on the island of Oahu. Here is his account of that eventful day:

"At 7:55 a.m., we heard machine gun fire and explosions outside. We ran out to see what was going on, only to see the sky filled with Japanese planes, which were strafing our barracks as they headed for the big air corps fighter plane base at Wheeler Field adjacent to our barracks. The Japanese planes were so low that we could see the pilots waving to us as they made their strafing runs. It all happened so suddenly it was hard to explain any reaction I may have had, for they were on their way to the main objective—the air base."

From his humble beginning as a private in the Army, Jim was transferred back to the United States, sent to officers' training, and became an officer. He had extensive service in the European Theater of operation. While participating in the Battle of the Bulge, he was seriously injured. He eventually finished his career with the high rank of captain in the US Army Reserve.

The bridge of the LST was inaccessible to me, so I had no idea where we would anchor. We passed many types of crafts including a cruiser, a destroyer and merchant ships—but I didn't see any LSTs. I found out later that they were anchored at West Loch. Amphibious ships were not important enough in the Navy chain of command to occupy a dock, or for that matter take up space in the main section of the harbor.

West Loch was in the far reaches of the harbor. The LST didn't have a liberty boat so we relied on a base-operated shuttle boat service. We made it ashore and from there, "Leaping Lenas," or tractor-drawn flatbeds moving slightly faster than a walking pace, took us from place to place. The Leaping Lenas were interesting. If you wanted to get somewhere, you had to jump on and off them while they moved. Each had her own route. To get from place to place, we hopped from one to the other until we found our way to our destination. It was quite a process. Officers and enlisted men had the same transportation unless you had three stripes on your sleeve. Those officers had their own vehicles to get around.

I was anxious to see Pearl City, which was a short distance off the base. After much confusion trying to find my way riding the Leaping Lenas, I finally got there, and when I did, I was a little disappointed with it. Atlantic City, New Jersey, or any other seaside resort on the East Coast was far superior to this place. I spent the rest of my time in Pearl Harbor aboard the LST. No more shuttle boats and Leaping Lenas for me.

On January 12, 1945, the captain ordered the anchor up. We proceeded out into the main portion of the harbor passing many ships that were either anchored, docked, or underway. Seeing all the ship activity impressed me, but soon we were at the mouth of the harbor and out into the open sea. Then we lost sight of land. As we had approached Hawaii, it seemed to take a long time to get into the harbor, but when we left the land, the islands disappeared quickly. It could have been my mindset too; I wasn't ready to be back on the open sea so quickly.

Of course, I had known my first destination was Hawaii, but after that, I did not know where we were heading. The LST captain met with me, and I was informed that he was launching my LCT at Manus Island. Other than that, he didn't have any information regarding my orders or mission. Manus Island is only 180 miles from New Guinea. After I took a quick look at the map, I could see I was in for a long voyage—4300 miles—which meant another 17 days at sea.

This LST with me aboard was out in the ocean alone, not part of a flotilla of ships. The LST captain had never been on this voyage before and had very little experience at this command. Would he be able to find Manus Island? Were we in dangerous waters? Could we be attacked by a Japanese warship or airplanes? What if a huge storm came up and disabled the ship—who would find us? I did not want to dwell on these thoughts too long. It was best to put them out of my mind.

Nothing eventful happened in these 17 days. On this trip I spent more time with my crew talking about lots of things, such as where they where from, what they did in civilian life, and what we would be doing in the Pacific. These discussions helped pass the time and made for very interesting conversation.

We continued on our journey, and one day as I was sitting near the bow of the ship, I began to think about my high school days and my first experience of being in love.

CHAPTER 9
MY LOVE LIFE

I have often wondered how two total strangers who never met before suddenly fall in love. This is perhaps the most important fork in the road of many couples—especially when they decide to spend the rest of their lives together. The following is the story of how it happened to me.

I believe the personalities that emerge within us in our late teens have a lot to do with why two particular people meet and fall in love. When I was a student at Carrick High School, sports played an important role in my life. I was on the swimming, soccer, and track teams. Being involved in a competitive environment helped develop my character.

Learning to dance also had a major impact on my personality. Most young girls enjoy dancing, and a man who is an above-average dancer has an opportunity to meet more women. Where else can a man have an opportunity to hold a young woman in his arms, simply by saying the words, "Would you like to dance?"

I learned how to dance when I was a junior in high school. During lunch, some of the students would dance on the auditorium stage. Most of the other students (including me) would sit in the auditorium seats and watch the dancing. The kids on the stage seemed to be having a wonderful time, and after observing them for several days, I wondered why I hadn't joined them. Well, there was one big problem: I couldn't dance. No big deal, I thought to myself. I was going up on the stage anyway. My first couple of efforts resulted in much laughter from the audience in the auditorium. After a few days, I seemed to somewhat get the hang of it, and I started having fun. That is how I learned to dance.

Dancing made it possible for me to meet and become involved with my first love, Dot Hutchkins. I was a senior at CHS when I met Dot, and our common bond was dancing.

I had no idea what a powerful emotion love can be. Dot and I would meet each other at our various friends' houses. We also saw each other at Brentwood Park, where dances were held every Friday night.

In June of 1940, I graduated from Carrick High School. I lived in a neighborhood where very few men went to college. Perhaps they never realized that college could enhance their future. Most of the adult males in the neighborhood worked in the steel mills or in some service-type job like roofing or plumbing.

As the summer went on, I gave some serious thought to college. I talked it over with my friends, and I received the same ridicule from them as when I joined the Boy Scouts. I believe the reaction by my pals made me more determined to pursue higher learning. I approached my father about the possibility of going to college, and he gave me an emphatic, "No. We do not have the money to send you." Being a persistent person, I would not let the subject die, and finally, in exasperation, he said he would help me get started and maybe I could get a job and pay my own tuition.

I looked into local colleges and finally decided on Duquesne University for two reasons. First, the tuition was reasonable, and second, since it was in downtown

Pittsburgh, I could travel by streetcar to class. This also would be the best place to find part-time employment.

When the time came for me to enroll at Duquesne, I suddenly realized that they expected me to know what career I intended to pursue. Although I really wanted to become an engineer, Duquesne did not offer the program. As I was standing in line at the registration office, I became acquainted with Bob Lawrence, who later became one of my closest friends at the school. I asked him how he was registering, and he told me he was going into the School of Business. It sounded good to me so I registered that way as well.

It was not long before I was at ease at the university. I became friends with many freshmen and a few upperclassmen. Like all universities, an important social aspect of being at the school is joining a fraternity. The one I became interested in was Kappa Sigma Phi. Their members seemed to be more outgoing and had more social affairs than the others had. This fraternity seemed to have all the ingredients for me, so I decided to become a member. Being new at the school, I had no clue of how to go about joining the organization. I found out that one had to be pledged. Much to my surprise, one of my friends in the sophomore class asked me if I would like to be pledged for the fraternity. Without hesitation, I readily agreed to his offer.

There was one major drawback to joining the organization. Its hell-week was the most grueling of all the fraternities. Each day for a week, we had to dress up like Indians. We also had to obtain a two-foot paddle; I had no clue as to its purpose, but I found out on the first day of hazing. We were ordered by the members to do silly things; for example, one of the members was partially bald and another brother ordered me to call him "Baldy." I said I could not do such a thing. When I refused, the brother ordered me to "assume the position" and he put my paddle to use. Finally, out of frustration, I agreed to his demand.

"Baldy" did not take too kindly to my remark, and I was paddled again.

The brothers dreamed up other activities for us, including sideshows on the street corners of Pittsburgh, dressed in our Indian outfits. None of these shows seemed to satisfy the members so they ordered us to duck walk, which meant we had to walk around with bent knees, shouting "quack, quack, quack." Duck walking was so hard on my knees that for two weeks after hazing, I had to hold on to the railing and go down steps backwards.

Another evening, we were sent on a scavenger hunt. One of the requirements was to steal a live chicken. I knew the location of a chicken coop in my neighborhood. Opening the coop door, I reached in and grabbed a chicken. Unless you've ever had the experience, it is hard to believe how much noise a flock of chickens can make. The quest for the chicken was successful, and we managed to make a clean getaway.

One Friday night, all of the pledges had to put on a performance at a local nightclub. I thought we put on a good show and so did the patrons at the club, who all cheered and clapped for us. The fraternity members, however, were not impressed. In fact, they were impossible to satisfy. On top of all the things they made us do, there was one more night of abuse at the fraternity house I will not go into detail about. At the end of the evening, if we lasted through their torture, we were welcomed as official members in Kappa Sigma Phi. Two pledges dropped out during the week. Finishing the initiation was a real test of my endurance. Looking back at the week, I have to say it was worth it, for they all became very close friends of mine. In fact, one of them eventually became my partner in a business that we called Eiben and Irr.

You may wonder what a fraternity has to do with falling in love. The fraternity and sorority organizations were an important part of social involvement at Duquesne. Each fraternity interacted with the other fraternities and sororities in social activities. For a large portion of my first year in college, I continued to date my girlfriend Dot. We always had an enjoyable time at the school's social affairs— especially the major ballroom dances. One day, it occurred to me that she no longer had the passionate love for me that I had for her. As a result, my love for her faded, and I decided not to ask her for any more dates. At first I missed her, but not for long.

One day I was walking across campus, and I noticed two beautiful girls across the street. One was a blonde woman and the other, a brunette. Which would I ask for a date? I had to make one of my fast decisions. A big university dance, the Homecoming, was one week away, and I quickly picked the brunette. I had never met her or even seen her before, but I went across the street. I introduced myself and asked her what her name was. She said Winnie Winner. I continued to make small talk from there and asked what school she was in. It turned out that she was studying education, so it was no wonder I had never seen her around. I asked her if she wanted to go to the homecoming dance with me, and much to my amazement she accepted. Wow, it was quite a surprise that she agreed, considering it was our first meeting.

The next day when I saw her, Winnie told me that when she went back to the sorority house she yelled, "I've got a date with Mel Eiben." Little did I know that anybody cared. Up to that time, I did not hang out with mixed company at the school, so I had no idea that anyone would want a date with me.

Was it love at first sight? Absolutely, it was. I was infatuated with Winnie from the moment I laid eyes on her, and from our very first meeting, we could not get enough of each other. Within days, we knew each other's class schedules and met at the local diner when we had a break. This romance was not like my love for Dot. I could tell that

Winnie and I both felt real love for each other.

I was obviously very happy about my relationship with Winnie, but much to my surprise, she had another boyfriend. What did I expect—that with her personality and beauty nobody was dating her? After all, I was just another boy at the college. Her other boyfriend, John, was in ROTC like me and was in his senior year at Duquesne. Not only was he in the ROTC, but he was a student in the top command. I will never forget the day there was an ROTC parade. Winnie was the parade queen and marched alongside John. I was supposed to be in the parade, but I had a friend who said "here" for me when they had roll call. I can still see her surprised expression when I waved to her from the sidelines in civilian clothes. She thought I was marching behind her with the rest of the ROTC Company.

Our romance almost failed because she had no use for my friend Bob Lawrence. She thought he was a jerk, and at times, she thought I was not much different. Whenever Bob and I would see each other on campus, we shook feet instead of hands and said, "Beer, babes, and music. Plenty of leisure and lots of fun," along with our secret phrase. Then we pretended to whisper in each other's ears. After a few seconds, we would yell as loudly as possible, "We will do anything for a laugh; humor at any cost." Winnie didn't seem amused by our spectacle, but I guess her feelings for me were stronger than her displeasure with Bob because we never seemed to tire of being in each other's company.

During my college years, the United States was engaged in World War II, and since I was of age, I figured I would have to serve in the military in some capacity. That realization changed my whole attitude at school, and I thought only in terms of enjoying life. I never knew how long it would be until I was called up, so for me, college became a place I went to each day where I did enough school work to justify my enrollment. I didn't know what the future held or if I had any chance of coming out of the war alive.

I missed many classes. Bob and I would hop in my car, have a couple of beers, and drive out to the country looking for a hill to climb. Somehow climbing a big mound of dirt had a lot of appeal; maybe the danger excited us a bit.

Other times, Bob and I would skip class and swim instead. In the spring and fall of the year, we drove out to Mayer's Pond in Bridgeville, where we would take off our clothes and dive off a cliff at the edge of the pond into the cold refreshing water. Bob was a great friend to have. He was always willing to go anywhere and do most anything. Bob was highly intelligent, and it seemed like there was nothing he did not know about or have an opinion on. It was important to have such a friend, for I was determined to enjoy life to its fullest in the months I had left before being in the service.

The second Homecoming dance I attended with Winnie was at the swank William Penn Hotel in downtown Pittsburgh. My relationship with Winnie barely survived that night, no thanks to Bob. Bob somehow managed to change his driver's license so it appeared he was old enough to buy liquor. He didn't have a date for the homecoming dance because, as he put it, he had "business" to attend to. It turned out the "business" included renting a room at the hotel and "dating" a suitcase filled with liquor. He had many customers at his door that night, including me.

Winnie and I visited Bob at his place of business, and after several drinks, the three of us made our way to the balcony that surrounded the dance floor. When Winnie left us and went to the ladies' room, Bob said, "Mel, we have climbed mountains together; let's drop off the balcony and onto the dance floor." I was slightly inebriated from all the drinks, and I figured it would be fun, so Bob and I climbed over the railing and dropped onto the dance floor together. I am sure we did not notice at the time, but we happened to do it right in front of the university president.

Apparently, Winnie had found out about our caper. She seemed to be gone for a long time, and I kept waiting for her to come back from the ladies' room. I wondered where she had gone, and I asked her girlfriend where she was. Pam said the last time she had seen Winnie, she was on her way back to the sorority house. I ran out of the ballroom in search of Winnie, and by luck, I caught up with her in the lobby. She was annoyed by Bob's shenanigans and mine. I promised to behave myself. She said if I agreed to be a normal person for the rest of the dance then she would agree to join me for the remainder of the evening.

The next day Winnie told me how her brother Ed had had a talk with her about how it was best she no longer date me. Ed was also my fraternity brother, and said I should break off my relationship with his sister. Of course, telling two people who are in love not to see each other is just not effective. Fortunately, our love endured and became even stronger.

There was one more caper of interest at Duquesne. Winnie was out of town, so Bob, George Lake, and I went stag to a dance at the university. Out of nowhere, Bob said, "Let's go swimming at Mayer's pond tonight." It was New Year's Eve, so we waited until after midnight. Then Bob, George, and I headed to the pond. It was snowing when we got there. With my clothes off, I felt very cold. The way to dive into the water was either from the top of a cliff, 10 feet above the water, or else at the water's edge. We decided to dive in near the water level. Climbing down the hill, my logical mind said, "Don't do it." But my determination overcame the thought. I dove into the ice cold water, and immediately rose to the surface to get out of the water as fast as I could. I told Bob the water was literally ice cold, and he should get in and out as fast as he could. Like me, he climbed out immediately. We had only our undershirts to dry off with. No one ever warned me about hypothermia, and I shook for at least a half a day. It may not have been one of the smarter things we did together, but at least we beat the Polar Bear Club at the river that year.

Looking back on this occasion, I realize it was possible we could have died in the water. I wonder how George would have explained this to the police.

By this time, my schoolwork was going downhill. After completing the final in my law class, I was anxious to get the results so I asked the professor to mark my paper on the spot. My law professor was somewhat strange; he went to all of our fraternity parties and got drunk like the rest of us. He quickly graded my exam and told me I had failed. I desperately wanted a passing grade so I said, "But Frank, that is what I meant on the exam." He said OK and made some changes, but then he told me he was just kidding. I still failed the exam by one point. I was very upset that I had failed the test, but so did many other students. In fact, so many people failed the exam that the dean forced him to mark our grades on a curve which meant I passed.

That same semester, my physics professor would not allow me to take the final exam because I had missed too many classes. The test was to see if I would get a passing grade for the semester. I said to the professor, "Why not let me take the test? I know the material." He said no, but with my "never give up" attitude in life, I made a desperate plea. I said, "Give me the test. If I get a C, you can flunk me, but if I get an A or a B, I will pass the course." He agreed to the deal, and I passed with a B.

My job at Kaufmann's Department store left little time to date. I didn't finish work at my shift until 9 p.m., and Winnie had to be in the sorority house by 10 during the week. Our desire to see each other was so strong that on occasion, Winnie would climb out the window on the second floor of the house and go down the fire escape to meet me. Winnie and I would stand on the sidewalk at the university, high above the Monongahela River. There we spent hours in each other's arms, never tiring of the other's company. I even wrote a song for Winnie once to the melody of the song "For it was Mary."

"For it was Winnie, Winnie, just an odd and pleasing name, For up at Duquesne U, it was my cue, to fall for you, Oh, my dear Winnie, Winnie, you sure know that I love you, When I am away from you, please don't feel blue, For I love you true."

Not only was it a struggle to see Winnie during the week, it was also difficult to have any time together on weekends. Meeting at the campus diner and walking the streets together was OK, but we both desired surroundings that were more comfortable.

One evening, Winnie said, "I have a great idea for next weekend. My Aunt Maggie, said she would like to meet you."

Little did I know that that first visit would be an evening I would cherish the memory of for the rest of my life. When I arrived at the apartment, Maggie and Winnie invited me into the living room. I could not help feeling at ease with Maggie's warm welcome. She was an attractive woman in her early fifties. She had a bottle of wine and cheese and crackers on the table. We had about an hour of conversation, consuming the delicious cheese and drinking a couple of glasses of wine. Maggie wanted to know about how we had met and the happenings at the university.

It was a warm evening in the middle of May. A short distance from her apartment is Frick Park, and Winnie suggested that we go for a walk in the park. As I look back on the evening, I believe she planned the stroll in the park as part of our evening together. A short time into our walk on a secluded path, we embraced and had a loving kiss. Further along on the path, we were again in each other's arms. But it was getting late, and we felt obligated to return to the apartment.

Welcoming us back, Maggie asked us how we had enjoyed our walk. The three of us relaxed in the living room. And then, much to my surprise, Aunt Maggie said, "I'm going upstairs to relax. Feel free to have some wine and enjoy yourselves." Alone on the couch, we began kissing and found ourselves lying together on the sofa, and I experienced sensuous sensations I had never before felt. If I had any doubts about her love, tonight I was convinced that she was indeed in love with me.

It was getting very late; in fact, it was now 1:30 a.m. As much as I would have liked to stay longer, I had to leave. One last embrace and I was on my way. I had the trolley ride to Pittsburgh and then on to Mt. Oliver, followed by my half-mile walk home. It was 3 a.m. when I finally lay down in bed. I expected my mother to interrogate me in the morning for being so late, but there were no questions. I guess after her other three children's romantic experiences, she knew what to expect. Every three or four weeks, Winnie and I enjoyed visits to her aunt's house.

Unlike her displeasure with Bob, Winnie was impressed with my friend George Lake. In fact, she asked me if I thought George would like to meet her cousin, Peggy Spates. Winnie gave me a picture of her to show George. When I did, he didn't hesitate at all and quickly agreed to meet Peggy. One weekend, we double dated.

Then the time came when Winnie thought it appropriate to introduce me to her parents. The Winners lived in a small town outside of Uniontown called New Salem. It was a wonderful experience to meet them. I arrived at their home, and it was like a scene out of a movie. The Winners lived in a three-story colonial house with a large porch across the front. Cecilia and Joe Winner were waiting to welcome me at the door. At this very first meeting I could tell they were two wonderful, loving people.

Before dinner, we all drank a glass of wine and made small talk to get to know each other. Mr. Winner was a superintendent at the local coal mine, and Cecilia was a music teacher. Winnie insisted that her father get out his saxophone and her mother play the piano so we could all sing songs together. At one time, Joe had played in big bands. They both were exceptional musicians, and it was quite a fun way to start an evening.

After a few songs, we sat down to a dinner that was fit for a king. Mrs. Winner was an excellent cook. Cecilia and Joe made me feel very comfortable so conversation came easily for me. I even managed to come up with a few witty remarks to demonstrate my sense of humor. Joe, enjoying our conversation, looked up at me from over his glasses and said, "I see I'm going to have trouble with you."

Since I was always tired from work, school, and dating Winnie, I sometimes would doze off at embarrassing times. Well, this happened during my visit with the Winners. I woke up at two in the morning to find myself alone in their living room. I was supposed to sleep upstairs in the guest room, but my problem was I did not know where it was. For a minute, I thought that perhaps they left me alone downstairs to get a laugh. I looked around the downstairs and couldn't find anyone, so I quietly climbed the stairs and softly called "Winnie," hoping she would wake up before her parents did. Finally, she answered and escorted me to the guest room. This was very embarrassing especially since it was my first meeting with the Winners.

One time I went to Winnie's house to pick her up for an important affair at Duquesne University. Mr. Winner looked outside at my convertible; it had a towel tucked into one of the windows to keep the snow out, a piece of wire holding the tail pipe in place and four tires with no tread. I could see what was going through his mind…could it possibly make the 50 miles back to Pittsburgh? The next thing I knew, he handed me the keys to his car and asked me if I would please take his daughter to the dance in his car. I didn't argue with him and said, "Thanks. I will do just that."

1933 Chrysler Roadster

The memories of those wonderful times at the university and with Winnie were so pleasant that I felt I was in a trance. But I suddenly broke out of my reverie, for reality had set in, and I once again realized I was on an LST in the middle of a war zone. After two weeks, Manus Island had appeared on the horizon. I wish I had been on the bridge of the LST when Manus Island was positively identified.

The captain of the LST #778 dropped anchor and secured the engines. The next day my LCT slid off the deck of the LST. From then on, I was in charge of making all the decisions regarding the operation of my ship and crew. There was nobody I could turn to for advice.

CHAPTER 10
ZAMBOANGA

After several weeks of adjusting to life on Manus Island, I found myself anchored at a large staging area known as Seadler Harbor. On the morning of March 1, 1945, I was ordered to go alongside an LST that was to tow me to Zamboanga.

Once my LCT was alongside the LST in the water, huge hawsers were dropped over the side of the ship. An officer aboard the LST instructed me to attach them to the bow of my LCT. I ordered my bosin's mate and two others to attach them to two large rings on either side of the bow of my ship. I hoped my men knew what they were doing because I didn't know how to safely secure the hawsers. Much to my relief, a small boat from shore inspected the ropes to make sure they were properly connected.

Early in the morning of March 2, I was ordered to cast off from the side of the LST. The two ships separated and mine drifted about 30 yards behind the LST. The hawsers lay slack in the water. As I stood on the bridge looking out at the stern of the LST, I noticed the wake produced by the screws of the ship suddenly appear. The hawsers rose from the water, and with a sudden jerk I felt the movement of my ship being towed. It was another form of transportation, and it felt strange to be pulled by the huge LST. I had no control of my ship. The day we left, the sky was overcast, and it was very warm and humid. It felt good to go North, away from the equator.

I decided to meet with my crew and brief them about our destination. Despite all the time we had been together, I had had very little serious conversation with my men, partly because we had yet to participate in an actual invasion. I couldn't tell my men much—just that we were headed to Zamboanga, which was on the southern portion of Mindanao island. I knew Luzon Island (where Manila, the capital of the Philippines is located) had been invaded. Much of the fighting was concentrated on the northern islands. The only information I was able to gather at Manus Island was that no landing had occurred on the southern portion of Mindanao Island. This led me to believe that my LCT would be involved in some way with securing the island.

I told my crew that they shouldn't be too concerned yet since there weren't any troops on the LST. If we were to be part of an invasion force, we would have to pick up troops, tanks, and supplies at some location other than Zamboanga.

For the first three days of our trip to Zamboanga, low, ominous-looking clouds hung over us. With each day, the wind seemed to increase in intensity. Huge waves began pushing my craft from side to side while raising it up with each swell. On the morning of our fourth day at sea, the wind suddenly took on what seemed like hurricane proportions. The waves became enormous—their height reaching as much as 25 feet. I positioned myself on the top of the wheelhouse standing on the exposed deck, holding onto the railing. Waves cascaded over the bow of the ship, drenching me in salt water. I had seen scenes in movies where the water crashed onto ships, but never thought this would happen to me. One moment I was on top of a wave, and I could see the LST in front of me with its stern out of the water and the screws of the ship exposed. Seconds later, I was slamming down into the troughs of the wave while the LST disappeared completely from sight.

With a huge banging noise, my ship hit the bottom of the wave. The railing on the side of the deck bent out of shape as if never to be straight again. Now the hawser became slack, and with a jerk, the LST pulled me on top of the wave again. Not only was the LCT going up and down, we were spinning sideways too. LCTs do not cut waves; they ride them like corks. I questioned whether my ship would hold together under the tremendous pounding. I also thought about the men on different LCTs in our group. They had bolted the sections of their LCTs together and I wondered if they would stay in one piece in this formidable storm.

The towline of the LCT on my starboard side had separated from the LST and the boat looked helpless in the water. The LCT eventually became reattached, but not before the storm abated. We withstood about six hours of this banging around before the storm completely settled down. Much to my relief, I had survived my first major storm at sea.

The distance from Manus Island to Zamboanga is 2900 miles. At an average of 10 miles per hour, it took 12 days to arrive at our destination.

The captain of the LST ordered me to drop anchor in the harbor. Our towlines were disconnected and our ship rested motionless in the water. As on the day I arrived at Manus Island, I had no clue as to why I was here. It was obvious I had to do one of two things. I could drop anchor or beach the craft; I decided "terra firma" was a better choice.

After the usual procedure of dropping anchor a short distance from shore, I ran my boat up on the sandy beach. I secured the engines, and we all relaxed on solid ground. It felt good not to be at the mercy of the wind and waves as we had been for the past 12 days.

On March 12, 1945, I ordered the ramp down. I looked out on the beach. Evidence pointed to a recent invasion. I went ashore to try to learn what had recently transpired at Zamboanga. There were many cargo ships and various landing craft in the harbor. I went to the nearest dock area and saw a group of military officers talking on the beach. I walked up to them and asked if I could join their conversation. As soon as I got a chance to talk, I asked them if they had any ideas why my LCT was here. That is when one of the men pointed to a liberty ship and said it was the LCT's job to unload them.

I learned from my short meeting with these various officers that they had participated in the invasion that occurred on March 10, 1945. I went back to my LCT and told the crew what I had learned. We had missed the invasion of Zamboanga by three days. If it were not for the storm, we would have arrived in the midst of the fighting. The next day I waited for my orders. I decided that I was not going ashore to look for instructions; someone from headquarters could come and find me for a change. I waited on board until about 11 o'clock; then I decided to take Clarence along and survey the immediate interior of the island.

Up to this time in my life, I had never been in a foreign country, much less an Asian country like the Philippines. I was accustomed to seeing Caucasians of average height. It came as a shock to me how small the average Philippine native is. In fact, every animal and structure there seemed undersized. Even the caribou and horses used for farming seemed little to me. There were no paved roads, and the whole countryside looked desolate. Homes were thatched huts, built above ground to avoid the open sewers.

Looking a little further inland, I noticed a church on top

of a nearby hill. I asked an officer who happened to be nearby if it was a Catholic church. He said it was and that he was going to Mass there tomorrow at ten. This was great news. I was Catholic too, and I hadn't been to a Mass in over four months.

I went back to my ship and asked my men if any of them were Catholic. Three of them were, so I told them news about the church. All of them wanted to go to Mass with me.

The next morning, all four of us washed, shaved, and put on clean uniforms. It was a beautiful morning. There were a few clouds in the sky, and it was easy to forget there was a war going on. The short mile and a half walk up to the church was carefree and relaxing.

When we walked into the church, we quickly realized how gorgeous it must have been before it was partially destroyed. Much of it was still standing but most of the windows were gone and there were a lot of holes in the roof. Birds flew freely about the church, and almost all the pews showed evidence of their presence.

I looked behind the altar and saw one of the most impressive sights I have ever seen in a church. There were more than 20 beautifully carved wooden statues. To this day, I can still close my eyes and picture their beauty. In fact, the whole experience was surreal, with the birds flying all around and the priest holding up the chalice in this half-destroyed church. As we were leaving the building, I noticed there were no young men. Old men, women, and children were all I could see. I wondered if the native young men just didn't go to church or if they were all out fighting to free the Philippines of Japanese invaders.

After church, the crew and I relaxed as best we could, wondering what was in store for us next. The following day, I still had no news from the Navy, and it seemed strange to me, but since it had only been one full day since we landed, I was not too concerned.

After three days, an Army lieutenant came on board the ship. I introduced myself to him, and he told me his name was Jim Brady. He had a strong handshake; it was not an overpowering one, but one of control. That made me feel very comfortable with him. At first, I thought this was a friendly visit, but this was not the case. Officer Brady informed me that all my future orders would come from Army headquarters. It was his job to deliver instructions for unloading the liberty ships in the harbor. He said to be ready to be underway at eight the next day. I guess he assumed that I had experience tying up to these huge craft. In the morning, Jim saw to it that we identified the right liberty ship. Sliding off the beach, we were on our way. The experience of tying up to a liberty ship was awesome. Imagine the sensation of approaching this huge vessel, with no idea how I would get my hawsers up to its deck.

A liberty ship has a displacement of 10,000 tons. This may not seem large compared to modern cruise ships of 80,000 and 90,000 tons; however, a liberty ship made an LCT feel like a rowboat. These massive ships are 100 feet longer than the LST. As I approached the huge bulk of steel 25 feet above the water line, it became bigger and more massive. I think I subconsciously slowed the LCT down to delay the encounter as long as possible.

At Solomon Island training base there was no large ship in the harbor to practice on. In fact, no mention was ever made that I would be called on to unload the large ships. I didn't know how to communicate with the liberty ship. My ship-to-shore radio was useless, for I did not know his wavelength, so I had to get close enough for him to hear me. An officer on board the liberty ship shouted to come alongside. I maneuvered my craft next to the side of his ship, putting the engine in low speed from forward to reverse, trying to keep my ship stationary.

112

World War II Liberty Ship

The officer on board the liberty ship standing 25 feet above me was shouting some orders, but I could not hear him. The two steel ships banging together made it impossible to hear anything. My adrenaline was at its peak as I wondered what I was to do next. How on earth would I get my hawser up to his deck? He was probably thinking what a dumbass they had sent out to unload cargo from his ship.

Suddenly, I heard several objects banging onto our deck. They were round balls with lead cores. I had never seen them before so I didn't know what to do with them. Fortunately, Clarence knew what to do. He said, "Skipper they are known as monkey fists." He tied them to our hawsers, which were pulled up and secured to the side of the liberty ship. Wow, I was glad that was over. I could firmly secure the engine, as we were now stationary alongside the large ship. That is, if you can call going up and down with each wave that passed being stationary.

Huge arms from the ship's crane lowered many boxes onto my LCT. I had no idea what was in them. The horrible thought that they were high explosives did occur to me. Well, it was best I had no knowledge of their contents. The procedure for loading my ship—especially for the first time was not easy. Each box had to be unhooked and distributed on the deck by my men. Obviously, they had never done this before. After many hours, my ship was filled with its first cargo. I was actually doing something that had to do with the war effort.

I ordered my engine started and all men at their stations. I shouted to the seaman aboard the liberty ship to cast off. I was on my way to the shoreline. Beaching was no longer a traumatic experience. With each day, my crew and I became more experienced. Bruce, my anchorman, was ready for my command to drop anchor—now a routine procedure. Once on shore, Jim, the Army lieutenant, was waiting with two large army trucks. The four Army men with the help of my sailors loaded the trucks, and after many trips, my craft was empty.

After dinner, I set up the night watch—a normal procedure in the Navy. After telling the crew they had done a commendable job for the day, I went to my quarters. I sat down, and a feeling of relief came over me. At my age of 21 years, having all that responsibility was overwhelming. As they say, you do what you have to do. Each new adventure built my confidence for the next unexpected experience. I was beginning to thrive on the unusual while building my confidence to be a qualified skipper.

The next day, we went through the same procedure. I still was not at ease tying up to the liberty ship, but this time it was not as traumatic. The job went on for eight days but the "coming alongside" was never easy.

I am sure the reader has observed what the stern of a large ship looks like. The side of a liberty ship is almost straight up and down, but as you go back to its stern, it curves under dramatically. The structure on the starboard side of an LCT is tall and flat. The big danger with tying up was to avoid the back end of the liberty ship. If they collided, an LCT super structure would be caved inward. This happened to several of the LCTs on this operation, but I was determined that it would not happen to me. That is one of the reasons the "tying up" was never routine.

On one of the days of unloading duty, the harbor waters were very rough due to a storm occurring in the tropics. In addition to rough seas, a heavy rain was falling. I approached the liberty ship and knew that this was definitely not going to be routine. Out of range of voice communication, even shouting as loudly as possible, there was no way to hear each other. The only possible way to let them know my thoughts about coming alongside was by blinker.

Pete, my signalman, was on the bridge with me. He was an expert at blinker and signal flags. The way blinker communication is accomplished is with the dots and dashes of Morse code. A quick flash and a slight delayed flash on my large spotlight made up words.

I flashed the liberty ship that it was too dangerous to come alongside. The liberty ship ordered me to come alongside anyway. I reiterated that I felt it was too dangerous. About 30 yards separated the two vessels. Suddenly, the captain appeared on the side of his ship. From the distance, he looked like a very upset man. He again flashed me back to proceed with the tying up. As captain of my ship, I had the same authority as he had. There was nothing he could do to force me to listen to him. However, I decided to attempt carrying out his order. As I approached his ship, a large wave lifted up my craft and turned the sharp edge of the bow of my ship into the side of his ship. Imagine the scene: he was looking down on me, high winds, heavy rain, and a sickening crashing sound of tearing metal. I put a hole in his vessel large enough to walk through. The captain disappeared from view, and I did not see him the rest of the day. I finally got alongside and proceeded with the usual unloading. The excitement of the day was still not over.

When alongside a vessel this large, hawsers are almost straight up and down, holding the LCT in close. When I first saw the hawsers supplied with an LCT, I wondered why so large for a ship this size. They were as heavy as the ones used for battleships. On this day, I was to find out why they were so heavy. Due to the high waves, my ship was going up on the waves higher than usual. The hawsers would hang loose when on top of the waves. When the waves would go down, all of the tonnage of my ship was held by the ropes with little water underneath. Try to imagine the other problem of our unloading. Heavy boxes were being lowered to the deck. My men were trying to unhook the boxes with the ship rising and falling. It was a very dangerous job.

All of a sudden, one of the hawsers snapped; it had been held by only one rope. It took quick action on the part of two of my men to get another line up. My bosin's mate suggested we use cable. I had no idea of the danger of the use of cable. He proceeded to connect with the cable. All went well for a while; then suddenly, the cable snapped, flying across the deck and almost hitting one of my men. Had it struck him, he could have been killed. That was the last time I used a cable.

I was glad when we finally were able to cast off. It was still raining with a strong wind. On the beach, the back end of the LCT was heaving from the large breakers coming ashore, and unloading onto the truck was a difficult task. The crew and I were exhausted. Back in my quarters, I got into my bunk early. Very tired, I was wondering if tomorrow would be as traumatic as this day's event. I know that this day strengthened my confidence to react to adverse circumstances, but I was sure glad it was over.

It seemed odd to think of it this way, but was I training the crew to be efficient operators of the craft, or were they training me to be a captain of the ship? I knew little of the skills of Pete, my quarter master. I didn't know the simple task of how to tie a knot, much less his many boating skills. Eighteen-year-old Larry, an expert on radio, Walt, my gunner's mate and Randy, the motormack—all were experts at their jobs. Despite my lack of knowledge in these areas, I was their leader and I seemed to have gained their respect. Regardless of how it evolved, I was somehow becoming a qualified leader, and they were meshing as an efficient crew.

I had two more days of unloading liberty ships. This part of my Navy career I was glad to have over. I hope I never again have to look at the 25-foot high bulkhead of a liberty ship. They could now tie up to the repaired docks at the city of Zamboanga. I thought that my assignment to the Army would be over once the cargo ships were empty. Not so; Jim Brady, my Army liaison, was back on board March 28. As before, it was not a social visit. The reason was to give me my next assignment.

I was informed that for four days I would have no duties to perform. At the start of the fifth day, however many of the supplies I had unloaded would be back on board my LCT to be delivered to small towns up the peninsula. The Army had disengaged the enemy, leaving them in the jungles of the interior. This meant that roads between the towns were not secure. These towns had no dock large enough to handle large ships, so LCTs provided an ideal way to supply these army bases.

The date was March 29, 1945. Knowing we had no duties for four days, the crew pretty well had a free reign to go ashore and visit other LCT crews. They also found their way to the Army base to visit with Army enlisted men. At the end of the first day, Frank Sloan was nowhere to be found. I never knew what to expect from him, given his penchant for doing the unusual. I became very concerned as to his whereabouts. It was already about 8:30 in the evening and dark outside when suddenly he drove aboard in a jeep. What a surprise! I asked him where the jeep had come from. He had found it at the Army base, unattended with the keys in the ignition. He said it was as if nobody wanted it. He said the Army had a lot of them, and they would not miss this one.

World War II Jeep

My first thought was to have him return it at once. Then I thought, "Why not wait until morning?" I told him to drive it onto the back of the ship and put a tarp over it. That night in my quarters, I could not get the jeep out of my mind. It sure would be great to have transportation other than our legs. As I lay awake, I was fantasizing about the jeep. I wondered what the Navy punishment was for car theft. All of a sudden, I realized I was an accomplice to the crime — certainly not a happy thought. We could always say we found it abandoned on Manus Island. It was not in running condition; however, my motormack was able to repair it. I had seen a movie once where a man was accused of a crime and there were 13 men in the vicinity. When asked who did it, all 13 hands went up. How could they discipline all of us by throwing us in the brig? They would have no one to sail the ship. I was sure my men would agree to this caper.

As bad as all the negatives were I couldn't resist the major plus of having mobility. By morning, I had made my decision to keep the jeep.

I looked for Frank and told him we were going to take a chance and keep the jeep. The first day, we left it hidden under the tarp. All day I expected some Army officer to come aboard asking if I had seen a jeep anywhere on the beach or on board an LCT. In the evening, we painted out the number. The next day, the tarp became the garage. We removed the jeep from the garage and went for a ride. If stopped, we would claim the jeep had come with us from Manus Island. I figured that if the Army saw me use it, they would figure I was on some type of official duty. After all, we were assigned to the Army. At the end of the day, it went back under the tarp garage and out of sight.

Having transportation at our disposal was great. It was no longer a hassle to procure food and supplies. In fact, it was gratifying to have a jeep just for rides now and then.

The second day of my off duty gave me time to analyze a pressing problem on my LCT. We had no running water. All of the water had to be pumped from a tank below deck. We had to wash our clothes in a container like a dishpan. We had to physically pump the water to be able to take a shower. Other LCTs in our group solved this problem by installing a large circular tank on top of the upper deck. By gravity, water was supplied to the water system. My crew put pressure on me to install the same system.

One of my personality quirks—that I could not stand clutter—made me resist their demands. The tank just looked ugly. Remember Clint, the 38-year-old crew member who had put all the wrong answers on his drafting papers hoping he would not be drafted? He suggested that all we needed was a water pump and an electric motor for a running water system. As far as I was concerned, that was like finding an iceberg in the tropics.

Clint suggested that we go into the bombed out town of Zamboanga. It was just possible that such equipment could be found in a damaged building. It had been only three weeks prior that the town had been devastated by the Navy ships and Army Air Force. This was a long shot but there was a possibility we might find what we needed.

Clint and I removed the tarp from the jeep; it was about to be used for the first time on official business. We proceeded down the beach and onto the road to Zamboanga. I had the uncomfortable feeling that at any time I would hear the siren of the military police telling us to pull over. The officer or the enlisted man responsible for the jeep must have had the whole base looking for it. The fact that I was an officer made me hope that I could get away with the caper—I might be less likely to be stopped.

Driving into town with Clint, I got to know him better. He told me he had been married for 20 years and was very much in love with his wife. They had two children. He sorely missed his wife. They had a good life. He lived in the suburbs of Atlanta with a good job as a rigger. The pay was adequate for a very comfortable existence.

We proceeded into the center of town, never having seen a bombed-out town before. Natives wandered the ravaged streets. They all had the look of devastation on their faces. I was overwhelmed. War is indeed terrible, especially when you know this destruction was caused by our own ships and planes. It is difficult to comprehend.

We went from building to building finding nothing. After two hours of searching, I was about to give up. Suddenly Clint yelled that he had found the pump and the motor. Sure enough, he was carrying the precious equipment needed to do the job.

We proceeded back to the ship, concerned that at any time we would be stopped. The next day with the help of the crew, they assembled the water system. To the delight of the crew, we could take showers and wash clothes without having to pump water. It was also a system that did not interfere with the look of the structure of the ship.

Another irritating problem aboard ship was that we had to wash our clothes in basins of water. One day, I saw Clint next to an oil drum and a piece of sheet metal. I asked him what he was doing and he said, "Making a washing machine." I replied, " Clint, you have to be kidding. There is no way you can do this." I saw him fashion the agitator out of sheet metal then bolt it to the shaft. Somehow, he either stole an electric motor or procured it from Army supply. A couple of days later, I was washing my clothes in a washing machine. He had done the impossible again. Thanks to Clint, we had running water and an electric washing machine.

It was now the evening of the fourth day of no assignments. The next morning I was to start my trip up the Zamboanga peninsula. If past experience was any indication, my new mission, would no doubt offer a whole new set of challenges.

CHAPTER 11
ZAMBOANGA PHASE 2: THE MEETING

The next day, April 2, 1945, one of my crew members told me that Officer Jim Brady was waiting to speak with me. As I stepped onto the ship's deck, I saw the ramp down and two army trucks driving on board, loaded with crates identical to the ones from the Liberty ships.

I invited Jim to my quarters to have a cup of coffee so we could talk. He immediately told me what I was to do with the cargo being loaded onto my ship. Officer Brady pulled out a detailed map of the Zamboanga peninsula and pointed to a town named Sibuko that was 65 miles north. "This is your destination," he said. "You are going to re-supply the Army at this location." I asked him if my LCT was part of a convoy headed to the same town, and much to my surprise, that was not the case. The other LCTs had different towns to supply. Each of us was on his own.

Just like unloading the Liberty ships, this was another assignment I wasn't prepared for. All of my training to date had been directed toward having army men aboard with

123

trucks or tanks poised for an invasion. I was about to embark on a solo mission instead of being part of an LCT flotilla directed by central command.

Not only was I not trained to carry out an individual mission, I did not have much equipment to navigate with. The LCT had a ship-to-shore radio and a magnetic compass, both of which were useless on this type of assignment. The most important thing I was equipped with at this time, was a detailed map of the Zamboanga peninsula. It had landmarks, land elevations, and most importantly, sea depths listed. Running aground was a constant threat, especially on individual missions since there was nobody to come to our aid if something went wrong.

I mustered my crew and gave the command to get underway. After all the trips to and from the Liberty ship, I was no longer as formal with my men. Everyone knew what he had to do in order to get off the beach. The ramp went up, the anchor cable was in, and I hollered orders down the voice tube to start the engines and put the motor in reverse. We drifted out into the bay. With the engine in forward and direction established, I ordered the rudder amid ship and steady as we go. We were on our way, on our first real solo mission, to the town of Sibuko.

We sailed out of the harbor, and once all the ships were out of sight, it seemed lonely out in the Sulu Sea. I stayed close enough to the shore to identify landmarks on the map. This was my only way to ascertain my progress up the peninsula. Most of the time the shore was nothing but rolling hills covered with dense foliage with no sign of inhabitants. This made me paranoid. As a result, I steered my ship far enough away from the shore to feel secure but still be able to identify landmarks just in case the Japanese had artillery installations. I even wondered about the possibility of encountering a Japanese patrol boat. With the speed and weaponry they would have on board, firing on us would be like duck hunting for them. Thoughts like these left me feeling very uncomfortable. But I had to maintain my composure so I blocked them out and turned my mind to enjoying the breezy sunny day.

We continued up the peninsula. Using the landmarks on the map and estimating by our speed the distance traveled, I figured we were close to Sibuko. The magnitude of my situation came over me once again. All major decisions regarding my ship and my crew were my responsibility. At times, I felt very immature, and these decisions weighed heavily on me. I was in the middle of the Sulu Sea looking for a spot on the map I had never seen before. Self-doubt reared its ugly head. I wondered if I had missed the town or would go ashore in the wrong place. I also questioned the odds of the Japanese having retaken Sibuko and the possibility of leading my men into danger. There was no way to communicate with the shore and it was difficult to really know where we were. After many hours at sea, we saw a town finally appear on the horizon. As we approached the shore, I was able to identify a church on a hillside as a landmark on the map. We had found Sibuko. The trip took nine hours.

I beached the craft and saw a couple of army trucks waiting on the shore for us. The sergeant in charge immediately ordered his men to unload the LCT. I invited him onboard, and he told me that his company had secured the perimeter around Sibuko. The Japanese made no effort to attack these defensive locations since they were occupied with Philippine freedom fighters.

When we left Zamboanga, we had been ordered to ship out immediately after the LCT was unloaded and not to mingle with the townspeople since there was no telling how desperate they were for food and supplies. They had been under Japanese control for over three years. Villagers began to converge near my LCT, looking desperate and hungry, and an uneasy feeling came over me when I saw them. I wanted to make a friendly gesture to say hello in some way, but since I didn't know their native tongue, I just smiled and tried to look friendly. The whole atmosphere, being on the shoreline and having the only ship in the vicinity, made me very uncomfortable. All army personnel were now gone, and the townspeople were very close to the LCT while the ramp was down. It suddenly occurred to me that a gang of natives could decide to come aboard and beg for food, putting me in a compromising position. After all, they had been liberated from the enemy for only three weeks.

I learned later that there was another good reason for not lingering on the beach. A large portion of the population living on the Zamboanga peninsula were Moros, a violent sect of the Muslim religion. Their dislike for Americans dates back to the Spanish-American War when the Philippines became a territory of the United States.

We shoved off, and my crew and I were in the open sea alone once again. I wanted to drop anchor until morning but decided to return immediately to Zamboanga instead. As the sun went down and darkness crept in, I realized that I had never sailed this ship at night. All my LCT training had occurred during the day.

Sailing under the bright moon at night was much easier than I expected. With my night binoculars, I had a very good view of the shoreline and I quickly adapted to the night sky. As we traveled on, I noticed cloud cover on our horizon. Visibility suddenly and dramatically decreased, and I was navigating through dense fog. The shoreline disappeared, and I used my magnetic compass to guide the LCT further away from the shore. Despite the fact that the compass could be unreliable, I had no alternative. It was too dangerous for me to keep the coastline in view.

Three of my men stood on the bridge, while I looked out

into the darkness for signs of other ships in the area. Running into another ship was a constant threat in the darkness. Despite the fact that we were in a war zone, I decided to turn on my running lights to avoid a possible collision. There was also a danger of running aground since I could not be certain how far off shore I was. As a precaution, I reduced the engine speed by half; that way, if I did run aground, I would have a better chance of backing off without sustaining damage or becoming stranded. Finally, around two o'clock in the morning, the cloud cover broke and the moon illuminated the sky. It was a welcome relief after spending the last five hours straining my eyes in the darkness. We arrived back at Zamboanga at 5 a.m. After beaching the LCT and securing the engines, I went to my quarters. I was exhausted and laid down in my bunk for a much-needed rest. I am sure the crew did the same.

On April 14, 1945, I had my usual visit with Lieutenant Brady, who said it would be three days before my next mission. The next day I relaxed on the bridge and watched the crew onboard a nearby LCI. Suddenly, I could not believe my eyes. George Lake, one of my best friends from Duquesne University, was walking down the gangplank! I rushed over to meet George, and he seemed equally astonished to see me in Zamboanga. I invited him aboard my LCT, and we reminisced about old times. I asked George how he happened to be in Zamboanga. He said his ship was involved in the invasion. He went on to tell me about the details of his involvement.

On March 6, 1945, at Mandarin Bay Midiron Island in the Phillipines, 166 soldiers and the officers of the Army's 41st infantry division boarded George's ship, LCI 1000. On March 8, along with 30 other LCIs, they joined the task force enroute to Zamboanga, arriving off the landing beaches very early in the morning of March 10. They stood by at the line of departure watching the bombardment of the beaches first by the guns of the cruisers and destroyers in the deeper waters behind them, followed by a plastering of the beaches with bombs from a series of flights by a Marine Corps air group, then rocket barrages by LCIs equipped with rocket launchers. After that, it seemed that nothing could have survived on those beaches.

At 9:15 a.m., the amphibious tractors (Amtraks) went into the beaches in the first few waves. George could see several of the Amtraks burning and disabled victims of mortar shells from Japanese positions in the hills behind the beaches. Some of the LSTs that beached after he did were hit and suffered casualties from the mortars, but George's ship discharged their company of troopers and got out of there quickly. The mortar fire continued on the day after the landing and then stopped after that, presumably because the United States pushed the Japanese back into the hills and out of range. On March 14, things had quieted down enough for George to dock safely at the Zamboanga city docks.

When I learned of the harrowing accounts of the invasion of Zamboanga, I was glad we had missed it. After describing the detail of the invasion of Zamboanga, George told me the most amazing news of all.

It just so happened that two of our other Duquesne classmates were in the area: Jerry Unites and Jim Egler. Jerry was on an attack transport at the pier, and Jim was stationed with the Army Air Corps. What a shock it was to find out that three of my friends were in the same area of the Pacific as I was. The last thing I expected was to run into one of my classmates, let alone three of them together thousands of miles away from our hometown. George suggested that we all meet on his LCI the next night.

George Lake (center) on the LCI he served on

That afternoon I needed fuel and water for my ship. I went to the fuel dock, secured the LCT to pilings, and walked to a small building at the end of the pier. I went inside to meet with the army sergeant in charge of refueling. To my amazement, it was John Russell, another friend from Duquesne.

The two of us could not believe we were meeting under these circumstances. The last John knew was that I had entered the Naval Air Corps, and here he was refueling my LCT. He laughed to learn I had gone from the Air Corps to commanding one of the slowest ships in the United States Navy.

John and I began talking. I told him about George Lake, Jerry Unites, and Jim Egler being in the area as well. He told me he thought I was having a crazy dream or hallucinations of some sort because it was impossible to run into four men, all in different branches of the service, thousands of miles away from Pittsburgh. I told him it was true, and we continued to exchange stories for a couple of hours. We talked about the war and how the five of us had made our separate ways to Zamboanga. I told him about George's plan for us to meet on the LCI the next night. John was concerned that he might not be able to make it since he wasn't an officer. Depending on how strict the captain of the LCI was, he might not be permitted into the officers' quarters on the ship. I told him not to worry; I would take care of the problem. I informed him about one of my crewmen stealing a jeep from the Army, and I said I'd pick him up at four unless he was squeamish about riding in a stolen jeep.

I left the refueling station and headed back to my ship. Along the way, I thought about what my friends and I had been doing when the war broke out. Most of us had looked for training where we could become officers—except for John. He did not pursue officer training as the rest of us did. I can remember him saying he was waiting to be drafted. In a short period, he was called up and assigned to the Army, where he became involved with fuel supply and now had a high enlisted man's ranking of Master Sergeant. The next day, I picked John up as planned, and we went back to my LCT. I took him to my quarters, opened up my desk drawer, and took out two gold bars. I pinned them on John and said, "I have upped your rank. You are now an ensign in the United States Navy."

John and I left my ship and walked up to the LCI. We were escorted to the officers' quarters, where Jerry, Jim, and George waited for us. It is hard to describe the elation I felt meeting four close friends from our Alma Mater. Much to

130

my surprise, there were two bottles of whiskey waiting for us, so we all began to do some serious drinking. We talked about our service experiences for hours.

George had the most interesting story among us by far, not that the other men had not had some harrowing experiences in their various lines of duty. Here is the story as told by George; he took us back in time to early May 1944.

"After graduating from Midshipman's school, I had a week's leave in Pittsburgh while I was en route to pick up my LCI in New York. One day I took a trolley over to Oakland. As I walked through the town, I became aware of a lot of commotion. There were crowds gathering and bands playing in Schenley Park. I went over there to find out what was happening and saw a grandstand with the mayor, military personnel, and other dignitaries celebrating the upcoming launch of an LST built by the Dravo Corporation in Pittsburgh. The ship, named The City of Pittsburgh, had been financed by War Bonds subscriptions from citizens of Allegheny County. The speakers on the grandstand included the skipper of the new LST and a navy lieutenant. Both said a few words and thanked the people for giving them this ship and promised to use it to fight the enemy. My time in Pittsburgh ended, and I eventually made my way to New York, forgetting all about the incident at Schenley Park.

"About seven months later, in late December 1944, I was aboard my LCI in a convoy from Leyte Gulf to Mindoro. During the entire three-day trip, we were under constant air attack from the Japanese. They used kamikaze pilots, conventional bombs, and torpedoes to sink many of our ships. During the middle of the second night with the convoy under attack, anti-aircraft guns erupted and the sparks from the tracers filled the sky. We came upon an LST, which had been hit with an aerial torpedo and was burning and listing badly. Her crew was jumping overboard and clinging to the stern propeller housing; our skipper, a gutsy guy, shouted 'Let's save these guys,' and he pulled our ship alongside the LST and rescued many of her survivors. During the rescue, I was on the fantail deck with the radioman. He was a powerful kid and joined me in tossing lines to the men clinging to the stern propeller housing, which was protruding above the water's surface, and then hauling them onto our deck. After many were rescued, I went to the bridge to report to my skipper who was with the LST captain. As we were pulling away, the LST skipper leaned against the railing, looked upon the sinking ship, and said ruefully, 'There goes The City of Pittsburgh.' It turned out that he was the one I had seen on the grandstand during the ceremony at Schenley Park, and of course I told him so. I remember thinking that except for him, I was the only one in the crowd at Schenley Park who was destined to see the end of The City of Pittsburgh.

"The heroics of my captain were not over. He skillfully accomplished a very difficult maneuver and tied up to an LCI that had a doctor and a medic onboard. It is difficult enough to guide an LCI into a stationary dock, but to tie up to a moving ship is next to impossible. The captain managed to get next to the LCI, and after securing lines between our two crafts, the wounded men from the LCI were transported to the other ship. All this was accomplished while we were part of a convoy under Japanese attack. Despite the loss of many men from the LST, we did feel very good about saving the lives of a portion of the crew that would otherwise have perished.

"Our skipper did a hell of a job on that caper; he should have been given a medal. Anyway, I will never forget this experience."

The party broke up around two in the morning, and I drove John back to the army base. Driving back, I realized I had left my hat on the LCI, so I went to pick it up. Without thinking about their security, I walked right onboard the ship and retrieved it. The next day George told me I was lucky someone on night watch had not shot me while I walked onto the ship. I had no such formalities on my LCT.

After getting my hat, I headed back to the LCT. To my surprise, the tide had come in while I was gone. I stopped to look at the water separating me on the beach from the deck of the LCT. In my inebriated condition, the water did not look deep to me. I put the jeep in gear, pushed the pedal to the floor, and splashed right into the water where I quickly came to a dead stop. With water up to my waist and the jeep stuck, there was no moving it without the help of my crew. It was quite embarrassing for me to have my men see a drunken skipper stagger aboard, leaving a disabled jeep in the water. The men salvaged the jeep, and the next day the motormack had extra duty getting it running again.

I continued to take orders from the Army and made many trips up and down the Zamboanga peninsula with supplies. All of them went according to plan until April 25, 1945. On that day, a platoon of Army men came aboard. I was to transport them to Siracon, a town 75 miles up the peninsula.

My accommodations for the men were not exactly first class; I don't believe even third class could describe the travel conditions. The Army men were on a flat metal deck that was 30 feet wide and had four foot railings on each side. Keep in mind: Zamboanga is only ten degrees above the equator; it has an intensely hot climate. The temperature that day was 98 degrees. Imagine how hot the metal on the deck and railing became. There was a section at the rear of the LCT covered with canvas. It was not much help to stay cool, but it was better than being on the open deck. The lieutenant in charge spent some time in my quarters, but a good part was spent on the bridge with me. He related to me the various invasions he was involved with on New Guinea. He was a seasoned veteran who had seen his share of men die in combat. Three of them were his close friends.

We continued up the coast, baking in the hot sun; the day finally started to cool when the sun set. Rain began to fall, but I did not think it was much to worry about. I figured the sea would get rough, but I could still proceed along at near normal speed. Suddenly, all hell broke loose. Huge bolts of lightening flashed across the sea, illuminating the night sky, and the rain poured down harder. We were in the middle of a tropical storm. A powerful gust of wind came up in the direction of the shore and threw me off course; I could not maintain my position because of the turbulent air and thrashing waves. I was concerned that we would be washed ashore. As I have said, the LCT didn't have a keel like most ships. It is just a big flat-bottomed landing craft and behaved like a metal sail in a strong wind. The wind was gusting at least 60 miles an hour, creating enormous waves. I had no training for a predicament like this. Huge waves 20 feet high were hitting the bow. One second I was on top of the wave, while the next, I was in the trough and nothing but a wall of water surrounded me. The LCT spun in circles on the water; it was completely out of control. I had no idea what direction the ship was headed. The only way I felt I could avoid being washed ashore was by heading into the wind. I thought if I sailed into it as much as possible, I could maintain some sort of course and escape running aground.

The Army lieutenant stayed on the bridge with me; he appeared very nervous and asked if I had been through these conditions before. I told him that I had and not to worry, the LCT was a solid craft, and there was no doubt in my mind that she could weather this storm. I kept the truth from him because it would not have helped matters any, but I sure had my doubts that the nuts and bolts holding her together would stay that way. I could barely see through the pouring rain. There was minimal visibility and it was pitch dark. Water gushed onto the deck and crashed against the bridge. The lieutenant and I hung on to the railing so we wouldn't be washed overboard.

Had I given in to my crew and installed a water tank on top of the LCT instead of an electric pump system, the storm would surely have brought it crashing down, putting my crew and the Army men in danger. The lieutenant continued to hold on. He was seasick, and so was everyone else aboard. I was too involved with controlling the ship to cave in to any squeamish feelings, so I continued to maneuver the craft.

After an hour of pounding rain and gale force winds, the storm abruptly stopped. Those 60 minutes in the tropical storm seemed like an eternity. No personnel were washed overboard. My crew and the Army men were all accounted for, and we proceeded to Siracon. I beached the craft, let off the platoon, and headed back to Zamboanga. Just another day in the life of a sailor.

In May of 1945, I had a big surprise. An ensign named Cliff Seare reported to my LCT. I now had an executive officer to help me command my ship. Cliff was a very likable gentleman. I was glad to have him aboard, and in a short period, we became at ease with each other. Before the ensign arrived, I had been very careful to maintain the fine line of always being the officer in charge. Consequently, I never felt totally at ease to discuss all subjects relating to running the ship. I feared it would be a sign of weakness. With Cliff, I had an opportunity to talk about the ship as well as personal matters like how I missed my wife, my family, and my friends back home, and he did the same with me.

Around the same time Cliff came aboard, I received a document from Navy headquarters. Much to my surprise, it was a promotion to Lieutenant J.G. I never knew if the reason for my promotion was to make clear that Cliff and I did not have dual leadership of the LCT. Now, there was no question. I was the captain and Cliff was my executive officer. It was nice to know that the Navy remembered I existed after I'd been part of the Army for so long.

Once I had an executive officer, I was able to leave the LCT for longer periods of time, knowing Cliff would be in command. This was a welcome relief from the pressures of being the only officer on board and this gave me the opportunity to do something I had wanted to do for a long time. My short time in the Naval Air Corps had left me with a strong desire to be involved with flying. The army air base was a short 15 miles away, and I decided that I would visit it as soon as I got the chance.

CHAPTER 12
ZAMBOANGA PHASE THREE: THE SULTAN

One particular day, I did not have an assignment, so I spent my time sitting on the bridge of the LCT. Planes were flying overhead, and I felt an urgency to visit the airbase. That evening I met with Clint and asked him to drive me to the airport the following day. He said it would be a welcome change from his usual routine aboard ship.

The next morning I left Cliff in charge and Clint drove me to the airbase. Upon arriving, I saw all types of aircraft, including fighter planes, bombers, and cargo planes. This was the first time since I joined the service that I had been this close to so many types of aircraft. I walked up to a serviceman and asked him what the name of the slick-looking fighter plane was. He seemed surprised that I did not know. He told me it was the famous P-51 Mustang. The P-51 Mustang was the fastest, most formidable aircraft in the United States' arsenal. I was surprised that I hadn't heard of the Mustang before, but after all, how would I? I was on an LCT and had no access to the news. It was an overwhelming experience for me to view all the planes and activity on the base.

My eyes were drawn to a twin engine DC-3 parked with a pilot standing next to it. The DC-3 was the first commercial passenger plane built with a pressurized cabin. I said hello to the pilot, introduced myself to him, and asked about his duties on the base. His name was Tony Martinelli, and he explained that his aircraft carried supplies and sometimes Navy personnel to various cities on the island of Mindanao. I told him that he was doing pretty much the same thing I did aboard my LCT; the only difference was that he made his deliveries by air. I told him about starting my career in the Naval Air Corps.

Tony told me he had a short trip to make to Dipolog. "It only takes four hours for the round trip including unloading the items I have on board. I have been waiting for my co-pilot, and he's thirty minutes late. Why don't you come with me?" he asked. "I would like to get up and back as soon as possible."

I asked him if he was kidding. The only training I had had was in a Piper Cub. He told me it did not matter; he would be doing all the flying. I told Clint to hang around the airport and guard the jeep; I would be back in five hours.

This was another one of my impulsive decisions that could get me into big trouble, but I was going anyway. I climbed on board, and down the runway we went. Sitting behind the co-pilot's wheel, I thought to myself, "What am I doing here?" Once airborne, Tony did some very strange flying. Instead of climbing to a safe elevation, he was flying in the valleys between the mountains. I asked him why, and he said it was more exciting that way. I informed him it was not my idea of fun; he just smiled and continued on his way—with me looking at the sides of mountains.

We arrived at Dipolog, and the cargo from the airplane was quickly unloaded. Tony seemed to be in some big hurry, which was all right with me. On the way back, we climbed to a safe elevation, which was a relief. If he had been trying to scare me on the trip there, he had done a good job.

We landed safely back at Zamboanga. It definitely had been an exciting experience, but I was glad to be back on terra firma. I thanked Tony for the trip and went to meet Clint who was manning the jeep. Upon my return, he said that being at the airbase had been a pleasant change from the usual. He had spent the day talking to the other men at the base and watching the planes fly in and out. We both agreed our trip had been a worthwhile experience.

On my next run up the peninsula, there was a very unfortunate occurrence. The ship's three engines were running at normal rpm's, but suddenly the engine did not sound normal. I looked out the stern and noticed that only two of the motors were working. I contacted Randy, the motormack, and asked him what the problem was. He said he did not have a clue. Back on the beach, he inspected the engine and reported that the pistons were frozen; the only solution was to replace the entire engine block. The next day, for the first time, I looked for Navy headquarters to report my predicament.

Up to this time, the army had supplied all our needs, but I was sure engines for LCTs would be available at the Navy depot. I found the headquarters, asked to see the officer in charge of procurement, and requested a new engine. I had no doubt that this would be no big deal; all small landing craft used the same type of engine. Surely, a base this large would have spare engines, but I found out that nothing was available. The procurement officer told me he would see what he could do and if he located one, he would let me know. This might turn out to be a break for me and my crew. They might have to repair the LCT in a dry dock, and we would have maybe a week of liberty just to relax. Days passed without a word about the engine. After a week, I revisited the procurement office and there was still no encouraging news.

Having a broken engine created several problems. First, my top speed was now eight knots versus ten, and my cruising speed decreased to six. It would have been much easier to control the ship with the center motor disabled. It was very difficult to dock with no starboard engine. In addition, I feared another motor would break, leaving us with only one engine. There was no way this massive LCT would make any headway at all with only one motor.

I was reasonably certain I could make some progress with one engine in still water but the ocean is not always calm. The tides create water movements, and every ocean in the world has currents you cannot see until a ship reacts to them; at any time a strong wind could take the ship out of control.

After a month, I gave up and realized I might never receive a replacement motor. I tried to convince the Army the ship was not seaworthy for any more trips. They simply said it would take a little longer, but I would get there just the same. In the service, you have no options. Orders are orders and you carry them out as well as you can.

After several trips with my executive officer at the controls, I saw no need for both of us to be on the bridge at the same time. I decided to sleep in for once, so I told Cliff to take the ship out the following day so I could get some rest. The next morning, I was lying in my bunk and heard the engines starting. I could tell the anchor was up, and I sensed the ship getting underway. I felt very relaxed; this was the first time I did not have to be on the bridge giving orders. A loud crashing noise suddenly interrupted my relaxed mood. The engines stopped and the ship quit moving. I rushed out on deck to see what had happened.

The bay we beached in had only one outlet; however, there was a short cut directly out to sea at high tide. It turned out that Cliff had decided to take the short cut, but it was not high tide, and he had crashed onto a reef. The LCT was taking on water, and I could feel it listing slightly. In the hopes we would break free of the reef before taking on any more water, I gave the order to reverse the engine full throttle, and I managed to get off it. We proceeded on our daily mission with the LCT leaning slightly to one side. LCT's are made of many waterproof bulkheads, so the listing was not very severe. I managed to get us back to our spot on the beach with the help of Clint and Randy, the motormacks. We found a way to take water on the other side of the LCT to bring it to a level position.

Cliff felt very depressed about his mistake, but I assured him it could have happened to me, and he should not worry about it. It would have been foolish to handle it any other way since we had many more months together. I realized he was second in command, and he had to maintain the respect of the crew as well. Any unnecessary censure on my part would have been self-defeating.

On May 2, 1945, a very exciting event unfolded. The Army informed me it did not need my LCT for the next couple of days. Two days prior, I had met an English-speaking native on the beach. Along with the various topics we talked about, he told me about a sultan whose home was on Basilan Island, 20 miles off the coast of Zamboanga.

The native told me the sultan was the leader of all the Moros who live in this part of the Philippines. Many of these people live in various parts of the Zamboanga peninsula, Basilan Island, and the Sulu Archipelago. (The Sulu Archipelago is a series of many islands extending 320 miles to the northern tip of Borneo.) The Moros are Muslims, and those peoples exist almost as a separate nation. The Philippines is a country that was a territory of the United States before the war, and now that the liberated parts of the Philippines were under U.S. control, this section was once

141

again a mandate of our country. Even before the war, these natives were very difficult to control.

I became excited about an idea that was germinating in my mind. Why not take the LCT on the short trip to Basilan Island and visit the sultan? I could not wait to tell Cliff about my great idea. I said, "Cliff, I am about to tell you about the great plans I have for tomorrow. You and I will have an experience that we will remember for a lifetime. We are going to Basilan Island to visit the Sultan of Jolo, the leader of all the Moro people in this part of the Philippines."

Cliff said, "Skipper, you must be nuts moving a Naval vessel without getting permission from some Naval authority." He said, "You can count me out; I am not going."

I pleaded with him, "What's the big deal? The Army said we have no job for tomorrow. If they see the LCT missing, they will figure the Navy may have had some use for the LCT. Why would the Navy be concerned now if I have not heard from them since I arrived at Zamboanga? If the Army and Navy both wonder where I am, they will assume I have gone to the fuel dock. They would never think I would be foolish enough to go anywhere without official orders from either the Army or Navy."

My pleading was to no avail, and we bedded down for the night with him saying, "I'm not going."

The next morning I was up at 8 a.m., and I proceeded to get underway with Cliff still saying he was not going. As I prepared to lift the ramp, he was standing on the beach. All of a sudden, he ran onto the deck, and we were on our way. En route, he never stopped saying, "You fool. You can't do this." He said the only reason he had hopped on board was to talk me out of going. Cliff reminded me that the Moros are savage people. It was hard for me to believe they would have any malice towards us since the United States had just liberated them from the Japanese. He said, "I am trying to save your ass. You could lose your command and rank as an officer." He knew how proud I was of having my own command and thought the fear of losing it would stop me from going to the island. Not so. I was determined to find the sultan.

I sailed to Basilan Island, beached the craft, and told the crew to stay within 100 yards of the ship. None of the crew knew why we were there. I sat in the jeep and invited Cliff to come along. He probably said to himself, "Maybe I can keep him from getting into more trouble by going along. After all, he is my superior officer, and I have the responsibility of staying with him."

Once on land, we proceeded into the small village near the shore trying to find someone who spoke English. As luck would have it, after about three tries, we located an English-speaking native. I asked him where the sultan lived and he said, "Go up that dirt road and you can't go wrong. Approximately 25 miles inland, you will find a very large thatched building. That is the location of the Sultan of Jolo."

I put the jeep in gear and we were on our way. I have to admit, I began to think Cliff was right. Why was I doing this? The road cut through a dense jungle adding to the suspense of the ride up the mountain. The 50-minute ride seemed like three hours. Neither he nor I said very much on our way up.

Suddenly, the huge building appeared. There were many small huts around it. Several natives were milling around, and none of them looked very friendly. In fact, they looked at us as much as to say, "What in the devil are they doing here?" They probably were not used to seeing two officers this far into the interior of the island. I parked the jeep and proceeded into the large building. In the center of the far wall was the Sultan. His clothes were very colorful and not of Western-style. Twelve native women dressed in similar attire sat around him. It was like a scene out of a movie. I began to feel very uneasy in the surroundings.

One of the natives approached us, and in broken English that was hard to understand asked me what the reason was for our visit. Befuddled by his question and before I could come up with an answer, he went over and spoke to the sultan in their native tongue. Now turning in our direction the interpreter shouted, "What is your proposition?"

His tone of voice made me feel very uneasy and fearful as to what would happen next. I knew I had to come up with some kind of reply, so I said, "I brought your leader a carton of cigarettes." Grabbing them from my hand, he gave them to the sultan.

There was not one smile or any sign that we were welcome. The interpreter said something that sounded more like a grunt than a word and pointed to the entrance. He followed us on the way out and pointed to a podium in the center of the room. He indicated for me to sign my name. Looking at the signatures, I saw General Douglas McArthur and Admiral Nimitz. My guess was he wanted to impress me with the importance of the sultan, who had such high-ranking individuals of the U.S. Government calling on him. I had no camera to prove it, but Cliff and I entered our names on the same page as McArthur and Nimitz.

Now I sensed why we were not welcome. My single silver bars and Cliff's single gold bars indicating our rank were not very impressive to the sultan. We proceeded out into our jeep and were about to leave when the interpreter ran out and asked if it was okay if the sultan's brother rode into town with us. The sultan's brother was standing next to the interpreter, and I indicated that he get into the back seat. He did so holding his rifle. About a mile down the road, I heard him cock the gun. I poked Cliff in the rib, stopped the jeep, and said, "Get into the back seat and cock your pistol." I proceeded down the winding dirt road. A few miles later, I heard the native uncock his rifle and Cliff uncocked his revolver. I will never be sure, but maybe the sultan had taken a liking to our jeep.

He probably had said to himself, "Who would care if these two idiots were missing in action? When McArthur and Nimitz came up to see me, they came with a small army."

When we returned to the village, many of the townspeople were very close, almost surrounding us. I could not see one happy, smiling face, and I was glad to get back on board the LCT. When the ramp was up, we were on our way. I said to Cliff, "Maybe you were right. It wasn't such a good idea to come to see the sultan."

I became concerned about whether any officers from the Army or Navy had noticed us missing. It seemed like it took a long time getting back to the beach, and I anticipated the worst. We arrived back on the shore. Apparently, no one knew where we had been, but this did not mean I had gotten away with this caper. I might get a visit the next day from the Army or Navy asking where I had gone. Days passed and I felt relieved that no one had caught us. This is one experience that I will never forget.

After the war, as I write this book, I realize how fortunate we were to get off the island alive. The Moros have hated foreigners for centuries, dating back 300 years from the time of the Crusades. The Spanish tried but could not conquer them. When the Americans took over after the Spanish-American War, they were a very difficult people for the U.S. to control.

Historically, the sidearm for the United States Army up to that time was a .38 revolver; however, it was not powerful enough to subdue the natives, who attacked with their swords. Because of this, the .45 caliber revolver was the new issue to United States troops, the same sidearm I wore in the U.S. Navy. As recently as June 2002, the United States has sent troops to the Philippines to train their soldiers to defeat a faction of the Moro people believed to be part of the Al Qaeda network.

The morning after our adventure, much to my surprise, I awoke to the sound of a dog barking. I walked out on the deck and saw Larry holding a dog—a very small, sickly-looking pup. Upon seeing him, I was taken back to being a small boy. He was almost identical to our family dog. Of course, I asked Larry, "Where did he come from?"

He said, "While we were on the Island, the dog just happened to wander aboard. As you can see, he looked like he was badly in need of a good meal. Well, we can't very well take him back to Basilan Island, so he will have to stay on board."

I asked Larry, "Did you give him a name?" He said not yet, and I suggested Pal, the same name as the dog I had when I was a youngster. Therefore, on this day we had a new member of the crew, a dog we named Pal.

It was strange how much a little dog helped keep up the morale of the crew. Having a dog was a lot better than what they had on LCT-805. They had a monkey. It was a very difficult pet to control, and he constantly crawled all over the men. As a result, the crew put the monkey on liberty at one of their beachings, and he did not return to the ship before they got underway. The Captain of the LCT-807 had his own private pet as well. He took on board a female native as a mistress. I wondered how he managed to control the morale of his crew.

Obviously, this group of six LCTs was a very loose operation. Navy regulations almost ceased to exist. As long as we did our thing for the Army, no one seemed to care how we ran our ships.

On my craft, we had rules of behavior, not as strict as the regular Navy, but strict enough to maintain order. We would have breakfast and lunch at no particular hour, but we had dinner at about the same time every day. I would always say a prayer before dinner. We would eat together, and everyone had to have a shirt on. Painting the ship was an ongoing task that was never finished, so the ship did have a neat appearance. That was not the case on some of the other LCTs. Some were a mess. I also would not tolerate things lying around. All equipment and personal gear had to be in its proper place.

One thing about the war and being in the Navy was that one never knew what the next day would bring. My Army career was about to end. I was again to become part of the Navy, and I was off to a new assignment.

CHAPTER 13
BORNEO

It seemed strange that Jim Brady didn't make his usual visit to give me my next assignment. Four days had passed without word from the Army. "Here we go again, I thought," and wondered what the Army had in store for me next. There was one constant with being under the command of the Army: I never knew what they might have me do. But it certainly was odd that so many days passed without new orders from them.

After waiting for two more days, I still had not heard from Officer Brady. As I was standing on the deck of my LCT, I saw a naval officer walking aboard. This came as a huge surprise to me since I had not had any communication with the Navy since arriving at Zamboanga. The officer walked up to me, and I noticed immediately that he was a lieutenant commander. We saluted each other in the traditional manner and sat down in my quarters to discuss business. Cliff joined us there, and the three of us had coffee. The lieutenant commander appeared to be in his 50s and looked like a career Naval officer. He was casually dressed like I was and wore no ribbons on his uniform.

Although his attire was plain, there was no doubting this man had seen a lot of action during his service in the Navy.

Considering the lieutenant commander's high rank, I figured there had to be a very important reason he came aboard my ship. My first thought was that my LCT was to be part of an invasion force since I didn't know if all of Mindanao Island was secure. In a short period of time, the lieutenant commander told me precisely what my mission would be. He handed me a map of the Sulu archipelago and pointed to Darrel Bay, which was near the huge island of Borneo. There I was to rendezvous with a seaplane tender. The bay was across from the last island of the archipelago. The lieutenant told me that sections of northern Borneo were still under Japanese occupation, but the area I was to sail through was allegedly secure.

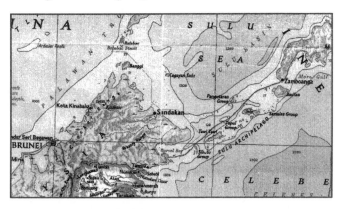

My Route to Borneo from Zamboanga to Darvel Bay

I asked the lieutenant commander how I would know which section of Darrel Bay the sea tender would be in. He pointed to the southern portion of the map where many islands were located. At the very tip of the land extension was a very small island where the tender was anchored between the island and nearby shore. From above, the tender was masked by dense foliage and vegetation, but from the water, it should not be hard for me to find it. Cliff suddenly looked very confused, and I am sure I did too after hearing what the navy expected us to do next.

I was very concerned about the task, so I asked the lieutenant how I could navigate to a place more than 350 miles from here with just a magnetic compass. He told me I should have no trouble if I used the islands in the archipelago as landmarks. That's easy for him, I thought; he isn't the one who has to carry out this assignment. I sat in front of him in a state of shock. How could he or anyone in the Navy expect me to successfully carry out such a mission? It also quickly occurred to me that I was responsible for 13 other lives aboard my ship. Despite this concern, there was no way I could refuse his orders. I had to do what the military commanded me to do regardless of whether or not I agreed with them.

Had I not been so shocked at the mission I was ordered to do, I would have told the lieutenant that my LCT had only two of its three engines working. I wasn't thinking clearly at the time. I was too overwhelmed with his high rank and his confidence in my ability to accomplish such a difficult mission. My newest assignment would be the longest solo run I had ever made. When it was over, I would have logged more than 700 miles round trip. I was ordered to report to the dock immediately to load up with barrels of fuel to deliver to the seaplane tender.

Before the lieutenant commander left, he warned me that under no circumstances was I to stop off at any of the islands en route to the tender. He told me that one place in particular, Jolo, was especially dangerous because it had a heavy concentration of Moros. I wondered what the big deal was and why I should be concerned about the Moros. After all, the United States had just liberated them from Japanese occupation so, as I said before, I figured they were friendly to Americans. That was not the case though. Apparently, after the Spanish American War, the Philippines had become a territory of the United States, and we had tried to subjugate the Moros to no avail. Their disdain for Americans stems from our controlling their land. During World War II, the Moros often gave the United States inaccurate intelligence information that led our troops straight into enemy traps.

As soon as the lieutenant commander left the ship, we set sail for the fuel dock. There, a group of seamen loaded the LCT with drums of fuel and oil for the seaplane tender, and I took three extra drums of diesel fuel for our ship. I was glad I remembered the range of a fully fueled LCT—350 miles. The actual mileage to the seaplane tender was 350 miles, assuming I had no difficulty finding the ship. Without the added fuel, it was almost a certainty that I would have run out.

We were almost ready to shove off on our mission when my old friend John Russell came over to talk to me. I told him where we were headed and with astonishment he asked, "What does a seaplane tender have to do with an LCT?" I told him I had to deliver fuel and oil to it. John shook his head in disbelief; he couldn't believe my LCT had to travel so far. We said goodbye to each other, and I could tell he was concerned for my safety. He probably thought he would never see me again after I left the dock.

I tried to analyze the mission to Borneo and decided the whole thing was crazy. An LCT was surely the wrong type of ship to carry out this job. There had to be some better-suited craft for this mission. A small Navy cargo ship with a keel and a cruising speed of 13 knots could easily accomplish such a job. There was not much I could do at this stage of the game but cast off and go on my way. By the time we set sail for the seaplane tender, it was 4 p.m. Fortunately, the weather was pleasant. It was about 90 degrees with a gentle breeze and a few clouds in the sky. The trip down the archipelago turned into a photographer's dream. We passed one island after another. I studied the details of the map in hopes of successfully navigating our way to the tender. It was a very detailed map. There were many landmarks indicated, and the mileage between the islands was listed as well. By analyzing the time it took me to travel from one island to another, I was able to estimate our mileage per hour, which in turn confirmed our position in the archipelago. Since my ship was again traveling alone in a war zone, I was acutely aware of the many dangers we could encounter. For this reason, it took total concentration on my part not to err regarding our location on the map. The most pressing danger was simply being lost and navigating into a Japanese-controlled area.

I sat on the bridge and relaxed somewhat, listening to the hum of the engines. Looking out over the stern of the ship and watching the wake created by the propellers mesmerized me. I kept thinking about the beautiful wife I had left behind, and I missed her terribly, so I went to my quarters to read some letters Winnie had sent me. It was comforting to read them; she always wrote how much she loved and missed me.

Winnie and I had been married for almost a year by now. We had a chance to spend weekends together for only five months before I had been shipped out. I wondered what she was doing now and if she regretted marrying me. It had to be hard for her back home, constantly worrying whether or not I would make it home alive and in one piece. One thing is certain, I was totally in love with Winnie and very happy that we were married. I hoped she felt the same about me. I couldn't get too caught up in these thoughts though; I had a mission to carry out. I had to find our way down the Sulu archipelago.

Navigating down the archipelago during the day was a lot

easier than I expected. Identifying the landmarks was not extremely difficult in daylight, but I was concerned about how I would do at night. I hoped there would be no severe weather conditions that would blow me off course or obscure my vision of the islands. I was glad Cliff was on board to assist me. Because I had an executive officer, I was able to take a nap now and then. Once nightfall came, the moon lit up the sky so clearly it was easy to identify the landmarks on the map. We sailed past the island of Jolo around eight in the evening. The direction we needed to head seemed to be southwest, but as I traveled toward my destination, I was unable to navigate in that direction for very long. The archipelago consisted of three main islands (Basilan, Jolo, and Tawi Tawi) and many smaller islands in between. On this mission, I was zigzagging around the small islands to avoid running aground while I constantly checked the map for the water depths. As a result of not traveling on a direct route, my estimated time of arrival at the seaplane tender was getting later and later.

Around seven the following morning, I passed the last major island on the map. From there, I figured it would take at least ten more hours before we would reach Darrel Bay. This meant we wouldn't arrive until five in the afternoon. If I could find the tender as soon as we reached the bay, it would still be daylight, and that would make the rest of our mission easier. I became very concerned about my arrival time. What would I do if I couldn't find the ship's location while it was still light? The sun was setting, and my chance of finding the tender in the daylight seemed hopeless. The last small group of islands I could identify on the map was the Subutu group. From there, Darrel Bay was across 50 miles of open water. Because of this, only the magnetic compass could help me find my way. There were no landmarks, just open sea.

The last 50 miles took longer than I expected. There was

no land in sight, and I had no idea how much headway I was making. If I missed the southern portion of the outer land mass of the bay, I could have hundreds of miles of open water with no idea who would be in control of the first village or city I encountered. I kept hoping that it was taking so long to get to the bay because some strong current was holding up my progress. Finally, I spotted land. It was 7 p.m. and dark because of the cloud cover. I discussed the situation with Cliff and decided not to beach the LCT. Beaching presented a risk, since I didn't know if the natives in this part of Borneo were friendly. The water near the beach could also have mines in it. After all, it was a war zone.

If the water was too deep, it might not be possible to drop the anchor since I had a limited amount of cable. I ordered Walt to drop anchor, and I heard the cable release from the drum. Finally, the cable became slack, meaning we had hit the bottom of the bay. A gentle breeze moved the ship forward, and much to my relief, we were finally standing still in the water.

I posted a two-man watch for the night because I had no idea what surrounded us. Some natives in this part of Borneo could decide to come out from the shore and become a nuisance to us. I also heeded the lieutenant commander's warning. He said the northern part of the island was under Japanese occupation. The seaplane tender was supposedly in a safe area, but I had no idea if I was even close to the ship. The crew settled in for the night, and Cliff and I went to our quarters.

Cliff and I talked about the mission before bedding down. I asked him what he thought our options were if we couldn't find the tender. He had no response, just a blank look on his face. This did not put me at ease. The only thing I was sure of was that we were off the coast of Borneo. It would be hard to miss that island considering it is nearly half the size of Alaska, but finding the tender was a different story.

I climbed into my bed and tried to fall asleep without much success. My mind wandered and worried over many things. Here I was, anchored off the shore of Borneo. No other ships were in sight. All of my decisions meant life or death for us. The last 50 miles of our journey had no landmarks, just open sea. Depending on the magnetic compass to stay on course was iffy since they are notoriously unreliable. If I went off course just a few degrees, I could miss Darrel Bay completely. And I was more than 350 miles from Zamboanga.

As the war progressed, Admiral Nimitz island-hopped from the Guadalcanal to Guam, then on to Saipan, and finally to Peleliu in preparation for a major assault on the Philippines. While this was happening, MacArthur was fighting the Japanese in New Guinea. This also positioned him for an attack on the Philippines. I kept thinking that these two men sacrificed more soldiers than were necessary because their egos pushed them to achieve quick victories. It was almost as if men were nothing more than an extension of the machines and guns they operated. Life to them was not very important. Winning their next objective in search of their final victory was all that mattered. That philosophy seemed to pass to the officers under their command. The lieutenant commander who sent me on this mission did not seem to care about our safety. He was concerned about getting the cargo delivered to the tender, regardless of the risk involved. He could have investigated other crafts in the area, but his only thoughts were to do it now.

I ordered the night watch to wake me at sunrise because I wanted to get underway as soon as possible. It would probably take us most of the day to find the tender, if I could locate it at all. The next morning, I studied the map carefully, looking for landmarks, elevation, and beach contours that would verify my position near Borneo. After several minutes, I still had no idea where we were on the map. Every part of the shoreline looked the same—rolling hills covered with dense foliage. I decided to head north and stay close to shore. After we sailed for nearly an hour, some islands close to the shore looked similar to the ones on the map. They almost touched the mainland. According to the map, I was about a half mile away from where I hoped the tender was located. Could this be true? It seemed like forever before I arrived at the part of the island near the shore. It must have been less than 50 yards when, sure enough, almost hidden by the trees was the tender. I can't explain how relieved I was to see this beautiful ship.

We were all elated when we saw it. It was as if we had achieved the impossible. The crew let out a loud cheer, and I even heard one of them yell, "Great job, Skipper." A sea plane tender seems small sitting next to a cruiser or battleship, but there are no words to describe how miniscule my LCT looked next to the tender. I put fenders over the side of the LCT, and we eased up next to the tender. Our hawsers were pulled up through the chocks and attached to the bits on the ship's deck. We were now motionless at the tenders' side, and the men on deck dropped a rope ladder down to us. Cliff and I climbed aboard immediately.

World War II Sea Plane Tender

The officer waiting for us on the deck greeted us and informed us the captain wanted to meet with us in his quarters. I could tell they were part of the "real Navy" by the formal way we were greeted. The tender looked like it had just rolled out of the shipyard. The deck and superstructure were immaculately clean. In fact, it looked freshly painted.

We met with the captain in his quarters and saluted each other. He invited us to sit down and relax because fresh coffee was on the way. He introduced himself to us. His name was Ed. I was impressed by his demeanor. Everything in his room was neatly in place. He looked like he was in his mid-thirties and very young to be in command of such a massive ship. I felt very much at ease around him despite his rank. He was a commander, a rank much higher than mine.

Ed told me he was surprised that an LCT had shipped the fuel. He had expected a more conventional ship designed for this type of delivery. I told him about our having one engine out, and he looked surprised and asked if it had broken along the way. I told him the engine had been out of order for over a month, and he could not understand why I had never told the lieutenant commander I was minus an engine. He was amazed my LCT made it to the tender at all and said that although we are trained to follow orders, sometimes we should say no and tell the commanding officer why.

We continued to talk about my mission. Ed asked me what the LCT's cruising speed was. I told him 7 knots. He said I could not have been going any faster than 6 knots since I was down one engine. He also complimented me on such a huge accomplishment. Sailing all the way from Zamboanga with a magnetic compass and a broken engine was astonishing. He remarked that there were times I had to be dead in the water if the tide, currents, and wind were all against my ship. I sure liked Ed; he made me feel really good about myself and my ability to captain the LCT. I was surprised at his comments. This was the first time anyone in authority had given me a compliment.

Ed stood up from his chair and said we had to get on with our mission. A crane would be lowered off the side of the tender to unload the barrels of fuel. I needed to return to the LCT to supervise. While the drums were hoisted aboard, I got a bright idea. With the last drum aboard, I signaled to the sailor on the tender to hoist me up. At first, he didn't understand my request so I stood on one foot, raised my other, and pretended to place it on the loop of a rope. He understood my attempt at charades and dropped the rope to my deck. I grabbed on and held tight as he pulled me up to the tender. This was definitely another thrill in my life.

Once the unloading was completed, Ed invited us to the tender for dinner. What a great invitation. My men and I had not eaten fresh food in months. It was several hours before dinner so Ed, Cliff and I talked about the beginnings of our military careers. I told him how I had washed out of the Naval Air Corps but had never gotten the passion to fly out of my system. Upon hearing my story, Ed got up and introduced me to a pilot named Jim.

Jim and I began to talk, and I asked him to show me his plane. We went up to the deck, and I asked him if I could sit in the cockpit. He gave his permission, and I climbed inside. Planes on this tender did not get airborne by catapult. They were placed in the water by a crane and had pontoons that kept them afloat. The planes then taxied out into open water and became airborne from there. I enjoyed sitting in Jim's plane. It reminded me of my brief flying days. I kept thinking that if the wind had not been so strong the day I washed out, I could have been flying a plane just like Jim.

During dinner, I had the honor of sitting next to Ed, and he told me about his mission at Borneo. He said that on this very day, fighting was to take place in Brunei Bay, which is a spacious harbor in British North West Borneo. The bay was located about 100 miles from the ship. The plane on the tender was used for reconnaissance flights over the bay area to help determine the strength and location of the Japanese troops before the invasion. Other invasions were planned on the East Coast of Borneo, and Jim made daily flights gathering information. After dinner, Cliff and I sat for several hours and talked to the other officers on board. They all had interesting experiences to talk about, which made for a very entertaining evening. Around eleven, I said goodbye and good luck to the crew of the tender, and my crew and I climbed down the ladder to the LCT.

At dawn the following morning, I ordered to cast off lines. The men on watch aboard the tender waved goodbye, and we were underway. I didn't expect to encounter any trouble on the way back. I thought it would be a relaxing 2 day trip. Cruising on the open sea up to the archipelago was uneventful. The magnetic compass was accurate enough to identify the first group of the islands in the Sibutu group. It took us only 8 hours to get this far versus the 10 it took on the way down. It was now 2 p.m. and the next major island we would pass was Tawi Tawi. We arrived at the island around 8 p.m. and everything was going smoothly. The next major island we were to pass was Jolo. It was 110 miles away. We continued on our way and were enjoying a relaxing return to Zamboanga. Visibility was good despite it being 10 p.m. so I decided to leave Cliff in charge for the remainder of the evening. We were approaching Jolo.

The next morning I awoke to the engines making their usual pulsating sound. I dressed and went to the bridge. I expected to be traveling open water on our last leg of the journey before Basilan Island appeared. Much to my amazement, we were only at the middle of Jolo Island. Cliff and I were alone at the bridge. When I noticed our location I lost my temper and yelled, "What the hell is going on here?

Did it occur to you that we aren't making any progress past the island, or did you doze off and head in the wrong direction? Maybe it isn't important to you that the terrain on the shore hasn't changed any!" Cliff said nothing after I yelled at him. He just stood there and stared at me with a blank look on his face.

I got to thinking that Cliff had never become a real part of the team that operated the ship. It should have been obvious to me when he ran us aground back at Zamboanga, and he did not seem to be overly concerned. He was just an officer putting in his time, hoping to make it home alive.

I tried to ascertain why we were not making headway. I had an instrument on the bridge of my LCT that allowed me to sight a landmark ashore. After a while, I could sight with the instrument on the same landmark; if the angle moved backward, this indicated I was going forward and vice versa. Much to my dismay, I was sighting a landmark on the island of Jolo, and it showed that I was making no headway. In fact, I was traveling backwards. I remembered Ed saying it was possible that if the wind, tide, and currents were all against me, I wouldn't make any progress. He was right. After checking the chart more carefully, I noticed the current off Jolo was indeed very strong, and I had the wind against me as well.

I called the bosin's mate to the bridge and told him to brief the crew on our situation and to tell them I wasn't overly concerned about it. I was sure the wind, tide, or current would change soon, and we'd be on our way. What a predicament. Here I was, off the coast of Jolo, making no headway. Moreover, the Moro tribes live there and the lieutenant commander had made sure to warn me to stay away from those natives. I quickly weighed my options. I didn't know if the Japanese were still on the island, but if I stayed at sea, something devastating could happen. I could lose another engine on the LCT. Any hope of seeing another ship was unlikely. I hadn't seen any other ships when I went down the archipelago; I doubted I'd see any when I went up either. The only boats in sight were sailing craft that belonged to the natives.

I discussed the situation with Cliff. We decided to proceed on course, hoping that some change in the current, tide, or wind would allow us to move forward. I still wondered what I would do if we couldn't make any progress. What a dilemma that would be. Beaching would be our last resort. Perhaps I could anchor and wait for some change, but this could be almost as dangerous as beaching because of the time it would take to raise the anchor to avoid any problems that may come from shore. I also thought about changing course so that we would go up the other side of Jolo. But, just as I was ready to change our direction, the backward motion stopped. Shortly thereafter, I was able to make headway. The motormack, who rarely ever spoke to me, told me how lucky we were to have the extra fuel on board. We had just finished the first barrel.

It was a relief knowing we were finally on our way back to Zamboanga. It was now the evening of June 21, 1945, and we were on our last leg of the mission. We had 100 miles to go before we reached Basilan Island. We had been fortunate to encounter such favorable weather during this next-to-impossible mission. We had clear sky during the days and nights of our mission. If at any time I had had trouble seeing the shorelines of the many islands, it would have been very difficult to avoid running aground.

Basilan Island finally appeared on the horizon. We all knew that in a few hours we would be beaching at Zamboanga. Around 4:30 on June 22, 1945, my LCT was finally resting on the beach. I expected the lieutenant commander or some other officer to come and congratulate me for a job well done. That never happened. No one greeted us on this day or any other. Either the commander or one of his men saw that we were beached or the tender's captain reported that our mission was accomplished.

After no word from the lieutenant commander, I realized I was right about him. He was a seasoned veteran who cared only about the bigger picture and getting his job done with no regard for the safety of the men involved. Nevertheless, the crew had the satisfaction of knowing we had accomplished such a daring feat. At dinner that evening, I told my crew how proud I was of them for doing their part in getting the job done.

After Borneo, I expected the Army to give me my next assignment. We sat idle for two weeks; the inactivity was a welcome relief. Finally, on the 15th day, the Navy lieutenant came aboard and informed me that the LCTs were no longer needed to supply the Army. All roads between the towns were now secure, and trucks delivered supplies. He said that on July 17 our group of six LCTs was to be towed by an LST to Hollandia, New Guinea. Hollandia was very close to Manus Island where my LCT had been launched in February.

The huge island of New Guinea is 1600 miles long and hosted many important battles on the Pacific front of the war. When the Japanese controlled large sections of the island, the Australians were fearful of being invaded. Port Moresby, an important city in New Guinea, was only 30 miles away. In April of 1945, MacArthur's army captured Hollandia. The harbor provided the Navy with a large staging area for operations in the Pacific.

The towing procedure was the same as before. Hollandia is 1700 miles from Zamboanga. The trip was much quieter than the one going to Zamboanga. We had 8 days of cloudless skies and very little wind. Each passing day we were coming closer to the equator. I remember lying in my bunk with sweat pouring off me and thinking about all the early years of my life. I went all the way back to the day I was born.

CHAPTER 14
MY YOUTH

My family history is as follows. My grandfather on my father's side came from Germany. He had four children; three were born in Germany. Only my father was born in the United States. A picture shows my grandfather and grandmother, their oldest son, my uncle Casper, and my dad with his hand on his shoulder. This picture was taken in 1894.

My Grandparents, their oldest son, Casper, and my father, Frank

On my mother's side, all the children were born in America. My grandparents on her side were German as well, so I was of all German heritage. My mother's parents, had 11 children. My mother, Leona, was the first-born and their last, Beatrice, was the same age as my sister.

I have a feeling I was an accident. My parents may not have wanted another child. Up to this time, their children's birth dates had a pattern. Lois was born in 1915; Paul, in 1917; and Maurice, in 1919. I was born four years after Maurice, which leads me to believe I was unplanned.

Our family doctor at the time of my birth was Dr. Bowman, a very compassionate man. He told my parents I was born with a hernia that required an operation as soon as possible. If this was not done, chances were that I would die.

An operation was impossible because I was dying from starvation. I refused my mother's milk, and she tried various formulas to no avail.

Every night Dr. Bowman would stop at the house and suggest some other baby food, none of which would I eat. My parents and the doctor were very frustrated with this dilemma.

I was fading fast and the situation looked hopeless. My stomach was extended, and it looked like I was about to die. After six weeks, my parents were at their wits end and pleaded with Doctor Bowman for some other solution. He had no answer, just a blank look on his face. I am sure that during his working day I must have been on his mind. What could we feed that child that he would consume? Somewhere in the recesses of his mind, he remembered reading about fresh cow's milk that saved an infant's life.

The next evening when he stopped at the house, he asked my mother if there was a cow in the neighborhood. She told him there was. A family down the hill from our house had a small farm with a cow. After Dr. Bowman left, my mother told my father to take the next day off and go see Mrs. Prokopovich for the milk. They knew little about this family. They barely spoke English and kept to themselves. I am sure my dad went with much trepidation, since he never met the family, and he did not know what to expect. They understood my dad's explanation of the need for fresh cow's milk, and were glad to provide us with it.

I can just imagine my mother's delight when she saw my dad with a container of milk. As instructed, she filled a bottle with the fresh milk and I had my first good meal in six weeks. Three weeks later, I was strong enough to be operated on. The doctors had a little surprise for my parents after my surgery. When operating on my hernia, they decided to remove my appendix too. I may have been the youngest person ever to have this done.

As weeks turned into months, I seemed to progress normally. My parents were delighted. By this time, I was eating food a normal child would be expected to eat. After two years, I had uttered no sound that resembled a word. My parents consulted with the doctor again. My parents asked him if there was any reason why I wasn't talking yet. Dr. Bowman told them there was no reason to be concerned. I was simply not ready to talk. Months passed and at four years old, I was still pointing to get my message across.

My parents insisted to Doctor Bowman that there was some problem with me. He stuck by his diagnosis that they should not be concerned. He told them I was getting what I wanted by being an expert finger pointer, so there was no need for me to talk. Doctor Bowman told them that he was certain that when I was ready to speak I would, and that it would probably be in sentences. This is exactly what happened.

Once I started, I would never be quiet. When I was five, my two brothers and sister were in school. My mother probably thought what a peaceful place her home would be if I was in school also. I do not know if I was a hyperactive child, but I suspect I was. I more than likely followed her around wherever she went and did not sleep until I fell over from exhaustion. In the fall of 1928, when I was five years old, my mother enrolled me at St. Joseph's grade school. As I remember it, I had no problems with the new environment. I looked forward to each new day and enjoyed all the new surroundings and friends.

Mel Eiben. Age 4   My Father, Frank Eiben. Age 5

From the very beginning, I enjoyed the learning process. I also liked going to school because it let me out of the confines of my house and yard. After school, I would roam the neighborhood visiting my newfound friends.

This section of the neighborhood also included a ballpark free of grass. On three sides of the ball field was a dense wooded area in which there was a creek with a small pond that had fish, frogs, and water spiders. At this early age, it seemed that each day was a wonderful new experience.

There were no organized sports to speak of, so we made

up our own games. Soon I was playing catch with one of my street buddies.

One day, one of the kids in the neighborhood came with a softball and bat, and within a few weeks, we had enough boys to play a pick-up ball game. In the fall, we would play football with no supervision, and fights would occasionally occur. Many times, I would be a participant in these neighborhood brawls. I felt like I was able to compete physically in these conflicts as well as the rest of the kids in the area. That confidence came to an abrupt end. My friend Bob Kautsman outweighed me by at least 15 pounds, and one day we got into an argument that resulted in a fistfight. It was not much of a contest. I was beaten so badly that when my mother saw me, she could not believe how battered and bruised I was. She asked what happened. I told her, and she had no comment other than for me to take a bath and get ready for dinner. There were no words of sympathy from her. Her silence was my mother's way of telling me this was just another lesson in growing up.

I never thought about the fight until many years after the war. One day at a restaurant in downtown Pittsburgh, I saw Bob, and we had lunch together. We reminisced about our childhood, and he asked me if I remembered our fight. I told him I did, and it taught me a lesson that with my type of physique, I shouldn't fight for I would probably lose. Bob said he felt bad about the beating he gave me, and he had never fought after that. I guess it turned out to be a good learning experience for us both.

There were also times when my aggressive spirit would get out of control. That is when my mother would say, "Wait until your daddy gets home."

When my father would arrive from work, my mother would give him a report on my behavior for that day. My dad would direct me to the basement and say, "Assume the position." He would take off his belt and give me a few hits on the rump. In the future, it made me think twice about being out of control. In today's world, the law for child abuse could censure my father. I have to say it was a bit painful, but it taught me to think twice about displeasing my parents.

On my eighth birthday, I received a wonderful present— a dog. I knew from the first day he arrived that he would bring much joy to my life, and I called him Pal. I never knew how much happiness a dog could bring by just being there to pet and play with. He was a great companion.

One never knows how early experiences in life may have a major impact on future decisions. Each year a group of Catholic parishes banded together to arrange a cruise down the Ohio River on board a huge excursion boat. We would board the craft in the morning. My mother and father would be carrying two large baskets of food. My first such trip must have been when I was eight. Every aspect of the experience is vivid in my mind. The gangplank rested on the edge of the wharf, moving slightly with the motion of the river water. The first part I saw of this enormous riverboat was the lower deck. Picnic tables took up a large section of the first deck, and by luck, my father laid claim to one of the tables on the outer section so we had full view of the shoreline.

Lois, Paul, and Maurice went off to inspect the rest of the boat. Much to my dismay, they did not take me along. My dad noticed my disappointment and took me on a walk around the boat with him. We were off to the top open deck, just in time to hear the loud piercing music from the calliope that always played before they cast off. After that, we went to the stern of the lower deck and watched the huge paddle wheel pull us away from the wharf. We sat in a deck chair; the boat moved out and headed down the Ohio River. I noticed small pleasure boats riding the waves created by the huge paddle wheel.

I still remember going through a river lock on this trip. The excursion boat entered the lock and sat in the center of the lock. The employees dropped lines down to secure the craft in place. Huge iron gates closed behind us. In front was another set of iron gates. The riverboat inside the enclosure slowly dropped about 20 feet. It was an eerie feeling being boxed inside the enclosure with concrete walls on each side and iron gates in front and back. Suddenly, the gates in front of us opened. The crew cast off lines, and we cruised out into the middle of the river. The riverboat continued on its way. The ever changing view of small towns, factories, and farms made for an interesting trip. At ten in the evening, the boat was back at the wharf we launched from. To an eight-year-old, this was quite an experience. Perhaps this was one of the seeds planted in my young mind that made me want to join the Navy years later.

My address was 505 Fisher Street. At the bottom of the street was a grocery store. Though it was small, it had all the necessary meats and groceries to maintain a family. My mother never bought large quantities of food. As a result, I was sent to the store almost daily to fetch some food. Since it was the middle of the Depression, the owner of the store seemed to be the only person with any wealth. He bought his son a 1933 Chrysler Roadster with a rumble seat. At that time, I had never seen a more beautiful automobile. When I passed the store, I often saw the son working on his car. I always wondered if it were possible for me to someday own such a car. There was no way of knowing that I would become owner of that very car years later.

Swimming was always a thing for me. When I was about ten years old, I located a public pool on Arlington Avenue. It was the nearest one to me in the city, about a mile from my home. With no public transportation and no family car, my legs were the only way I could get there. A couple of my friends and I decided to go swimming, and it became a daily occasion. I had no idea how to swim, but when I ventured into the deep water, I found out I could swim "doggy" style and stay afloat. It was not very long before I was swimming free style. I also spent many hours learning how to do fancy dives.

My dad and I liked to take long walks together. One of these long walks was to visit with his brother, Father Conrad. He was pastor of St. Michael's on the South Side of Pittsburgh, two miles from my home. To a ten-year-old Catholic boy, a priest was of great importance, commanding great respect. Walking into Father Conrad's office and seeing him in his religious garments was an awesome experience. He was an excellent painter and many of his pictures hung on the walls. One partially-completed painting was resting on an easel.

Father Conrad was very well known in the city of Pittsburgh; he was instrumental in starting the passion play still being performed to this day at St. Michael's. Being that close to him made me feel very proud that he was my uncle.

As early as the first grade in school, I found I enjoyed art class. After doing my necessary studies, I would enjoy drawing various animals. My dad enjoyed working with wood. He was always making or fixing something. I was around a good part of the time, either helping him or getting on his nerves. When I was about ten, he bought a scroll saw. I would draw the animal on a piece of plywood and cut the shape out on the scroll saw. One day I cut out a small dog from a piece of plywood. I had a burning tool and inscribed my mother's name on it. I decided to make a pin out of it for her and asked my dad how to do it. He told me I could use special glue to put a safety pin on the back. After I glued the pin on, I varnished the dog pin and gave it to my mother. She was very pleased and proudly showed it to her friends. I asked my mother if she minded if I took the pin to school to show it off in art class. Several of the girls in class liked it and asked if they could have one. As a result, I took orders and charged them ten cents each. The nuns took an interest in my business venture and let me go to the other classes to sell them. This was my first experience in retailing, not to mention jewelry design.

Our home was a half mile from the streetcar line in Mount Oliver. When it was raining, my mother would say, "Melvin, grab two umbrellas and go to the car stop to meet your father." I never refused to do what she said; in fact, it was enjoyable walking home in the rain with my dad. Mount Oliver served the same purpose as today's strip malls. Each side of the street had small businesses like hardware, bakery, candy, clothing, and other types of small stores. At the end of the business district was a fruit market owned by my maternal grandfather. His wife did almost all of the work, since he was the town's burgess and spent most of his day in his office with his cronies.

My Grandfather Kraus and My Mother Leona

Every year, March was kite-flying time. Today's parents simply go to a store and buy a string and kite, but when I was young, we made our own. My brother Maurice showed me how to make my first kite using the wood from an orange crate my grandmother saved for us from the fruit market. Maurice and I walked to Mount Oliver and carried it home. The wood split easily into long sections, which became the kite's frame. We then attached string to the frame and glued newspaper to the string to make the kite. From there, we attached some old rags that we tore into long sections for a tail. My dad made me a wooden kite wrapper that was the envy of all the other kids in the neighborhood. Once the string was attached to the kite, everything was in place to get airborne. It was wonderful to see our homemade creation soaring in the air.

In the winter time there was sled riding. I had a store-bought sled I received for Christmas when I was ten. Our street was excellent for sledding. We made skis to use on the street. They were made of bamboo. Back in the thirties, rugs were delivered with a bamboo pole in the middle. My brother Maurice would cut off a foot-and-a-half long section and file the bottom flat. He would then split it in half and place the end in the coal furnace in the basement, which made it possible to curve up the end of the pole, making it a small ski. After a snowstorm, cars would go up and down the street and flatten out the snow. Placing a ski under each foot, we would go down the street at a surprisingly fast speed. As I look back, I wonder if my dad knew what we were doing at the furnace.

My parents never told me what to do (other than I had to go to school), and the only rule I remember was having to be home when the streetlights came on. I guess they accepted the pattern of my older brothers and other children in the neighborhood.

My desire to have more money than the meager allowance from my parents inspired me to get a paper route when I was about 15 years old. I got a job delivering the morning paper. I had to get up at 6 a.m. in order to complete my route before school. Not only did I have to deliver the paper, I had to collect the money for it once a week. I had to go to each house and punch a card if they paid for their papers. If they did not pay, I had to make up the difference.

The job was no fun in the wintertime. My mother kept a bottle of liquor, Rock and Rye, in the cupboard. I would take it out of the cupboard, look at it, and say to myself, she will not miss one more shot from the bottle, and it will make me feel warm. I was right; she never missed it. After the war, I was visiting with my mother and told her about my caper. She said, "I was wondering why it was evaporating so fast."

On February 23, 1936, my father heard about an ice jam in Rochester, Pennsylvania. He said to his three sons, "Why not drive down and look at the ice jam?" It was unbelievable. The Ohio River was stacked high with huge chunks of ice all the way across. If this was the case on the Ohio, then the Allegheny and the Monongahela also had to be covered with ice. As the weeks went by, the area had a very warm spell; in addition, we had heavy rain for seven days. The ice holding back the water broke loose on all three rivers. I vividly remember that week because it was so miserable that after school I would just stay in the house out of the rain.

Ice Jam, 1936 Pittsburgh Flood

The day during the flooding, March 17, 1936, I will never forget because my dad did not come home from work. We did not hear from him, but we knew that he had to be in Pittsburgh, for that was where his office was. In the morning my father was still not at home. The date was March 18 — my birthday. Finally, around three in the afternoon he came home from work. He had spent the night and most of the day passing out food to the emergency workers at the Pittsburgh Railway Company where he worked. What a relief to see his smiling face. In a short period of 42 hours, the river had gone from 22 feet to 46 feet high. It was five days before the rivers were below the flood levels. The town was devastated, for it was the worst flood in the history of Pittsburgh.

When we would go to the various amusement parks in the area, I would enjoy playing golf with my dad. When I was about 12 years old, I actually built a golf course on the vacant lot across the street. I tried to make my friends pay to play on it with no success. We had a lot of fun playing on it for a while. About a month later, it was vandalized beyond repair.

Mel's Miniature Golf Course

My parents always wanted to know where I was going and what I was doing. They allowed me a lot of liberty, and

I am sure it developed my character to face adversity later in my life.

In the year 1935, there was an event that had a big impact on my life. My oldest brother, Paul, bought his first car. Until then, the only ride I ever had in an automobile was when my Uncle Martin came to visit.

When Paul drove home in his 1930 Ford Roadster, it was definitely a major event for our family. The Roadster was not much of a car, but it did have a steering wheel, four wheels, and an engine. I had a lot of fun sitting next to Paul in the front seat while patiently waiting for him to start the engine. With a turn of the key, the four-cylinder engine began to hum, and I could feel the car's gentle vibration beneath my feet. I can still remember the sense of elation I felt when the car began to move.

Brother Paul, 1930 Ford Roadster, and Maurice
leaning on the fender

My father was a rather quiet man, and he didn't seem very impressed with Paul's purchase; however, I believe it planted a seed in his mind. Sure enough, the next year, my dad bought his first car. It was a brand new 1934 Chevrolet. Back then, it cost

$700. It is hard to believe, but a similar car today would be at least $17,000. I will never forget the day my father drove his first car home. He and Paul pulled up to our house, and both of them had very proud looks on their faces. What a major event it was in our family—the car made a huge difference in our lives.

After my father became the owner of an automobile, there was no stopping him. We were always on the go. Almost every Saturday we would be on one-day trips. Hard to believe that we would go to Lake Erie and back in one day, the distance of 300 miles. The highways at the time were not as they are today. This is still vivid in my mind. There was a road in Ohio where one section of the highway was paved only on one side. When a car approached in the opposite direction with the right of way, the other car had to move off onto the unpaved side.

We had our first family vacation in 1936 when I was 13 years old. Back in the mid-thirties, cars had no trunks for luggage. If there had been no fenders or spare tire, there would have been no place to secure the luggage. It had to be quite a feat to find a way to attach enough luggage for six people. My parents rented a cottage in Conneaut Lake Park. This was quite an experience for me, for this was the first time we were ever away for a week as a family. At home, the family was close but on vacation we got to know each other as never before, for it was just us, no outside friends to distract us.

First Family Car, 1934 Chevrolet

Many family vacations followed the one we took to Conneaut Lake. In 1938, my parents rented a house in Wildwood, New Jersey. Up to this time, I had only been to lakes. Gazing out onto the Atlantic Ocean for the first time was mesmerizing. The New Jersey shoreline seemed to go on forever. I was awestruck by its magnitude. Lake Erie is impressive to see for the first time, but it doesn't compare to the enormous beaches at Atlantic City. I had my bathing suit on and ran into the ocean and dove into one of the large breakers. The waves crashed over my head, and I got my first taste of the ocean water.

My uncle Clarence and his son come to the shore with us. Uncle Clarence was a very knowledgeable fisherman, and he suggested we go on a fishing expedition. My brother Paul, Uncle Clarence, my cousin, and I all went on a tourist fishing boat. We were told to drop a fishing line over the side of the ship. Each line had six hooks on it, and the crew provided us with a large basket to put our catch in. In no time at all, Paul and I were pulling in three to four fish at a time. We quickly filled the basket to the point that we could hardly carry it. Each fish was 12 to 15 inches long.

That fishing expedition was quite a memorable experience.

Result of Fishing Trip

In 1939, we vacationed at Geneva on the Lake. My dad told me that he went there on vacation in 1911, long before he was married. In September of that same year, my family went to see the World's Fair in New York City. I was 16 at the time, and it was an awesome experience for me. All of the huge displays depicting what the future might be stimulated my impressionable mind.

New York City was massive compared to the town I grew up in, and its size overwhelmed me. My dad drove down to the section of the city where the cruise ships dock and we walked down to the pier where the French cruise ship The Normandy was docked. It was the largest ship in the world at that time. Another wonderful experience brought to us by the miracle of the automobile.

When I finished the eighth grade, my parents decided to send me to Knoxville Junior High School, a public school. St. Joseph's High School was only a block from my home but now I realize they must have switched me over because Catholic schools charged tuition. I wondered how I was going to get to school, and it turned out that I had to walk. At the age of 13, walking over a half-mile alone to school seemed overwhelming to me.

Attending a public school was another fork in the road over which I had no control, but it did turn out to have its benefits. St. Joe's didn't have a swimming pool but Knoxville did, and I was able to join the swim team. This was my first experience in organized competition of any kind. Watching other kids attend the meets and cheer the team on was a new experience as was riding the bus to other schools for swim meets.

After two years at Knoxville Junior High, I transferred to Carrick High School. This was a difficult time at first because I had no friends. The school was over two miles from home. The other students seemed to have their circles of friends, and

I felt like a total stranger. To get to school, I had to either walk the distance there, or I could walk a half-mile to Mt. Oliver and take the street car the rest of the way. There were a lot of other changes I had to deal with when I transferred to Carrick. Making the swimming team was far more difficult than at Knoxville. My many hours of practice diving at the public swimming pool paid off. That was the event I participated in. I did swim in the longer distance event.

Swimming alone was not enough to keep me busy, so I went out for the soccer team as well. Before that, I had never played the game in my life. Many of the guys on the team had grown up in a soccer environment and were very skillful at this sport. As a result, I was lucky to make the second team.

Carrick also had baseball and track teams. I needed something to do in the springtime, and since my skills in baseball were very limited I went out for the track team. My daily two-mile hike to school had me in great condition, so I decided to compete in long- distance running. Participating in sports made it possible for me to become friends with many of the students.

One aspect of my life that had no importance up to this time was being friends with females. Learning how to dance made it possible for me to have some lady friends. Much to my surprise, I found being in female company was a relaxing experience. There was not a day that went by that I did not look forward to going to school.

In the summer of 1939, my father let me get my learner's permit. My dad told Maurice to teach me to drive. Maurice told me to drive down the alley, which was one lane with a ditch on one side. Once we got to the end of the street, he told me to put it in reverse, go back to where I started, and go down again. After four times of up and down, Maurice got out of the car. He looked at me and said if I did this ten times, I would know how to drive.

After some parallel parking lessons and driving in traffic

a couple of times, Maurice felt his student was ready for the driver's test. He was right, for I passed on my first try and received my license. It was a great feeling to be all by myself driving my father's car.

In the spring of 1940, I was a senior at Carrick. At this stage in my life, going to college never occurred to me. My grades at school were slightly above average, a combination of A's, B's, and C's. One subject I had great difficulty with was Latin. In fact, I had a failing grade up to the last exam. One day after class, Mr. Lions asked me to stay and talk to him. He asked me if I realized that without a passing grade in a language, my chance of getting into college was very slim. He said that just in case I had college in mind, he was not going to be the reason I couldn't get in. He told me to enjoy the summer because I had passed the class. What an important event this was in my life—an event I considered a major fork in the road of my life.

In 1966, when I joined the South Hills Country Club I discovered that my Latin teacher was also a member of the club. What a thrill it was to reminisce with him about that eventful day and thank him again for giving me a passing grade, making it possible for me to enroll in Duquesne University.

Once I started college I needed to make some money. Before my brother, Paul, was drafted into the army, he had worked many years as a suit salesman at Kaufmann's department store. I went to visit with one of Paul's old friends and he informed me that a stock boy was needed to hang up the suits. I applied for the job and was hired. The hours of work at the store did not interfere with the university. I worked from 4-9 p.m. and all day Saturday. This was my first employment out of high school. It gave me great satisfaction to place my card into the time clock. The pay was

33 1/3 cents per hour. My job at Kaufmann's was to hang up suits after the salesmen tried them on a customer.

I found out that the 4 to 9:30 employee in the cloakroom was quitting, and a replacement was needed. I applied for the job and was lucky enough to be hired. There was more to do than just sit and hang up coats. Back then, there were no bar codes or pre-strung tags for merchandise, so we had to string tags as well.

My schedule each school day was like this. Up at seven. My dad, Paul, and I would go to town in my father's car. I would be dropped off at the end of the 10th street Bridge with a long climb up the steps to the university campus. My school day was over at three and I walked to Kaufmann's and worked from four to nine. After work, I would go home—tough enough in the mild weather, but how about a cold snowy evening waiting for the 9:30 streetcar to Mount Oliver? Once off the trolley I had a half-mile walk to my home, arriving around 10:30 p.m. With this schedule, keeping up with my schoolwork was no easy task. I was living proof that one could get by with very little sleep.

One downside to the job was that I was not needed in the summer, for there was no need to hang up winter coats. This left me with the need for a summer job. I had no idea what to look for. My friend Bob Lawrence suggested that we apply to be city lifeguards. I had no training for the job, nor did he. The day arrived to apply for the job. There was no written exam. We were just asked some questions, and I must have had the correct answers, for I was told to get my swimsuit and be ready for in-pool tests.

Bob and I had no idea what skills this test would require. We decided to go to the end of the line and watch the other men qualify. The men were paired off in twos. One swimmer had to pull the other man the length of the pool. Fortunately, Bob and I were one set of twos. I said, "Bob, when it is your time to qualify, I'll kick a little to help you make the length of the pool; you do the same for me." We had no way of knowing if we were hired. They informed us that if hired, we would be notified by mail.

In about four days, I saw Bob at school, and he said he had gotten the job. Well, I guess I should not have been surprised that he was hired, for his Uncle Dave Lawrence was the mayor of Pittsburgh. Three days passed and the letter finally arrived telling me I was a city lifeguard. Maybe the reason that I was hired was that no one wanted to be assigned to the Oliver Street indoor pool. It was a bit of a disappointment not to be outside, but I was happy to have a job. The hours were from twelve to eight, seven days a week. The wages were $35 a week, more than double my Kaufmann's wages.

When the summer was over, I was back at school with a job at Kaufmann's and a summer job as a lifeguard at the city pools. I settled into a routine I could live with until I finished college. This routine suddenly ended with the bombing of Pearl Harbor on December 7, 1941.

This momentous event was about to make a major change in my life. I was enrolled at school in Army ROTC, but as you already know, I decided to join the Naval Air Corps. Since it was the middle of the war, most young men were already in the service or were working at jobs needed for the war effort. I could not understand why there was such a long delay of being called up for training. During the summer of 1942, I was back at the city pools. Having one year of experience, I was assigned to the large pool on the North Side of Pittsburgh.

The head lifeguard at the 22nd Street pool in the South Side was called into the service. I was transferred to this pool and made head guard. At first, I was pleased about the promotion until I realized what my responsibilities would be. For an additional $3.50 a week, I had to schedule the guards and control the filtering system.

Just when it seemed my daily routine would overwhelm me, I had a stroke of Luck. Remember my writing about the 1933 Chrysler automobile owned by the son of the proprietor of the neighborhood grocery store? Well, he was one of the first to be drafted into the service before our entry into World War II. He sold the car to a friend of my brother Paul. Not too many months later, he was drafted and my brother Paul bought the car from him, only to be pressed into the service a short time later. He gave the car to his girlfriend Bea Orient, to whom he was engaged and eventually married. When he came home on leave, he saw the car rusting away in a field at the Orient Farm.

This upset him, so he said that he would like me to have his Chrysler Roadster. Bea was not using it, and it was just turning to rust. The next day, Bob Lawrence and I drove to Bea's house to pick up the keys. In nervous anticipation, I went over to the car of my dreams. The car did not look like it did the first time I saw it when I was 12 years old and I wondered if it would start. Of course it didn't start because the battery was dead. Bob and I installed a new battery, turned the key, and the engine turned over. We both let out a sigh of relief and were on our way. A bit of panic came over me. The inspection sticker was outdated. Would it pass inspection? If not, where would I find money to have it repaired? Driving to Bridgeville, we stopped at the first inspection station. It was a small, one-man operation. He had an honest look about him, so Bob and I gave him a briefing of the circumstances involving the ownership, and asked him to inspect the car while we waited, regardless of how long it took.

The mechanic began to inspect the car. He had many interruptions during the process. He had to stop to pump gas and answer the phone a few times. Finally, he approached us and said the tires were questionable but close enough to passing. He put the inspection sticker on the windshield, and we were on our way.

I was now the proud owner of my first car. What a break this was to be able to drive to school and home from work in my Chrysler Roadster.

Back at Duquesne, I was settled into a more usual routine. I had my job at Kaufmann's and was waiting for the day the Navy would notify me to report. It seemed strange that almost all the men my age were already in the same branch of the service. There was a rumor that the Navy had signed up more men than were needed for the Navy Air Corps. In fact, this actually happened. A post-war friend of mine told me he was never called, so he volunteered for the regular Navy as an enlisted man. Finally, I was instructed to report for duty by June 13, 1943.

Recalling my enlistment brought my current situation immediately back to my mind and I began to wonder what duty on the island of New Guinea would bring. With these confused thoughts churning in my brain, I finally fell asleep.

CHAPTER 15
NEW GUINEA, WAR'S END, AND DISCHARGE

We arrived at Hollandia, New Guinea, on July 26, 1945. The LST released the hawsers from the ship, and we dropped anchor. The location was the very edge of the harbor. There were mountains on three sides of the anchorage. There was no sign of activity, just our LCT all alone inside this small inlet. I had the same lonely feeling I had experienced at Manus Island when I was launched off the LST with no idea why I was there. I feared that the captain of the LST had let me off at the wrong place. Of the six LCTs that were towed, Ours was the only one to be anchored at this location.

The next day was brutal. Never in my life did I experience such a hot day. An LCT has no insulation of any kind. It is constructed of all metal. The temperature must have been 110 degrees with no breeze of any kind. We were trapped inside these mountains. The heat came right through the soles of our shoes. Touching any part of the ship was like touching a hot stove.

Cliff reported to me that the crew would like me to go ashore and determine why we were in Hollandia. I told him I would wait one day to see if orders would be given to me. I decided to beach the LCT for a little relief from the heat. The shoreline would have to be better than just sitting in the bay.

The next morning I left Cliff in charge, in case someone might come aboard to let us know what our next assignment would be. I took Clint along to guard the jeep in case someone should take a liking to it. I drove down the road next to the shoreline, looking for some place that looked like Navy headquarters. I noticed a large number of ships of all kinds, anchored at the docks or on the beach. I then located a series of buildings and went inside the largest one. A yeoman was sitting outside an important-looking office and I asked him for a meeting with the commander inside. After an hour's wait, I was escorted into his office.

When we had saluted each other, I told him the number of my LCT and asked if he knew why I was at Hollandia. This tall, overweight individual had the appearance of a man who had spent his career behind a desk. He had a nonchalant attitude and was seemingly not much interested in my predicament. He said that headquarters was aware of all ships in the harbor, and they were all waiting for orders for the next invasion, giving me no indication as to what it might be.

One benefit did occur; he told me the location of the supply depot. I was able to make arrangements to procure some fresh food for the LCT. The crew would be happy to hear about this, since it would be the first time we would have seen real meat aboard the ship since we had arrived in the Pacific.

Everyone back on the ship was anxious to hear what I found out. Other than a requisition for real food, I had nothing to report except that we were to remain on the beach and wait for our orders.

I talked it over with Cliff and told him about this huge armada in the harbor. I did hear some rumors that this was one of the major bases getting ready for the big one—the invasion of Japan. It was July 30, 1945. One day went into the next, and no orders were given. We just sat in the intense heat of the harbor, killing time as best we could.

This is especially true in the service, but also in civilian life. One of the worst things that can happen is a group of bored men with no everyday duties to perform. I was very fortunate that my men seemed to get along well with one another. As I look back on their daily living on board ship, it was surprising that there were no major arguments. The living quarters were very small—only 48 feet long and 8 feet wide—and provided the sleeping quarters for 12 men and the galley as well. Try to imagine the everyday living conditions: the hot, humid climate and the cooking heat from the galley. I wonder what their thoughts were, knowing my space was the same size as their entire living area.

There was one exception to the apparently trouble-free relationship among the men. Much to my surprise, a small shipment of beer was delivered to the ship. I suggested that the men put their names on the bottles and store them in the refrigerator. We never had any use for the refrigerator since there was seldom any fresh food. The next day, I heard a lot of arguing originating from the crew's quarters. The honor system did not work very well, for a name on a bottle did not stop a thirsty sailor from consuming extra beers. Going over to see why there was trouble, I made a proclamation: "From this day on, hide your share and drink it warm." This system worked, for the beer thieves were reluctant to steal from anyone's personal belongings.

We did occasionally have a cocktail party. Bill, the cook, became an expert at converting canned fruit into an alcoholic beverage. He would allow the juice from the containers to ferment, and it became a substance that had quite a kick to it. Needless to say, the men preferred this beverage to canned fruit.

After several days of boredom, I decided to drive down the road near shore and invite myself aboard an LCI beached in the harbor. I decided on an LCI because the captain would be a lieutenant JG like me or one rank higher. Maybe he could give me some idea why we were here. I went up to the enlisted man on the ramp of the ship, and we saluted each other. Then I asked to see the captain. I was escorted to the officer's quarters and introduced myself to him. The captain was a lieutenant and seemed about 25 years old. He looked Irish and there was no doubt when he said his name was McDuffy. I was surprised at the ship's size and the number of men I observed moving about. I asked the captain what the complement of men was for this craft, and he told me 4 officers and 24 men. I then inquired if he knew why all the amphibious crafts were in Hollandia. He told me that he was involved with the landing in the Philippines at Leyte Gulf, Mindanao, Luzon, and Zamboanga. Then his flotilla of LCTs was sent to Borneo where they invaded Tarakan, Brunei Bay, and Balikpapan. After all these invasions, he was very content to sit in the harbor with no invasion to deal with. He went on to say that with each invasion, he knew nothing of his next operation until a few days before actually being underway. As far as my knowing the reason for being there, I could only surmise that a large flotilla of ships was being assembled for the invasion of Japan.

Landing Craft Infantry

After listening to his harrowing experiences, I realized how lucky I was that my LCT had never been used for an invasion. The captain invited me to lunch. It was a delightful experience to be eating with four officers in the wardroom. It was certainly a huge difference from the environment on the LCT.

Back on board my LCT, I was more content to wait for our next assignment. With each day that passed, I remembered the lieutenant saying he was satisfied to sit on the beach. Who knew? Maybe the war would be over soon, and I would be one happy sailor who came home alive.

I never moved from my isolated position on the beach in case headquarters needed to find me. I did not have the carefree attitude that I had at Zamboanga as part of the Army. I was now part of a huge staging area of many ships.

One of the frustrating things about my command was the lack of news about the war. On August 10, I joined a group of officers who were gathered on a pier. They were talking about how the United States had dropped an atomic bomb on Hiroshima on August 6 and another one at Nagasaki on August 9. Both cities were devastated beyond comprehension. I was surprised when I heard the news, and the other officers were just as surprised that I had not already heard about it. I told them the LCT was the Navy's only ocean-going ship that had only a ship-to-shore radio. The majority of the men believed that the war would be over soon. No country could expect to survive the massive loss of life in its homeland and continue with its war effort.

Back on the LCT, I was anxious to tell the crew about the bombings and how I thought this meant the war would be over soon. The crew was elated about the news and the feeling that the end of the war could be a reality.

The next day around 8 p.m., we observed much commotion down the coastline where flares and tracer bullets were lighting up the sky. This convinced us the war was over. Then suddenly all activity stopped. It seemed very strange that this happened, so the following morning I drove down to visit my friend on the LCI. McDuffy had a radio on board, and twice a day he was allowed to tune it in and listen for war news.

McDuffy told me it was a false alarm. Apparently, there had been confusion in the Japanese government as to how and when to surrender. Each day I met with the LCI skipper waiting to hear the wonderful news of Japan's surrender until finally, on August 15, 1945, Emperor Hirohito gave the order for his troops to surrender. This time, the activity on board the ships in the harbor didn't stop until well into the morning. Searchlights, signal flares, and tracer bullets lit up the sky. The spectacle of lights and colorful explosions in the sky had a deeper meaning for us than just an exciting display. Servicemen around the world must be reacting the same way we were knowing that the war was really over and they no longer had to fear that tomorrow, next week, or next month, they might be killed in action.

After the war, I read about what actually occurred between the men in charge of the Japanese government. The final decision had been made by the emperor himself. Up to this time, he had not been involved with any major decision regarding the fighting of the war. On August 15, 1945, Emperor Hirohito gave the orders for all Japanese forces to surrender.

Everyone on board wondered when we would get our orders to be discharged and be on our way home. We were back to our old routine of just sitting on the beach. On September 20, a second lieutenant of the Army and a Naval lieutenant came aboard the LCT. They informed me that the following day a platoon of Army men would arrive and we were to take them to a small island 52 miles away. The Navy lieutenant handed me a map and showed me the exact location. He told me that the intelligence at HQ believed that there was a group of Japanese soldiers on the island who did not know the war was over. The platoon sergeant's job was to find them and tell them about Japan's official surrender.

After the officers left, I thought to myself that this was crazy. Surely they would have a man who could speak Japanese with the platoon and maybe some large signs would be provided. They probably went to the other LCT captains and they all said to give the assignment to Mel, he's willing to do anything. After all, he went on a solo run to Borneo.

It was difficult for me to tell Cliff and the crew about this dangerous mission we would be on the next day. In the morning in my quarters, the more I thought about this ridiculous assignment, the more concerned I became about what dangers we might encounter. The following morning, the sergeant whose name was Jerry arrived with his platoon. No Japanese linguist and no signs were provided. Looking at the Army men dressed in battle gear carrying rifles and hand grenades made me realize that this could become very dangerous for the Army platoon, for my crew, and for me.

On the way to the island, I invited Jerry to join me on the bridge. I told him what I thought about this mission. I have twelve men and myself that have survived this war. You probably have been exposed to many dangers and have seen men under your command lose their lives. I can't help but feel common sense dictates we do not expose ourselves to unnecessary dangers on this ridiculous assignment. We both agreed to keep the possible danger to a minimum, by beaching the craft, while he and a small number of men would step onto the beach and return back on board as soon as possible. Jerry and I gathered the men together and made them aware of our decision. The island came into view, and my adrenaline was at its peak.

As we approached the island, much to my surprise I noticed some men on the beach. My first thought was that they were natives of the island. When we were close enough to see the men more clearly through binoculars, I passed them on to Jerry and he confirmed they were indeed Japanese troops and seemed unarmed. This could be a decoy and armed men could be hiding in the jungle. I stood exposed on the bridge where an expert marksman could pick me off with a rifle shot. As we approached the beach, it occurred to me that I should be in the pilothouse, where armor plate could reflect small arms bullets. Too late now, for the anchor was released, and we were about to land on the beach. My thoughts centered on Jerry, who was at the front of his men, waiting for the ramp to come down. He and his men would be exposed to mortar shells that could be fired from concealed foliage a short 40 yards away from our landing position. What about my four men manning the 20-millimeter guns? Up to this time, I had not been involved in any invasion, and with the war over, I was about to have my own private invasion.

All of these thoughts went racing through my mind. The ramp went down, and Jerry and his men were face to face with the Japanese. There were no words spoken and the Japanese held their arms in the air indicating surrender.

There were only eight of them and they were escorted on board. I had the anchor winch engine in idle, and I ordered Frank to activate the motor. We were pulled off the beach with the ramp only partially elevated. Now safely away from the island, Jerry came to the bridge and we both felt relieved that we were on our way back to Holandia. Jerry said he would report back to Army headquarters that after a thorough search of the island, we could find only these few Japanese. Apparently, HQ was satisfied with the report because no one came to see me the next day.

With the war over so suddenly, there must have been a lot of confusion in Washington as to how to disband the military, especially the Navy, since they had ships all over the world. Men cannot just walk away from a ship; someone has to stay to run and maintain it.

Frank and Clint holding Japanese Flag
LCT 804 in background

After a couple of weeks with no activity, all the skippers of our group of LCTs were summoned for a briefing at the naval base. We expected some sort of information as to when and how we would be decommissioned. Once this was accomplished, the officers and crew could be reassigned or sent back to the States to be discharged. We were all in for a big surprise. The officer in charge told us we were to dump massive amounts of Army equipment into the ocean; the trucks would be at our LCTs in the morning.

At 8 a.m. the following day, an army sergeant with two men backed a truck onto my ship. Lucky me. My craft was picked to dispose of ammunition. Sometimes I thought that whoever was in charge gave me all the dangerous jobs because I never complained. Each day we dumped thousands of rounds of all types of ammo and explosives into the water. After two weeks of dumping, I decided to find out if we'd ever be discharged. My crew was restless, and we all wanted to know when we could go home. This was especially true of my two older enlisted men.

I visited various offices, and nobody had the answers I was looking for. I finally located the place that had the detailed information I needed. The key to being discharged rested with a point system the military had devised. Points were awarded according to how much time we spent in the service, and we received extra points for being overseas. A quick calculation showed I had enough to be discharged. In fact, my entire crew had the necessary points. That was the good news, but he informed me of a snag. There had to be men to replace me and the crew in order for us to be discharged. The officer gave me papers to fill out for my crew and me. I walked out of his office thinking I had no problems. Cliff was my replacement. I was elated with the happy thought of going home to my wife.

Each of the men came to my quarters and filled out the necessary paperwork. All of them had the points needed for discharge, but I warned them that before they could be released from the service, they needed replacements. I had no idea when this would happen, but I had reason to believe it would not be very long. I returned the papers that afternoon and was told to come back in two days for a response. I left Cliff in charge and went back as instructed two days later, only to find out that Clint and I were the only ones to be processed for immediate discharge. We could move ashore as soon as transportation was arranged.

Even though I was thrilled to think of going home soon, I was disappointed that there were only two of us who could be discharged, and I wasn't looking forward to telling my crew the news. I figured Clint was being discharged because of his age. The decision to discharge me was probably easy since I had Cliff on board to take over my command. Randy the motormack would probably be the most upset because he was the second oldest on the LCT. I figured that despite his age, the LCT needed an expert to stay on board and service the engines. He was the only member of the crew I felt never had any respect for me because I was much younger than he. I never forgot the time I woke up after an assignment, and the engines were still running. I asked him why he hadn't turned them off, and he retorted that had I failed to order him to secure the engines as per proper procedure. He was definitely going to be the most unhappy sailor of all my men.

The crew was anxious for me to tell them good news. All I could say was that when the Navy sent replacements they could go home, but there was no exact time for that. It made me sad to see the depressed looks on their faces, knowing they had to wait indefinitely to go home.

We had a day off from dumping the ammo, and Cliff asked if I minded if he went ashore a few hours. There was no sign of Cliff all afternoon and into the evening. I began to worry, but I had no idea where to begin looking for him. Since the following day was a Sunday, I would have a whole day to try to find out why he hadn't reported back to the ship. I didn't want him to be considered AWOL, since it was such a serious offense in the service. I had no clue where he could be, and I was concerned that he had fallen victim to foul play. The first place I thought to look for him was at the base hospital, and sure enough, that is where I found him. When I walked into the hospital, there was Cliff lying in a bed. He immediately told me he was being sent back to the United States.

I was worried about his health and said, "Good grief Cliff. This must be serious, what is the problem?" He told me that he had acne, and he was being treated for it in the hospital. He then went on to say that he requested to be treated in the United States. It is still to this day very hard for me to believe, but a doctor signed the necessary papers to get Cliff shipped back to the states. I think the doctor thought he did this for Cliff as a favor, but without realizing it affected someone else.

After Cliff told me he was being shipped home because of acne, he could barely look me in the eye because we both knew what it meant. He was going home instead of me. If the situation were reversed, I would never have done to him what he did to me. What a joke. To this day, I often wonder if this unfair move of his bothered him at all throughout his life. This was easily the most depressing experience to happen to me in my lifetime, and I wondered how I could cope with such a drastic turn of events. I now realized I was right about Cliff's lack of enthusiasm with regard to operating the ship. His only thoughts were how he could get back home.

I went back to the LCT and told my crew of the change in plans. They all felt sorry for me and tried to cheer me up by saying a replacement was probably on the way. I continued with the various jobs the navy assigned to me and tried to keep my spirits up. I was still in charge of 11 men and being despondent was not going to be the best for me or the morale of my crew. The disposing of the Army ordnance proceeded for weeks. There was no sign of our replacements anywhere. I saw trucks, bulldozers, and all types of equipment being dumped into the ocean.

One eventful day an Army sergeant came aboard with a cargo of ammunition. There was one exception to the usual ordnance though. Two men were about to place a phosphorus bomb on the LCT. The bomb was used to light the sky over a target. There was a parachute attached to the casing to delay its drop to the ground, which made it possible to illuminate the sky for a longer time. One of the men unloading the truck must have been curious about the bomb because he pulled the parachute away from the casing, which ignited the bomb. A loud swishing noise came out of the bomb, and it generated massive heat on the back of the truck. Next to the bomb were several cases of 50-caliber ammunition. As fast as I could think, I yelled out my crew members' names to get out the fire hose. Six of us remained on board, including the sergeant. The rest of the crew climbed over the side of the LCT and ran off the ramp in front of the ship—including the two who were unloading the cargo from the truck. Frank Sloan, who had procured the Jeep, had the hose in his hands, and Walt, the gunner's mate, was helping him. In a matter of seconds, water poured into the back of the truck where the bomb was.

Surprisingly enough, the water had no effect on the flames streaming from the bomb—though it did reduce the possibility of the ammo exploding. The sergeant hopped into the cab of the truck and backed it off the LCT and onto the beach. The bomb burned a huge hole in the bed of the truck, but the ammo never exploded. What luck. We could all have been killed. The sergeant was very brave for moving the truck, and we all thanked him for his part in avoiding disaster.

In retrospect, I was a fool to attempt to put out the flames from the bomb. I should have given the order for all of us to abandon ship. The war was over and one less LCT would have made no difference to the Navy. I guess it was instinct to try to save the ship since it had been in my command all these months. If I had let the ammo just blow up the ship we could have all gone home.

The following day, I expected a high-ranking officer to come aboard and congratulate me on how I reacted in preventing a disaster. No one ever appeared. It was as if the incident never occurred. Again, I thought the Navy had little concern for the men who served on amphibious crafts. Now that the war was over, they could not care less about us 90-day wonders.

Occasionally I would have a day off, and on one of those, I took a walk along the shore. I noticed an LCT beaching. Down went the ramps and a couple of enlisted men came ashore. The next thing I noticed were some very dissipated, sick-looking men appearing on the ramp. They could hardly walk, and none of them looked like they weighed more than 90 pounds.

It turned out the men had recently been released from a Japanese prisoner of war camp. What harsh treatment they must have experienced. I am sure many soldiers perished in the camp. Seeing them was a sight I will never forget. This made me realize how brutal the Bataan death march must have been.

Most of the Army ordnance and ammunition must have been disposed of, for now the LCT was being loaded with different cargo, which consisted of generators and other equipment that the people in Hollandia needed. I had other trips to various villages along the coast close to Hollandia. On many of these trips, my freight was sacks of food.

The crew was very discouraged about our being stuck in the Pacific with no word from the Navy as to when our replacements would arrive. On Christmas day, 1945, I had never seen my men more dejected. They pleaded with me to do something about our being discharged. My many trips to HQ were met with no positive results. I wondered if anyone outside the Hollandia Naval Base even knew we were still here.

On February 20, 1946, my ship was once again loaded with food destined for Hollandia. I was to dock at the main pier, but upon my arrival, they ordered me to anchor offshore because they had no personnel to unload the cargo. Two days went by, and we faced a severe rainstorm with high winds, which allowed the water to soak the food. Days went by and there were still no orders from the dock. The food began to ferment and smell rancid. Finally, after one week, I was permitted to tie up to the dock.

I got to thinking about my predicament of not being able to be decommissioned or being relieved from my command. I called the crew together and announced I was going to do something drastic to get us discharged and sent back to the States. I was going to wait until high tide and run the LCT up the beach as far as possible. This would expose the hole in the side of the craft. Since we already had one engine out, I thought we could convince some authority that the LCT was no longer seaworthy, and we could all be sent home.

The following morning, I had breakfast and was on my way to headquarters. As I walked past the ship, it did look like it was in decrepit condition. Our pride in keeping the craft rust-free no longer existed. One engine was out, and the large gash in the side made it look like it was ready for the scrap heap. I proceeded up to headquarters, determined to convince an officer with authority to decommission LCT-804. I walked into the main office and encountered a Lieutenant JG. I explained my situation, and he disappeared into the inner office. He came back and told me he had relayed my message to the officer in charge. After about an hour, I was escorted into the inner office and introduced to the commander, who was sitting behind a desk. He listened intently to what I had to say. I explained that my men and I had enough points for discharge, and I thoroughly described the condition of the LCT. Much to my relief, I did not get the usual Navy, "Sorry, my command does not have the authority to help you." Instead, he got up from his chair, and we went to examine the damaged LCT.

The commander looked at the huge hole in the side of the ship. We walked back to the base. He said it wasn't up to him to make such a major decision, but he would plead our case to the captain in charge of the base. He told me to return to his office in two days, and in the meantime, he would see what he could do.

Early on the second day, I waited with nervous anticipation to hear what the commander would say. There was no waiting in the office this time. I was immediately escorted to him and there was a big smile on his face. "I did it," he exclaimed. "In a few days, you will be discharged." I never thought my executive officer Cliff would help me get out of the service after the selfish move he pulled, but he did. It was Cliff who had run the LCT onto a reef at low tide and put a hole in the ship.

I was instructed to leave the LCT on the beach where it was. I returned to my weary crew with the good news. When I told them they were going home, they were ecstatic. What a bunch of happy faces I was greeted with. They either hugged me or shook my hand and said, "Thanks skipper for making it possible to get out of here."

The next day we shut down all the equipment and walked away from the ship, never to see it again. It was no longer the beautiful dark green craft I had climbed aboard at New Orleans more than a year ago. Everything happened so quickly that I made no record of the addresses of my crew. After all the months we had spent together, I never heard from or saw anyone from my LCT again.

After spending four days ashore, on March 26, 1946, I climbed aboard a cargo ship. My six months of duty in New Guinea were over, and I was finally going home. I stood near the stern of the vessel and watched the city of Hollandia disappear into the horizon. "Thank you, God, for allowing me to survive this brutal war."

CHAPTER 16
HOME AT LAST

After ten days at sea, we finally saw Hawaii on
the horizon. I did not feel the excitement I experienced when
I first arrived here. We stopped for two days and then the
ship got underway once more. I couldn't believe that in
seven more days, I would see the Golden Gate Bridge in San
Francisco, California. I can't describe the anticipation of
actually seeing the good old United States of America.

The navigation officer told me the Golden Gate Bridge
would be visible around 7:30 in the morning. I asked the
night watch to make sure I was up by 6:30 because I didn't
want to miss the bridge. The next day, as predicted, the
bridge came into view over the horizon. What a feeling of
elation to actually see the high bridge; it seemed to stand
taller and larger as we sailed toward it. As I neared the
bridge, I imagined there was a big sign draped over its side
which read "Welcome home Mel Eiben." It may seem like it
was a ridiculous thought; however, the bridge was a symbol
for many servicemen and announced to us that we were
home. The ship completed its pass under the Golden Gate
and into the harbor where it prepared to dock.

The cargo vessel eased next to a large pier and hawsers were attached to the pilings. We stood motionless in the harbor, and I was about to step onto United States soil for the first time in over a year. I walked down the gang plank with my sea bag and stood on America's solid ground. Since leaving New Orleans on an LST such a long time ago, I definitely had enough of going up, down, and sideways on a ship to last me a lifetime. One thing the Navy did for me was remove any desire I had to pursue a career with anything concerning life at sea.

By this time I was used to not knowing what I was to do next. Logic dictated that I look for some building that looked like headquarters so that I could find out what to do.

I looked around the base and picked the most impressive looking building to enter. I thought surely this was headquarters. I walked into the office and asked the corpsman inside how I could be officially discharged from the Navy. He looked at me with disdain, and told me I was in the wrong place; I needed to go one block down to the amphibious headquarters building.

I left the office and made my way to the designated building. By this time, my bag was getting heavy, and the spirit I had when I stepped off the ship was somewhat deflated. I walked into the amphibious headquarters; the building was a very ordinary-looking structure. I presented my papers to the enlisted man behind the desk. He welcomed me back to the States, and it sounded very routine. I am sure he said it many times before. It was not exactly the type of welcome I expected after my many months overseas. He escorted me to the inner office and introduced me to the officer inside. The lieutenant immediately stood up and shook my hand. His attitude was very different from the other Navy men I had encountered up to this time at the base. He seemed interested in the details of my command on the LCT and wanted to talk about my experience in the Pacific.

He struck me as a person who had something to sell. Sure enough, he had a proposition for me. The lieutenant asked me if I wanted to join the reserves. I did not have to go to additional training, and there were no meetings to attend. It didn't seem like a bad idea, so I signed up for the duty. I thought surely there would be no more wars like this one again in my lifetime. As it turned out, in the not too distant future, many men were called to serve in the Korean War, but luckily for me, LCT captains were not in demand. The lieutenant gave me a mustering out pay of $100 and a mileage allowance of $27.84. It never occurred to me to tell him it was barely enough to get me home to Pittsburgh.

It was April 18, 1946, certainly a day to remember. Now that I was officially out of the service, it was up to me to make my way home. A mere 3,000 miles separated me from my beloved wife. I went to the railroad station and bought a ticket, but the train didn't leave until the next morning, so I spent the night in a second-rate hotel.

Although sea travel is slow, it is clean. Sleeping and eating is almost always done in a relaxed atmosphere. As I learned before, this was not the case with land travel, especially on a railroad car. But I was desperate to get home to my wife and family, and that was the only way I knew to get back to Pittsburgh. It took over three days to get there, and I spent the entire time sleeping and eating in a passenger seat.

Finally, on April 21, 1946, I arrived in Pittsburgh and walked into the beautiful rotunda of Pennsylvania Station. I took a deep breath of fresh air, flagged a cab, and went straight to my parents' house. My brother Maurice was the only one there. It was the first time we had seen each other since our chance encounter at Manus Island. Maurice had been home for four months already, and he had not changed a bit. He was still the same exuberant brother I knew him to be before the war. I was dead tired and covered from head to toe in soot from the long train ride. We talked briefly about how great it was to be home. Maurice asked me when I planned on seeing Winnie. He had always been fond of her and was pleased about our decision to marry. I told him I would worry about seeing her tomorrow; I needed a bath and a good night's sleep first. Indignantly, he looked at me, and yelled, "Like hell you are; we are going right now!" So with that, and completely covered in soot, I hopped into his car, and we were off to see my wife. I did manage to make a quick phone call to tell her we were on our way.

Maurice's driving was far more harrowing than many of my war experiences. Maurice and I had a few beers before we took off, and the ride proved to be very dangerous. He was a wild man behind the wheel of a car and loved to speed. I will never forget, as long as I live, the stomach-churning drive up the valley with him.

Maurice and I talked about things on the way to Brownsville, and I asked him about his girlfriend Connie. She was a real beauty with an outgoing personality. He sarcastically replied, "What girlfriend?" It turned out their relationship was history. He had loved her very much and had planned to marry her. He sent her all of his extra service pay while he was overseas for her to save for their future. Unfortunately, when he returned, he found out she had another boyfriend, and all the money was gone. She refused to return any of it. I was shocked to hear this news, and I asked him how he coped with her doing all these terrible things to him. That is when Maurice responded in his true fashion and said with a huge grin on his face, "All the sex was worth it!"

After a little more than an hour on the road, we made it safely to the Winners' house. Winnie was waiting on the porch for me, looking just as beautiful as I remembered her. I rushed up the steps and hugged her tightly before either of us could say a word. I felt both of our hearts pounding as we embraced, still without speaking. Finally I broke the silence and said, "Winnie, I love you more than words can say, and there is no way to tell you how much I have missed you." She responded with "I love you" over and over again.

Once Winnie and I had embraced, her parents welcomed Maurice and me inside. Winnie's brother Ed was there. He was an officer on a cargo vessel during the war. Mr. Winner pulled out a bottle of Old Granddad whiskey, and we all toasted together, thanking the Lord that we all made it home from the horrible war alive. After about half an hour, Maurice excused himself, said goodnight to the Winners, hugged Winnie, and said goodbye. I thanked him for insisting that we drive up to see my wife right away.

The five of us continued to talk for another hour, but all I could think about was being alone with my wife. I excused myself by saying I needed to shower to get off the layers of soot from my train ride and change into clean clothes. My in-laws had a knack for always saying and doing the proper thing. When I was done showering, Joe, Cecilia, and Ed retired for the evening. Finally, I was alone with Winnie. It was the first time we were alone since I kissed her goodbye on December 2, 1946, and left for New Orleans. Now, 17 months later, I held her in my arms again. It felt incredibly wonderful to finally be together.

Needless to say, it was not long before we headed upstairs to get "re-acquainted" and fell asleep in each others arms.

The following morning, Winnie and I awoke to a bright sunny day. We walked downstairs together where Joe and Cecilia greeted us with their smiling faces. Mrs. Winner served a breakfast, the likes of which I hadn't experienced in a long time, and it was even more enjoyable since I had my beautiful wife sitting next to me.

After breakfast, I decided to call my parents. Winnie and I had already determined we'd drive to Pittsburgh the next day to see them. I dialed their number, and after a few rings, my mother answered the phone. She was as excited to hear my voice as I was to hear hers. My mother asked if I could come and see them as soon as possible, and after a few minutes of talking, she put my father on the phone. It was so good to hear his voice again, and I told him we'd be there by mid-afternoon the following day. My mother asked what I wanted for dinner; I told her nothing special, just ground meat and mashed potatoes. She was surprised at my simple request, so I told her how much I longed for that meal while I was overseas. After telling my mom how much I missed her and my father, I said goodbye and assured them I would see them the next day.

I sat back down at the table, and the Winners brought me up to date on the many happenings while I was away. There were two major changes in their household since I was gone. First, Winnie graduated from Duquesne University and was looking for a teaching job. Secondly, Mr. Winner no longer worked as a coal mine superintendent. His brother owned a jewelry store in Brownsville and couldn't find good help, so he asked Joe to be his partner. Joe wasn't a co-owner, but he shared in the profits. The new job turned out to be a perfect fit for Joe. He was a very good salesman and excellent at repairing clocks. I didn't know it at the time, but Joe's career change would greatly impact my future. Cecilia asked me what I wanted for dinner, and I requested beef stew. Next to my wife, I could not think of anything I missed more while I was in the war than good food. I sorely missed the great home-cooked meals I had before I joined the service.

Winnie and I spent the afternoon sitting together on the front porch talking about pre-war times. After that, we discussed what she had done during my absence, and I told her more stories about my experience as Captain of LCT 804. One thing certain about our romance was that we were never at a loss for words when we were together, and our conversations flowed easily.

When Mrs. Winner returned from work, she immediately began cooking dinner. She refused any help from Winnie and insisted we spend more time alone together. Mr. Winner came home shortly, and the three of us sat in the living room while Cecilia prepared our dinner. Joe told us how much he enjoyed the jewelry business and how he had grown quite fond of it. It was a relief for him not to have to go into a dreary coal mine each day. Instead, he had a nice place to work, he enjoyed dealing with the customers.

The aroma of beef stew simmering in the kitchen found its way into the living room, and Cecilia finally called us to dinner. We gathered around the immaculately set table. It was a sight to behold. We took our seats, and Mr. Winner said a prayer before we ate. Not a drop of wine or a mouthful of food was consumed until he finished. I then proposed a toast, and we raised our glasses as I said, "Thank you, dear God, for allowing us to be together this glorious evening." We passed around the food. The stew was mouth-watering, and the enticing meal was topped off by Mrs. Winner's tasty homemade apple pie. The home cooked meal I had that night and the relaxing evening afterward is a part of my life I will never forget.

It finally occurred to me that I promised my parents I would visit them, but I had no way of getting there. Joe told me not to worry; he and Cecilia would find a way to get to work, and we could take their car. Since we now had transportation lined up, I suggested to Winnie that we have lunch at the Summit Hotel. It was only a few miles from Brownsville, and it would be a nice treat for us.

The next morning we were on our way at 10 a.m. Driving the car through Uniontown and past Hopwood; viewing the landmarks I hadn't seen in years was a relaxing experience. On the steep mountain outside of town, we stopped at the viewing platform and gazed at the valley below. The sight of the Pennsylvania forest was completely different from the landscape of the jungles in the Pacific islands that I viewed for so many months. What a gorgeous sight to see the pine trees intermixed with the oak trees below. From this vantage point, we could see into the next county.

When we arrived at the 19th century Summit Hotel, its old world charm was a sight to behold. The lobby was filled with period furniture, and beautiful tapestry lined the windows. In the dining room each table was set with elegant china, flatware and crystal. Though our order was nothing unusual, it was very special for me. A bacon, lettuce and tomato sandwich with butter pecan ice cream for dessert was food that did not exist overseas and I savored every bite.

We continued on our trip and made it to my parents' house around four in the afternoon. I climbed the front steps that I had climbed hundreds of times before and rang the bell. Seconds later, my mother and father greeted me with smiling faces. I hugged them both tightly; it was a thrill to see them after being away for so long. The first thing my father said was how relieved he was that his three sons made it home from the war alive. It had been almost three years since I left for training. Seeing my parents again and hearing their caring voices made me very happy.

Not too long after our arrival, the doorbell rang and in walked my brother Maurice, my brother Paul and his wife Bea, and my sister Lois and her husband Chuck. What a wonderful reunion! I hadn't seen Paul since he was drafted five years before, and I hadn't seen Lois or Chuck for at least three years. This was indeed a very delightful surprise, and it was quite a homecoming for all of us to be together again. After a lot of exciting conversation, Maurice reminded me of how we said back at Manus Island that we couldn't wait for a moment like this to happen again. Now, here we were at 505 Fisher Street, safe and sound.

Paul, Melvin, Lois, Maurice
Dad and Mother

My mother and Lois went to the kitchen to put the finishing touches on dinner. My mother, like Mrs. Winner, was very proud of her china, crystal, and silver. Whenever there was an opportunity to use them, she loved to show them off.

The ground meat, mashed potatoes and many side dishes combined for an excellent dinner, followed by delicious strawberry shortcake for dessert. The whole experience reminded me of the many times we gathered here for family dinners in the past. My parents liked to serve after-dinner drinks on special occasions, and we all settled into the living room for a small glass of amaretto to cap off a wonderful meal.

Before leaving for the Navy, food was not that important to me. I grew up eating wholesome, well-prepared meals, but this abruptly ended when I joined the service.

After dinner, we settled into the living room. My mother was so excited to see us together again that she left the table full of dishes and joined in the conversation. We had a lot to talk about since we had been separated for so many years.

My brother Paul saw action in what was probably the most gruesome battle of World War II, the Allied invasion of Normandy on June 6, 1944. He was also in the Battle of the Bulge. In the service, Maurice's welding talent was put to good use. He helped build air fields and docks that were needed on the many island invasions in the Pacific. I, of course, had many stories to tell about my command of the LCT in the Pacific.

My sister Lois was busy having babies while I was gone. She had Wayne, Dale, and Darlene before I went into the service. While I was away, she and Chuck added two children to the family tree, Donald and Charlotte.

The evening was certainly one to remember. All of us were together as a happy family once again after many long years of separation. The conversation went well into the morning. Around 2 a.m., Lois, Chuck, Paul, and Bea left for their homes, and the rest of us retired for the evening.

The following day, Maurice and my father went off to their jobs. Maurice was a welder, and my dad worked for the Philadelphia Railways Company. My mother prepared a wonderful breakfast for Winnie and me; it was French toast like only she could make. There was no question about it, she was a wonderful cook.

Around 11 in the morning, Winnie and I headed back to Brownsville. It occurred to us that we needed to buy a car of our own; we couldn't keep borrowing the Winners' car. I discussed my dilemma with Joe, and he recommended a used car dealer in town. That evening, Winnie and I went car shopping.

All my life, I had been very impressed with the look and style of Packard automobiles. Winnie and I decided on a big black 1939 model with a chrome grill. The car was already eight years old and had 60,000 miles on it. One has to remember that no passenger cars were built during the war, so all of the used cars had high mileage. Gas was running about 15 cents a gallon, and even though the Packard only got 8 miles to a gallon, we didn't care. We paid $300 for the car, which was quite a deal considering a brand new one would have been at least $1100. Although the purchase put a big dent in my savings, it was a necessity for us—in fact, having a car was a necessity, not a luxury, in the post-war economy.

Winnie and I drove off the lot as proud owners of our 1939 Packard. Winnie suggested we go visit her Uncle Eddie, whose daughter, Peggy, was a bridesmaid at our wedding. It sounded like a great idea at the time. We didn't really have anything else to do, plus it gave me a chance to drive my "new" car through the scenic mountains and into Maryland.

We got to Uncle Eddie's house, and Winnie was delighted to see Peggy again. They hadn't seen each other since our wedding day almost two years before, and it had been longer than that since Winnie had seen her aunt and uncle. After hugs and kisses at the door, we were escorted to the living room. There was the usual talk about how they missed each other, the war, and how their lives were affected by it.

Peggy had two teenage brothers. Both had their driver's licenses, so I saw no reason not to let them borrow my car. After being gone about three hours, they returned with dumb looks on their faces. I asked them if they enjoyed their ride; they said it was fun, but the engine overheated. They said they noticed steam pouring out from under the hood, and the oil gauge showed no pressure. They managed to get the car back home, although the engine was making strange noises the whole way. I instantly marched out to the car and turned the key in the ignition, but the engine would not turn over. I figured it must have frozen from not having any oil in it. I popped the hood and steam bellowed out. The engine block was covered in oil. I called a local mechanic that Winnie's uncle recommended. I hoped the problem was minor and we'd be on our way to Brownsville in no time. Unfortunately, the mechanic had very bad news. The oil line had broken loose from the engine block, and it turned out to be a major problem. He hooked my Packard onto his tow truck and off he went. Winnie and I simply stared in disbelief as the car disappeared down the street.

A few hours later, the mechanic called to tell me my car needed a new motor because it was impossible to repair the old one. Using one he found at a junkyard, he could have it fixed in two days for $100. Now, $100 may not seem like much, but it was a third of what I had just paid for the entire car. I was devastated. Not only did I have to shell out for the car repair, but we were stuck in Frostburg, Maryland, for two more days. To top it off, Winnie's uncle made no effort to pay any part of our repair bill. It was difficult for Winnie and me to maintain an upbeat spirit and enjoy ourselves under these circumstances.

Two days later, we were on our way back to Brownsville. It was nice to be at the Winners again. Each day was filled with one happy occurrence after another. We visited Winnie's many friends and relatives, and one evening, Cecilia's cousin Bob asked us to baby sit. I thought it wouldn't be that big a deal to honor such a request. It might even be fun to be in the company of a 4-year-old for a few hours, and after she went to bed, Winnie and I could have a relaxing time alone.

By 10 p.m. the baby was asleep in her bed. I spotted a bottle of wine, and Winnie said she was certain Bob wouldn't mind if we treated ourselves. I poured two large glasses. Neither one of us drank much wine, so the taste did not seem odd to us. Hours later, Bob and Del came home and were quite shocked to see two drunks caring for their child. I apologized repeatedly to Bob and told him I didn't understand how one glass of wine could be that potent. Well, with that Bob broke the news; it was his homemade moonshine that he colored to look like wine. Winnie always suspected that Bob sold moonshine to supplement his income. It turns out she was right.

After the car fiasco, I knew that I had to be prepared for the many unexpected problems that pop up in life, as well as the serious circumstances Winnie and I now faced. We were married. Neither one of us had a job, and we had no place to live. The money I saved up while I was in the service disappeared fast, and the cost of fixing the car highlighted challenges we'd face together. Winnie asked me about my future career plans. I told her I wanted to complete my degree at Duquesne. After that, I figured I would look for an accounting position or something in the business field. I really had no clear vision with regard to a job. I told her that I figured her parents would let me stay at their home for the summer. Then I would find some type of work and go back to college in the fall. I thought between Winnie's teaching and my working part-time, we'd be able to get by. In two years, I'd have my degree, and then I could get a position somewhere. Maybe it sounded like a simple plan, but it was my idea of our future.

One day, Joe and I were talking about post-war politics. I could tell he had something else on his mind, though, and he did—Winnie. He bluntly asked me how I intended to support his daughter, and I told him of my college plans. He seemed to be satisfied with my answer, and we moved on to talk about something else.

Another week passed with Winnie and me hanging around her house visiting her relatives. Our future began to rest heavily on my mind. A few days later, I found myself back in the living room with Joe. He came right out and asked how I intended on supporting his daughter now.

Dumfounded and taken aback by his remark, I told him I didn't have a solid, definitive answer to his question. Joe abruptly made me aware of the awesome responsibility I had of being Winnie's husband. It was now my job to take care of his daughter. Our marriage released him of that role. It was a rude awakening, and it helped me become a more responsible husband.

Joe must have spent the week pondering what he was going to say to me next, and that is when he suggested I become a hand engraver. This came as a shock to me. It hardly was the type of work I had envisioned for my future. I asked him what type of job that would qualify me for. I didn't realize then how important engraving was in the jewelry business. Mr. Winner went on to explain that there was a huge shortage of talent in the engraving field. Most of the engravers were getting along in years, and there weren't too many young men who wanted to replace them. He told me I would be a natural at learning the trade considering my wood carving talent. I figured it was a pretty crazy idea, but Joe planted a seed of thought for me to dwell on.

Apparently Joe did more than just think of my future as a hand engraver; he researched it. He checked into engraving schools and found the one with the best reputation. It was called Bowman Technical School in Lancaster, Pennsylvania. He handed me a school pamphlet with information on their program. It turned out the United States government would pay my tuition because I was a veteran. Joe seemed very enthusiastic and excited about my going to the Bowman school, so much so that I couldn't ignore his request to give it a try. This would turn out to be a major fork in the road for Winnie and me.

CHAPTER 17
POST WAR CAREER

It is absolutely amazing how small decisions seem so unimportant, yet they can have a major impact on one's future. When trying to decide what clothes to wear on my trip to the school, Winnie suggested I wear my Navy dress uniform. At first I said no way. I didn't like wearing a uniform when I had to, and I liked the thought even less now. To me, my career in the military was behind me and so was wearing a uniform.

During dinner with the Winners that evening, we discussed my pending trip to Lancaster. The three of them ganged up on me and insisted I get my uniform cleaned and pressed for the trip. Mr. Winner also suggested I take some of my woodcarvings along. I told him it wasn't necessary for me to do so, and again I was out-voted by them.

I left for Lancaster Thursday morning dressed in my Navy blues and carrying a briefcase filled with woodcarvings. It was about a six hour drive to the school, and the whole way there I kept wondering why I was doing such a thing. At this point in my life, I really wanted to go back to Duquesne and graduate from college.

Lancaster is not a very large town, so I had no difficulty finding the school. The entire trade school was housed in a building that was a far cry from the universities and naval bases I formerly trained at. Winnie and her parents were right on the money when they insisted I wear my uniform and take my carvings along. The dean, Mr. Bowman, could not have been more patriotic, and it turned out he had a woodcarving hobby as well. And what's more, he was German. He even had a slight accent and reminded me of my Grandfather. Mr. Bowman had a slightly receding hairline, large bushy eyebrows, and a conservative moustache.

It seemed like forever before we discussed the school, because all he wanted to talk about was my time in the service and carving wood. I liked this man, and I could tell he felt the same about me. I was getting anxious to discuss the particulars about the school, particularly the engraving department and when I could enroll. He told me he would be glad to put me on the enrollment list, but there would be a two-year waiting period before I could begin. He said he had been offered as much as $1000 to let a jeweler's son move up on the enrollment list. My heart sank. I could finish college by that time. Well, that is really what I wanted to do anyway, and Mr. Winner would be satisfied that I at least had tried to be an engraver.

The school had three divisions: watch making, jewelry repair and engraving. Students were required to complete all of them. He asked me if I would like to visit the classrooms at the school. The first room we visited was the watch making class. It did not have much appeal to me seeing students working on the small movements of a watch. The next stop was the jewelry repair department. I never saw anyone working on jewelry before. It was impressive to see each student with an acetylene torch, all kinds of files, and an amazing number of grinding wheels and other equipment. I never realized how much equipment was needed to work on jewelry. It was certainly impressive but had little appeal as a future for me.

Finally, we moved over to the engraving class. Each student had an engraving block. It is a heavy piece of iron about the size and shape of a cantaloupe. The top portion is flat with holes to hold various attachments used to secure the jewelry. At each bench were about six different tools the engravers used to cut the metal. I had to admit it was an intriguing process, cutting the metal into various shapes and letters. I said to Mr. Bowman, "How long does it take to finish this class?" He replied, "Six months." I told him I was not interested in all three courses; it was only the engraving I cared about. I saw an empty chair in the back of the room and asked if I could learn to engrave only. He replied that this had never been done. All the students were here for all three courses.

Back in his office, I asked him how students progress at the school. He told me that it was according to their ability. My next question was what the average time was to learn to engrave. He again said six months. I knew I had three months left to enroll at Duquesne for the next term and that six months would set me back one semester. Without much thought as to what I was about to say, out popped the words, "I could do it in ninety days." Mr. Bowman had no reply. He just seemed taken aback at my remark. There was a brief moment of silence as if he was in deep thought. He then said that my kind of guts needs to be rewarded and that I could start tomorrow.

On May 26, 1946, I was sitting in the engraving class at Bowman Technical School. That evening at the desk in the room that I rented, I tried to figure out how I could possibly do in three months what takes six months for most students. This town had many ties to the jewelry industry. In fact, the Hamilton watch factory was located here. There must be a place I could buy used engraving equipment. The next day after school, I located such a place and bought a used engraving block. The other tools I needed were small, and I could borrow them from the school each day. Now I could engrave all day and many hours into the night. I graduated from engraving school in three and a half months. Mr. Bowman was amazed because no one had ever accomplished what I did in such a short period. He congratulated me, and I was on my way to Brownsville with my diploma.

Back at the Winner house, the big question was what would I do now? It would be another semester before I could enroll at Duquesne. Just what did my new talent qualify me for? How would I get a job engraving? I had difficulty sleeping on Saturday night thinking about what my next move would be. What did I know about the jewelry business, and how did engraving fit into the scheme of things. I kept hearing in my subconscious mind Joe asking how I expect to support his daughter now.

It suddenly dawned on me that I bought my diamond engagement ring for Winnie at Frank Becker's jewelry store in the Clark Building in Pittsburgh. Frank was a close friend of my father's going back to his teenage days. Back in 1946, the Clark Building was the center of the wholesale jewelry industry. It was also honeycombed with the different facets of the jewelry industry. Small retailers, jewelry repair shops, watch makers, and engravers were all in the Clark Building. Why not make my first move by going to see Mr. Becker? On Sunday, I talked it over with Winnie and her parents. Mr. Winner confirmed my vague memory that this building was the hub of the jewelry industry. We all decided that I should go and visit Mr. Becker. Very firmly, I told them I was not going in my Navy uniform.

On Monday morning, I was on my way in my best Sunday suit to visit Mr. Becker on the fourth floor of the

Clark Building. I explained that I'd just graduated from Bowman Technical School and was looking for a job in a jewelry store. He asked me if I knew how little engraving each store needed to have done. I said I had no clue, so he went on to explain that the only way I could succeed as an engraver was to own my own business with a minimum of about twenty stores sending me work.

I had the horrible thought that I had wasted three and a half months of my life learning a trade that I would never have any productive use of. Frank was trying to tell me that most engravers made a good living and seemed to be well off financially. They need the least amount of space and tools to do their work. "What you need, Mel, is to find a jewelry manufacturing business willing to rent you space from them." He said, "There have to be at least a dozen of them in this building, and they don't all have engravers. Any one of them would be glad to rent space to you."

I was hardly listening, for it seemed out of the question for me to seek out this option. To me, college was still my most promising way to have a successful future. All of a sudden, I heard this awful loud swearing and racket in the hall. Frank told me that it was Nutsie Friedman, a man in the building otherwise known as the "mad Russian." "Don't be concerned. I am used to his outbursts, but this time is a little different because he is yelling at the engraver who leases space from him."

The argument moved out into the hall, and engraving tools were thrown out the door. Frank calmly said it looked to him like Nutsie Freidman needed an engraver since his was just eliminated. If you have the guts to rent from him, you have a business. Some of the accounts the engraver has will become your customers, and you will have space at a very low cost.

I told myself that if I could make all the decisions when I was Captain of an LCT in WWII, I ought to be able to take

223

advantage of this opportunity. I took a deep breath, stood tall, went over, and introduced myself to Mr. Friedman. I told him I was an engraver looking for space to rent to set up my business. In a very gruff tone of voice, he said there is a desk and space, the rent is $35 a month. I immediately agreed, which was hard for me to comprehend since everything transpired so suddenly. I had a hard time believing I was in business for myself this quickly.

My lessor was a man of very few words. He went back to his bench and said he would see me in the morning. I went over and thanked Frank for his help. He seemed very surprised that I actually decided to start my own business so hastily. I left the city and headed to Brownsville.

Arriving back at Hibbs Street about six o'clock, I was met by Winnie and the Winners. Of course, they were anxious to know if I found a job as an engraver. I went on to explain how hopeless working for a jewelry store was because each store had few engraving jobs. I put on the most depressing look I could muster, stared Joe in the eye, and said engraving school was a big waste of time; I really saw no future for me in this profession. They all had very sad looks on their faces, especially Joe, for he knew it was all his idea. I told them that what really upset me was that I missed a semester at Duquesne because they all wanted me to go to engravers school instead. Joe said that he was sorry he recommended the school, but he was sure that my engraving talent would serve some purpose in the future.

I then gave them the most elated look I could manage and said I could not find anyone in the Clark Building to hire me. Winnie asked why I had such a happy look on my face. I told her that since I could not find a job, I opened my own engraving business. Winnie said, "Come on, Mel, quit making another one of your silly jokes." "I kid you not" I said, "I am now in business, at 717 Liberty Avenue, Room 408 in the Clark Building. I then told them the story about meeting with Frank Becker and how I leased space from Nutsie Freidman. They just looked at me in disbelief, as if I had done the impossible. Joe was a little upset at me for the joke I played on them, but he did commend me for my acting performance.

On September 23, 1946, I was sitting at my engraving desk. I unpacked my engraving block and tools and said to myself, "Wise guy, what is your next move?" I found a piece of brass in the bag I carried my tools in and put it into my engraving block. I engraved my name on it to show I could engrave in case a customer came in.

The owner of Sieger's Jewelry Store in the south side came in with some work for Mr. Friedman. He noticed me and said it looked like I just opened shop today and needed some business. It was rather obvious, for my desk was bare except for my tools.

He opened up his briefcase and left a cigarette lighter, an identification bracelet, and a locket for me to engrave. He said he would be back in two hours to pick them up and walked away. This was the first time anything was in the engraving block except for the brass plates. If he knew that I had never engraved a piece of jewelry in my life, I am sure he wouldn't have left it with me.

To say I was nervous would be an understatement. I did the lighter first, and the results looked great. I took a deep breath and cut letters on the other two items. Al Seiger came back, looked at my work, and said "You have a customer."

The next day, I walked the halls introducing myself to everyone in the various businesses within the building. One has to know how difficult it is for a new salesman to sell a product by making a call to a company who has never seen him before; this is known as a cold call. It is especially difficult if it is a service one is selling. At each stop, I was given the similar reply that they already had an engraver they sent their work to. Some owners were very gruff and upset that I took up their time. I was very discouraged. It looked like the only exchange of money would be when I paid my rent each month for a net loss.

One favorable event did happen. On the sixth floor was an engraver; I passed his space many times. His desk was packed with engraving jobs that needed to be done. With much trepidation, I decided to introduce myself to him. He was deeply engrossed in his work, so I was careful to wait until he finished a piece and was about to pick up the next item. I wondered how he would react to my being a competitor in the same building. I knew his name, Web Best, because it was displayed on the window of the office. I said, "Excuse me, Mr. Best. I would like to introduce myself to you. My name is Mel Eiben. I recently opened up as an engraver on the fourth floor."

Much to my surprise, he got up from his desk, shook my hand, and said he was very glad to meet me. His manner was such that I immediately respected him. He was a dignified-looking man, probably about 56 years old. He seemed to be in no hurry to shorten our conversation. I could tell he was very proud of his work, and he showed me some of his finished jobs.

The job that intrigued me the most was a crest ring he had just finished. It represented the coat of arms, which is a symbol of the origin of a family's name. Only another engraver could appreciate the detail and depth of cut. It was hard for me to comprehend that it was possible to cut so much detail on top of a ring. I thanked him for spending time with me. In parting, he said, "Mel, if you have any difficulty with engraving a piece of jewelry, do not hesitate to come up, and I will help you with your problem."

I left him, overwhelmed by what he just said. I was a competitor of his, and he was willing to help me over any difficulty I might encounter. The rest of the year, I made many trips to the sixth floor for his help. Without his assistance, I doubt I would ever have been successful as an engraver. It did not take long for me to discover that my skills were very limited. Engraving on flat brass plates for three months was not much training for all the items eventually dumped on my desk. How would I go about engraving stainless steel watches, sterling silver flatware, and tea sets... inside rings and trophies? I don't know why Web wanted to put up with me, with all the time I spent with him. He was never too busy to stop and help me solve my problems. Many times, he would do the whole job and would refuse any money for his time.

After one month, it became obvious that at my present rate of income, making a living for Winnie and me was not very realistic. I had some built-in accounts from the previous engraver. The Clark Building being the hub of the jewelry industry provided me with a few more customers, but not enough to make a living. I visited various jewelers around the city and did add to my customer base. It still was not enough. I was hardly making minimum wage.

There was one type of engraving that was relatively easy to do. It was trophy engraving. Almost all of the work was done on flat brass plates. An engraver with the skill level of Web Best did not like to do this type of work. At this time in my engraving career, my only concern was to have enough engraving to convince myself that this profession had a future for me.

Each day I would wander around town, and I did manage to get some new accounts. There was one account that turned out to be a major surprise. It was an old traditional-type store, in existence for at least 90 years. It had been passed from father to son for three generations. They filled my desk with sterling silver hollowware worth hundreds of dollars. I was to engrave family monograms on the tea sets.

This is by far the most difficult type of engraving to do. One slip of a tool can cause irreparable damage. With much embarrassment, I carried these back to the store explaining my lack of experience in doing these difficult jobs.

On Liberty Avenue at this time was a sporting goods store named Honus Wagner. From the display in the window, I could tell that trophies were a big part of this business. I thought, "Why not go in and speak to the owner about doing his engraving?" Entering the store, I went up to a man who looked like he might be the owner, only to find out he was just managing this department. I asked him if there was a need for an engraver. In a very curt reply, he said he already had an engraver. Rather than just walking out of the store with this answer, I pleaded with him to go see the boss and tell him I was here to speak with him about doing engraving on his trophies. He finally agreed to go to his boss and ask if he would meet with me. I was introduced to Mr. Spellman, and I told him I was a new engraver in the Clark building. I could tell he was deeply involved with a pile of papers on his desk and was not very happy at being interrupted. He asked me how much I charged per letter. I knew the going rate was 5 cents per letter, so I figured a lower price might open a door of opportunity for me, and I told him 4 cents.

Much to my surprise, the two of us went down to the first floor to talk to the man I met when I entered the store. Mr. Spellman told him to give me some work. I walked out of the store with a boxful of trophies. The going rate at this time was five cents a letter on almost all types of engraving, but engraving on jewelry was much more difficult than trophy engraving. I knew I could engrave three times as fast on this flat plate as on regular jewelry. If it was that easy to become the engraver for Honus Wagner, why not other stores selling trophies? I called on Wilson Sporting Goods, Pittsburgh Sporting Goods, and Union Supply Company, three big trophy stores in the city. They all started to send me trophy engraving. It seemed as if I was engraving almost every trophy that was won in the city for all types of sports.

The one sport that gave out a tremendous amount of trophies was bowling. In April and May, it was almost impossible to stay on top of the workload. I would start to work at home at 8 a.m., and then leave for Pittsburgh at 10 to miss the traffic; I would engrave until one and then go to lunch. Back at 2 o'clock, I would now work until 7 p.m. to miss the traffic going home. About nine o'clock, I would be back at work at home until as late as 2 a.m. I worked six days a week on this schedule and all day Sunday at home. I had the same workload in the month of December as well. With this killer schedule, I made almost $3000 in my first full year of business. Not too shabby an income for the first full year in my new business. The average yearly income in 1947 was $2900. It is hard to believe, but with inflation over 50 years, my $3000 would be at least $30,000 today.

Part of my income came from selling jewelry to my friends. They would come to visit me and ask where to buy jewelry at a reasonable price. One of my engraving accounts was Baggard and Company. Baggard and Company was a huge operation occupying the entire 21st floor. They were a full line wholesaler selling all types of jewelry. The owner suggested that I bring customers to his showroom, and I could sell to them from his inventory. At this time in the jewelry industry, wholesalers were very strict about selling to the public, so the only way my friends could gain access to Baggard and Company was for me to be with them. As a retailer, I could take the merchandise off the shelves without the help of a salesman and present it to a customer. I would make the sale, and Mr. Baggard would give me a cut of the profits.

One of my engraving customers was John Keppie and Company. John sold only diamonds and wedding bands. He had a great personality, and it was always fun to be around him. At times, I would take a competitor's diamond for him to see. I would say, "Look, John, this diamond is the same quality for less money." He would look at the diamond, raise out of the seat of his chair, throw the diamond on his desk, and say, "How can you sell this junk?" He would then show me that the difference is in the cut characteristics of the stone. The diamonds from Keppie's business were only of the finest cut. In fact, his company was a pioneer in emphasizing the importance of an ideal cut. John and I became very close friends, and my visits to his office were like going to the Gemological Institute. He taught me about carat weight, color, clarity, and cut and its relation to a diamond's price. I could not bring my customers into his showroom because his company was very strict about selling to the public. In order for me to sell his merchandise, I would have to determine the price range and quality of the diamond and mounting the customer wanted to buy. Then with this information, I would procure samples from his inventory on memo to show my customer.

I now had access to a diamond inventory larger than the stock of any jewelry store. John gave me a present of a ten-power eye loupe and tweezers and said with these two tools and his inventory I was ready to start a jewelry business. He said the best way to sell a diamond in the jewelry business was by first teaching the customer about the 4 c's and their relation to price: carat weight, color, clarity, and the most important, cut. He told me to be especially diligent in my sales talk about the cut of a diamond. The next step was to show the customer a loose diamond magnified 10x power with an eye loupe. Most customers have never seen a diamond magnified. The final procedure was to place it on top of a selection of mountings. John said never hurry a sale, be patient, and if I followed his advice, I would sell a lot of diamonds. He was right. To this day, I use this procedure in my diamond selling.

John's friendship and my business dealings with his company indeed became a very important fork in the road in my life. The more I visited his office and worked with his instruments, the more I became intrigued with diamonds.

John Keppie's honesty and integrity impressed me from the very beginning. My association with John embedded in my mind that honesty was the best way to run a jewelry business. There are many honest jewelers, but since it is so difficult for a customer to determine the value of the merchandise, it is also very easy for a jeweler to deceive and cheat a customer.

My dealings with J.C. Keppie Company made it necessary for me to obtain a retailer's license. The document made me feel very proud, and it opened up a whole new world for me. Having this document made it possible for me to go to any wholesaler and procure the merchandise on memorandum. I could show it to my customers and return the unsold samples. I now had access to all the wholesalers in the building and could buy from out-of-town manufacturers.

My space at Nutsie Freidman's was not ideal. His personality made it very difficult for me to do my work. After about six months, I moved to a jewelry manufacturing business by the name of Kuni and Brown, Suite 617.

This turned out to be a perfect fit for the retail phase of my business. At Freidman's, it was impossible to see how jewelry was made. Kuni and Brown never objected to my seeing them work. This gave me a chance to learn how to adjust stock mountings into different configurations. I began to design original pieces of jewelry and they became very pleased with their tenant because I gave them additional business.

I had much more space in my new place of business, and I learned a lot about how jewelry was repaired and manufactured. This was very helpful in developing my talent as a jewelry designer, which was about to become a big part of my future.

Things had started looking up and I thought to myself, "As small as this business is, 15 square feet, it is a jewelry store. I have a retail license and am dealing with everything jewelry stores deal with." That made me feel good, knowing I had the embryo of a store that could someday be a major business.

Almost all my efforts had been concentrated on my new business. This gave me limited time to deal with a very pressing problem. Due to the shortage of living space after the war, I was forced to live with relatives. I could not go on like this, imposing on their family life. Somehow, this difficult problem had to be resolved.

CHAPTER 18
A PLACE TO LIVE

During the first three months of being in business, I traveled from Brownsville to Pittsburgh each working day. The drive was a killer, especially in the winter. It was just a matter of time before I would fall asleep at the wheel and I knew this arrangement could not go on. I had to have some place in Pittsburgh to live. After the War, finding a habitable apartment in a middle class neighborhood that would satisfy our basic needs was next to impossible.

My sister lived in a small house located just 15 minutes from downtown Pittsburgh. Despite the fact that she had four children, she found space in the attic for Winnie and me to live, and in the middle of January 1947, we moved to 804 Stiner Street. (Our new address was the same number of the LCT I lived on for 16 months.) Life now had a bit of normality to it. After work, I had a place to go that was close to my business, and the first two months there were very pleasant. Winnie helped Lois with the cooking and cleaning. My sister's husband Chuck had a great sense of humor. He was a fun person to live with, and their children seemed to enjoy having an aunt and uncle around.

Lois never complained, but our presence there had to be a strain on her and the family. Both Winnie and I felt our welcome was wearing thin, and it was time to move on. I wanted to be sure to leave before some incident would happen that would mar our friendship with the Riethers.

Winnie arranged for us to move in with her cousin Mary Martin in mid-April. She lived in Homestead, which was about 20 minutes from downtown. Here we were able to live in a room on the first floor. Mary had two children, and the conditions were not as cramped as they were at the Riether house.

One month later, my wife told me she was pregnant. It was marvelous news, and I was very happy to find out that we were going to have a child. The timing, however, was not too wonderful. I had no permanent place for us to live. My engraving business was very new, and it left me with many loose ends. I had to press on with my life and do the best I could to provide for our future, one that included our first child.

The Martins gave us no reason not to feel at ease in their home, but I knew this arrangement could not last indefinitely. Winnie and I were looking for an apartment, but none of the ones I felt we could afford appealed to us. I decided that we needed some type of permanent residence at a reasonable price. I discovered that a mortgage on a small house was less than monthly rent on an apartment half its size, so, in the middle of July we started looking for a house to buy. This fork in the road was about to send me on another roller coaster ride.

Trying to buy a house right after the war ended was depressing. Quality homes near schools and public transportation were in short supply and extremely overpriced. After looking for a few weeks, we realized that our plan of buying a finished home was hopeless.

In my usual decision-making fashion, without thinking

ahead, I decided to buy a lot to build on. I found out later that this was not the way to go when getting a house constructed. My first move should have been to get an estimate on the total cost of each segment of the project. There were other fundamentals I should have looked into as well, such as what builder I should use, was I eligible for a veteran's loan, and how much would the bank let me mortgage. At the very least, I should have considered what type of house Winnie and I wanted to build before buying the land. One would think I would have dealt with at least some of these issues. I did not and it was as if I bought an automobile without a steering wheel, engine, or drive shaft when I chose to buy the land first.

Without researching what building a house entailed, Winnie and I went looking for a dream location in some newly developed neighborhood, near a Catholic school and public transportation. We searched everywhere, and the section of the suburbs we kept coming back to was Pleasant Hills. Driving around the borough, we spotted a plot of ground one-half block from a bus stop. St. Elizabeth's School and Church were within walking distance, and the name of the street had a relaxing sound to it, Broadway Drive in Pleasant Hills. Winnie and I were incredibly excited about this spot. Armed with the number, we went to the nearest pay phone and called the real estate office. Of course, there was no answer since it was Sunday. There are some things in this world that are unique, and this particular plot of land was one of them, which is why Winnie and I were so anxious about it being sold before we could make an offer.

First thing Monday, I called to make an appointment to arrange to buy the lot. The real estate agent was able to see me that morning, and the price of the lot seemed reasonable at $1500. What a joke! How would I know what a reasonable price was considering I had never bought land before? I met with the agent, told him he had a deal, and I would get back to him with the financial arrangements.

That afternoon, I stopped at Mellon Bank where I had my business account. The real estate agent had given me a survey of the lot along with the price to show to the bank. The bank officer said I needed a down payment of $300, and they would lend me the remaining balance. On July 14, 1947, Winnie and I became the proud owners of land in Pleasant Hills. Now Mr. "Quick Decision," what do you do next?

On my next trip to the bank, I asked an employee if he knew how to go about getting a house built, and he said that I should first contact a builder. I called Bill Roth, a friend of mine from Duquesne University. His dad built houses, and I asked him to arrange an appointment for me.

A few days later, I met with Pete Roth. I told him I desperately needed a place to live and asked if he could build me a house in six months. He told me it was very possible, but first I had to decide what type of home I wanted. Once I made up my mind, he would give me an estimate, and I could go to the bank and procure a construction loan. Pete showed me several designs for a seven-room house with two baths and a connected garage. The entire layout looked great except the dining room was next to the living room. I told him I did not want a dining room and to make it into one large living room instead, and that way Winnie and I would have one large room the length of the house to entertain in. Winnie and I agreed on the design, and Mr. Roth said he would go by the lot to check out the property and get back to us in a few days.

One week later, I received Pete's estimate in the mail. It was $9500. Winnie and I compared the price with some of the finished homes we looked at, and the cost was comparable. At the time, $9500 was a lot of money; the average income that year was $2900. Pete suggested I take out a 30-year veteran's loan where my payments would be approximately $80 a month. I figured I should be able to make that payment without too much trouble.

I talked to my friend Bruce. His father worked at Western Pennsylvania Bank, and he led me to believe that they had more liberal loan policies than most other banks in the area. From our conversation, I thought this bank would more likely approve a questionable loan, and there was no doubt in my mind I was in that category. I stopped by the bank and made an appointment to see a loan officer.

The days before my appointment with the loan officer were filled with doubt. I constantly wondered if I had a chance at procuring a loan. Would the officer laugh at me when I said I wanted to borrow $9500? I had no idea what would transpire. Little did I know that even a veteran's loan required a down payment, and the only money I had went toward the lot.

I went to Western Pennsylvania Bank for my appointment. Finally, the loan officer appeared, and we made our way to his office. He looked like he was in his mid-sixties, and his demeanor suggested that I had no chance of getting a loan. I thought to myself, if a lieutenant commander in the navy did not overwhelm me, then why should this man. We began to discuss the purpose of my visit, and I presented my business card to him and a list of companies I did business with. I also told him I had a retailer's license, and I sold jewelry as well. He seemed impressed with the size and quality of the companies I worked with despite the short time I was in business.

Much to my surprise, we got down to processing my loan when suddenly he hit me with a bombshell of a question and asked how much cash I was going to put down to secure the loan. My answer required some fast thinking, and I was trying not to act flabbergasted. I told him I did not think I needed a down payment since I had a valuable lot in

Pleasant Hills to build on. Luckily, he didn't ask me how much I owed. I was completely astonished when he said I could use the lot to secure a construction loan. I told him the cost of the house, not including the lot, was $9500, and he approved a construction loan for me. The bank would pay the contractor the amount needed for each phase of building the house only after the previous section was complete.

Once the bank approved the mortgage and Pete got his money for the first phase of building, his construction team broke ground. I especially enjoyed watching them dig the hole for the foundation, and it was a thrill knowing this was to be our house in a mere six months.

In September, Winnie told me that she wanted to be near her mother since she was now seven months pregnant. As a result, she went to live with her parents, and I went to live with mine. It was next to impossible for me to commute from Brownsville to Pittsburgh each day, and this arrangement seemed logical for now since our house was supposed to be finished by mid-January. Despite the fact that I was not living with my wife, thoughts of our first child and our new home made me very excited and happy for our future.

As if life were not chaotic enough, I ran an engraving tool into the palm of my hand. I was not worried about it and went to work anyway. The wound began to fester and looked very ugly. I decided to go to a doctor in Pittsburgh; he did not seem overly concerned with the gash in my hand and did not discourage me from going to work. I became very concerned when a bright red stripe developed on my arm. That is usually the first sign of massive infection. My parents became very alarmed because along with the immense soreness, I felt very sick. In early October, my mother called Winnie and told her of my condition. That very night, Joe and my wife came to Pittsburgh and took me to Brownsville.

As soon as we arrived in Brownsville, Mr. Winner called Dr. Williams, whom the Winner family had used as their physician for many years. Dr. Williams was in his early sixties, partially bald, and dressed as if he were about to go to a baseball game. Despite his casual appearance, he had a warm, reassuring look about him that put me at ease. Dr. Williams diagnosed me with a severe case of blood poisoning. Penicillin was relatively new at this time, but despite this, he injected me with a large experimental dose in my arm. A few days later, I felt much better.

Dr. Williams later told me that I had been a lot worse than he led me to believe. In fact, he said he gave me the largest dose of penicillin he had ever used on anyone before and was concerned how my body would react to it. Nevertheless, considering my condition, he said it was a chance he had to take.

Little did I know that in such a short period my life would take so many twists and turns. After all, I had only been home a year and a half. At times, I thought that being back on the LCT and sailing up the Zamboanga peninsula would be a welcome change from all the complications of my post-war life.

Once I was over my blood poisoning, life seemed to settle into somewhat of a normal pattern. The main aggravation I had was wondering when our house would be finished. All the builder had constructed in twelve weeks was the foundation, and it seemed highly unlikely that the house would be completed in six months.

I had more on my mind than the house. Winnie was over eight months pregnant, and I knew the baby would be born any day.

At six o'clock in the morning on November 3, Suzanne Cecilia Eiben was born. Much to my relief, all of her bodily functions were as normal as those of a healthy baby should be. I spent Sunday and Monday at the hospital. As much as

239

I hated to leave my new family and travel back to Pittsburgh on Tuesday, I was a one-man business and had engraving to do. What a farce the saying "own your own business, come, and go as you please" is.

After Suzi was born, I became more focused on getting our house completed. I was also overwhelmed with my work. December was the busiest time of year and confusion surrounded me; I had to satisfy my customers, my wife, and a new baby. On Saturday nights around nine o'clock, I would drive past my house to check on its development. It was now month five of construction, and all I could see was a roof supported by a bunch of two-by-fours.

I called the builder to ask about the progress on our house and got a horde of excuses. "The weather this time of year is making work difficult," and "It's hard to obtain building materials because of all the new homes going up after the war" were some of the reasons I was given for why the house wasn't done. I sensed something was not right about the progress on the house.

I decided to check into it and went to the bank to ask how much money Pete Roth had received. I found out that the amount forwarded to date was for the third phase of construction including the plumbing, and drywall work. I told the loan officer that none of this was being worked on and asked why they released the money to Pete. His only reply was that they had many of these types of loans on the books and did not have enough personnel to check on the progress of each home. I emphatically said, "This is crazy. I certainly do not have the knowledge or time to do your job for you."

Shortly thereafter, I ran into my friend Bill (Pete's son), told him about my problem, and asked if there was anything he could do to help speed up the completion of my house. He said his dad was very busy and was building more than one house at a time. We drove past one of his dad's other building sites. Bill said the home was not sold yet; his dad was going to put it on the market when it was finished.

I talked about my dilemma with one of my engraving customers who was familiar with building houses. He told me about unscrupulous builders who might be building three houses at a time. Construction loans like mine would finance two of them, while the third one would be built using materials from the other two jobs. The builder counts on selling the third house in the middle of constructing the other two so he can have enough capital to complete all three and make some money on the side. The only trouble, my customer said, is it could delay the completion of my home for several months.

I went to the bank, told them about my concerns, and asked what they would do about it. The loan officer said it was a practice they could not control and all they could do was to make sure my home was properly finished before the builder would get his final payment.

I decided to be more aggressive in harassing Pete regarding this matter. I told Pete I knew the amount the bank had given him so far to build the house, and what he was doing could cause him some serious legal problems. I kept on him about finishing the house and noticed a lot more progress.

Finally, in the middle of April, ten months after we broke ground, the bank inspected the house and said we could move in. There was still one minor detail not completed: A large boulder in the middle of the back yard needed to be taken out. We moved in anyway, and Pete asked me to release the final payment. I told him there was no way I would do such a thing until the big rock was gone, and three weeks later Pete and his son showed up. They spent most of the day removing it.

The day I moved into a brand new home with my wife and daughter was one of those wonderful days in my life that I will never forget. The following day, I worked until four and drove home to my new residence for the first time. It was thrilling. As I pulled up, Winnie was standing on the front steps with Suzi in her arms. What a remarkable sight. I gave my wife a kiss, took my daughter into my arms, and went into the house where I smelled a delicious aroma coming out of the kitchen. "Winnie" I said, "this can't be true...you cooked my favorite meal, ground meat and mashed potatoes!" As we sat down at the table, about to enjoy our first home-cooked meal together, a fly landed on my dish, and I waved it away. Seconds later, our food was covered with flies, and swatting at them was hopeless. We could not eat one bite, and Winnie was incredibly disappointed because she wanted so much to please me. We found out after that this often happens with new construction because flies like to lay their eggs in fresh wood.

Family Residence - Broadway Drive, Pleasant Hills

Life for the next year took on a pattern of typical suburban life. My neighbor to the left was an elderly man in his late sixties. The neighbors on the other side were in their early forties and had a daughter who was twelve and a son who was ten. Mrs. Reher was a wonderful, outgoing person while

Mr. Reher was a quiet individual with little to say. If Winnie had any questions or concerns, Mrs. Reher was always there to listen or lend a hand. Paul, although subdued, was always glad to help me with any electrical or mechanical problems. I cannot tell you how many times he saw me frustrated and yanking on the cord to the lawn mower. Without my asking, he would come over, make some minor adjustment, and with one pull, the mower would start.

On December 6, 1949, Cynthia Lee Eiben was born. Our second-born brought new pleasure into our home along with many sleepless nights. The two children and my demanding work hours kept me very busy. For the next two years, Winnie and I were very content and enjoyed life in our new home.

In the fall of 1951, a friend of mine convinced Winnie and me to join a bowling league. Up to this time, our circle of friends was limited to our neighbors and some of the people we became acquainted with at St. Elizabeth's church. As I remember, this was one of the happiest times of our married life. Our next-door neighbor's daughter babysat for us so we could go out and enjoy our newfound friends. We also joined the American Legion, which was a great place for us to relax after bowling. The Legion had a billiard table, and I enjoyed shooting pool as much as I fancied bowling. To add a little excitement to the game, there was usually a small wager involved.

As I look back on all the evenings of pleasure, I like to remember how each couple's unique personalities influenced me. All my life I was very fortunate to be around interesting people. Boredom was not part of my existence. The most fascinating person I befriended was a man named Bill O'Hara, who looked and acted like Jackie Gleason. Similar to Gleason, he was an excellent pool player and very good at golf. Bill and I had many enjoyable rounds of golf together.

CHAPTER 19
GOLF

Golf had a major impact on my life in so many different ways. The four to five hours it requires to play a round of golf has always given me an opportunity to relax and remove myself from the everyday concerns of living. It was also a way to spend quality time with friends and business associates.

From the very first time I had a golf club in my hand, the game of golf had a fascination for me. This was on a family vacation at the age of 12 playing miniature golf. Holding the club in my hand and sensing how it could be used to strike the ball hard or with a very sensitive touch to guide it into a small hole was an intriguing sensation.

Then one summer day when I was 16, four of us decided to play a round of golf on an official 18-hole course, just outside of Pittsburgh. We managed to borrow clubs from some older men in the area. They were a mixture of old clubs long discarded.

Bill, the oldest one in our group, had a driver's license and had the use of his dad's car for an afternoon a few days later. Off we went to the golf course.

I could see the owner looking at the four of us in tennis shoes with beat up looking bags and about 6 unmatched clubs in each bag. He said, "Did you ever play golf before?" Bill, the smooth talker in our group, replied, "Don't let the look of our bags and clubs deceive you." It must have been a poor day business-wise, or he would not have allowed us to start.

Following us out to the tee, the owner watched as Bill was the first to tee off. The ball went a reasonable distance, slicing in a sharp right direction into the woods. The next man up dribbled the ball about 50 yards on the ground. Third to tee off had a high pop up. Now it was my turn, and guess what? I missed the ball completely. The owner just shook his head and walked back into the clubhouse.

When we started to play, there wasn't anyone behind us, but by the time we proceeded to the eighth hole, a foursome caught up to our group. We were so involved with trying to move the ball in some forward direction and looking for the lost balls that it never occurred to us we were aggravating the players behind us.

They put up with us for about two holes. Suddenly, they were hitting balls landing too close for comfort and yelling for us to speed up our play. Looking back at four powerful-looking men with mean looks on their faces, we decided to pick up and move to the next hole.

On this first day of golf, I learned a lesson on the lethal possibilities of physical damage from a golf ball. My friend Bill was in a sand trap next to the green, and I was holding the flagstick. After several attempts to remove the ball from the trap, in frustration, he took a full swing. All of a sudden, the ball came flying past my ear. This could have been the only game of golf I would ever play. I learned a very important lesson the first day—always stay behind the golfer.

The first time I played golf with Winnie's brother, Ed, I had no idea of his playing ability. I brought my friend

Chuck, and Ed brought his neighbor Pete. Three of us teed off with typical Sunday golfer results, meaning the shots were nothing to brag about. Then Pete teed off, and his shot went 200 yards down the middle of the fairway with a slight fade, indicating that we were not up to his playing skills. It made me wonder how he would put up with playing 18 holes with three duffers. (As I would find out through years of playing golf, the disparity of players' skills never seems to affect the enjoyment of a foursome.)

On the ninth hole, Pete was approaching the green and picked a club that he felt would send the ball high in the air, then drop softly on the green. He took a full swing, and the ball rose majestically into the air. The shot cleared the green by 20 yards, crashing through a rusty screen door into the men's room located near the back of the green.

After Pete hit his shot, he examined his club and discovered he had used a six iron instead of a nine iron. Going into the men's room to retrieve his ball, he heard a man who was sitting on the "john" shout, "God damn! I thought I was safe from a bad shot in here."

One of Winnie's closest friends, Velma, owned a cottage on the shore of Lake Erie near the city of Erie, Pennsylvania. One evening when we were visiting with them, they suggested we rent their cottage for a week. Velma explained that it was a perfect location for children, with an amusement park nearby, and the beach only a hundred yards from the cottage. Knowing I liked to play golf, she informed me that Geneva municipal public golf course was only a mile away. I tried not to act too excited about renting the cottage for fear Winnie would think she would be a golf widow for a week and decide this would be the wrong place to go on vacation.We told them we would think it over.

The next day I told Winnie that from Velma's description it would be a wonderful place for the children to have a vacation. Winnie, with her wonderful smile, said, "You mean the golf course is not part of your desire to go to Lake Erie?" "Well," I said, "I have to admit it might have a little to do with my decision."

I can't tell you my excitement thinking about playing golf for five days in a row. The only problem was I had no one to play with. Arriving on Saturday afternoon, we unpacked and settled in to what was really a home, not a cottage. I told the family I was going to take a short walk down to the beach, not letting on I was looking for some evidence of a golfer in one of the nearby homes. Sure enough, luck was with me. I noticed a man taking his clubs from his car. I introduced myself and struck up a conversation about my looking for golf games in the coming week.

His name was Hank Helnan, and I could tell by his golf equipment he was a serious golfer. How lucky could I get, for he needed me to round out a foursome for the coming week. The first game was on Monday, and our tee time was 9 a.m. What could be more perfect? I would have the afternoon to spend with the family. To make the setup more ideal, I could leave the car for Winnie.

Hank told me a little about the course. It had a bit of notoriety in that Jack Nicklaus had won the amateur Ohio State Championship there. Monday morning could not come soon enough. By this time in my playing career, I played well enough to be comfortable with almost any golfer, so I felt at ease with the thought that I would fit in with the foursome.

Monday arrived, and we went in Hank's car. The other two gentlemen had great personalities, so the four of us had a very pleasant day of golf. To add to the enjoyment, it was the best golf course I ever played on. I played each day the rest of the week.

Friday's game did have some unusual happenings. After playing 18 holes of golf, we stopped at a local bar. The two players who lost, me being one of the losers, argued that it was a fluke that we did not win. Just to prove it, why don't the four of us go to Erie Shore golf course and play nine holes.

On the number one tee, the first man up whiffed 3 shots in a row before moving the ball about 20 yards. The next man up did pretty much the same. What a couple of jerks. This couldn't happen to me. Sure enough the results were the same. Then the fourth man, Hank, approached the tee. Hank needs a short description. He is a rugged, good looking individual about 5 feet 8 inches tall weighing about 200 pounds. He flew B-17 bombers in World War II; his natural voice was as if he were shouting over the noise of the bomber's engine. Standing over the ball, the golf professional at the course tapped him on the shoulder and said, "Would you mind if the next foursome hit first." In a loud booming voice he said, "This is the first damn time a foursome hit through me on the first tee."

The golf course had very peculiar carts. Each player had his own cart, and you rode them as if on a horse. It was quite a sight to see the four drunks going in all different directions on the fairway and into the rough. The results were never determined, for no one was sober enough to keep score.

The week was so enjoyable for my wife and the children that we returned to the same location for many years.

Even though I did not continue my education at Duquesne University, I kept in close contact with my acquaintances at the school. I was asked to organize an annual golf outing for the alumni of the school. One of the graduates, Norm Weidner, was a member of Wildwood Country Club. He agreed to arrange to hold the outing each year at his club.

I chaired the affair for five years. Being in charge of the outing helped me keep in contact with my fraternity brothers and other friends from college years. At the time, I did not realize it, but their contacts later became important in my business career.

It made me feel very proud when they presented me with an enamel plaque of the seal of the University. To this day, it hangs in my office.

One year after a round of golf, sitting at the bar, the entire group was feeling good about the day's events, and it was suggested that we all go on a golf trip in the spring of the next year.

Tom Grealish, with his very outgoing personality, signed up 16 golfers for a trip to South Carolina to the famous seaside town of Myrtle Beach. He researched accommodations and rates and decided on the Sea Pine Golf Resort. It was April, the spring of 1954; we had just arrived at the hotel and been assigned our rooms. Tom decided to call the pro shop and find out our tee off times. Much to his dismay, he discovered that when making reservations he had failed to arrange tee off times, a rather important detail for a golf trip. Sixteen frustrated golfers looked out over the beautiful number one tee of the Sea Pine Golf Resort, wondering if there was any solution to this sad situation.

Tom called the Pine Isle Golf Resort in Georgia, further south. Much to his delight, starting times were available. A quick meeting resulted in a split decision. Half of the group decided to rent a van and go to the other course, me being one of them.

Chuck Nelson was in the group heading south. He had flown down in a four-seater single engine airplane. He was learning to fly and had his instructor George with him. He asked if I would like to go with him and fly to the other resort. I had no idea what was in store for me on this eventful day. The hotel courtesy car dropped us off at the Myrtle Beach airport. It seemed like a perfect flying day, 80 degree temperature, a few cirrus clouds in the sky, and very little wind. But viewing the airplane, I wasn't so sure it was such a great idea to go by plane. It looked pretty much the same as the Taylor cubs I flew in the Air Corps. On board the plane, there was little room for me in the back seat with three sets of clubs to keep me company. They had a nonchalant conversation about the possibility of the plane being overloaded. Was this to scare me, or was it a real danger? Not much I could do about thinking this was a bad decision, for the engine was running, and we were on our way down the runway. Was it my concern about being overloaded that made me think that it seemed like forever before we were airborne? We were in the air at a cruising speed of about 100 miles per hour at an elevation of 1000 feet. It is hard to describe if you have never been in a light plane flying at this elevation; what an exhilarating sensation it is viewing the scenery below. The trip also brought back memories of my flying days in the Navy Air Corps.

After two long hours in the air, we circled what looked like a couple of dirt roads that I had to assume was an airport. The only way I could be sure was I saw a wind sock indicating the direction of the wind. Landing an aircraft is more difficult than taking off. The student was at the controls, which left me with an uneasy feeling about having a safe landing, but he seemed to execute the maneuver very well, for we were now at rest on the runway.

George went over to the pay phone hanging on the outside of a small office building and phoned for a cab. We had a short 20-minute ride to Pine Isle Golf Resort. In the hotel, we arranged tee off time for the next morning. Chuck decided to call our friends up north to see if they decided to join us at the resort. Norm Weidner said there was no reason to, for they now had tee times for the rest of the week and said why not come back and join us. When the rest of the men arrived by van, we had a quick meeting and decided to go back to the other resort, but we decided to have dinner first.

Back at the airport at 8 p.m., it was dusk, although the visibility was still good. It didn't take much thinking to know it would be dark before our landing at the airport after a two-hour flight. In the airplane, the engine revved at its maximum speed with the brake still on. I looked out the back of the plane and saw a cloud of dust flying in the air. It was an entirely different experience than the take off from the concrete runway of the Myrtle Beach airport.

In the air at 9:30 p.m. as we are approaching the airport, the instructor said, "Chuck you are about to make your first night landing." Chuck said, "Are you sure I can do it?" He replied, "Why not? This is a well-lit airport. The maneuver is pretty much the same as a day landing. There is very little wind, so there should not be a problem."

I remembered Chuck and George having a drink at the dinner table; I hoped they only had one. I had to say I was much relieved when we finally came to a stop. It was indeed a very eventful day.

In the morning, we met for breakfast and made wagers for the day's events. It was a clear day, 80 degree temperature with a mild wind, a perfect day for golf. I experienced the usual elation of anticipating a day of golf.

The day had no disappointments. It is difficult to describe the enjoyment of a game of golf on a professional golf course such as this at a seaside resort. You can forget the everyday trials and tribulations of family and business and totally enjoy the day's events.

Back at the hotel, we were all set to have a gourmet dinner. We had reservations and met in the lobby. We were dressed in much the same attire we would wear on the golf course. The maitre d' told us we could not be seated. Protesting, we argued that we had reservations. He said that is not the issue; you need a tie and a jacket. What a disappointed bunch of hungry golfers.

One of the men in the group, Father Gary, was a talented

artist. He had the habit of always having a dry marker in his pocket, and he asked for volunteers to paint a tie and jacket on their shirt. I for one said "OK," and three other men volunteered. The four of us walked up to the maitre d'. Seeing the painted shirts, he broke out into laughter and said we could be seated and have dinner.

The week went by too fast, as it always does on a vacation. It was Saturday, the last day of our golf trip. At dinner that evening, we began thinking about Monday morning when we would all be back in the usual everyday routine of traffic jams getting to work, arriving on the job with a pile of details to work out. We'd be happy to see our wives and families, but then the every day problems of living would occur. There would be the never-ending task of paying bills and living within a budget.

As the evening passed, one of the men wondered if it would be possible to play one more round of golf on Sunday. We called the airport and learned there was indeed a 6 p.m. flight to Pittsburgh, and seats were available. However, there was one glitch: almost all of us were Catholic, and we had to attend mass.

Several of the men gave the assignment to me to see what could be done about this problem. At first there seemed to be no possible way to go to church and still play golf. Suddenly it occurred to me there was an easy solution. Father Gary in our group is a priest. Why couldn't he say Mass? He said it was impossible, for he had no religious paraphernalia with him. The determined person that I am, I racked my brain for a solution.

I decided to call the local parish and ask the priest to come to the resort and say Mass. I consulted with Father Gary, and he said it could be possible. On a hunch, I figured he might be a golfer and would jump at the opportunity to play golf on the pristine layout. To give him an added incentive, I took up a collection of $20 from each person, thinking the tidy sum of $320 plus a golf game would be hard to pass up.

Fortunately, the priest I got on the phone seemed to be young. I told him about my proposition, and he said it is a very enticing offer, but there was one big problem. Church law has a rule that I can only say three Masses on the weekend. He went on to say he did have a solution to our predicament, knowing how much you all love golf. With that much love, you must also have a portion left over for the love of God. With that in mind, I have decided to give you all special dispensation; you do not have to go to church this Sunday.

I said, "Father, hold on till I give the wonderful news to my friends." I then told them that I arranged through the good father for special dispensation, and none of us have to attend Mass. Tom Grealish said in a loud voice, "Come on, Mel, this is impossible." Telling the priest that one of our men said "This is impossible," the priest now asked me his name. I said, "Tom." He then replied, "I should have known his name would be the same as St. Thomas who doubted Jesus. Even Tom was now convinced, so the next morning we teed off for one more day of golf.

The flight out was at 6 p.m. We knew this, but it would still get us in Pittsburgh by 9 p.m. and home by 10 o'clock. Our wives, who were expecting us late in the afternoon, would be a bit upset. Jim, the one who called the travel agent, failed to ask if it was a direct flight to Pittsburgh. Much to our dismay, we discovered there was an hour-and-a-half layover in Washington. Finally in Pittsburgh after some luggage delays and difficulties finding a taxi, I arrived home at three in the morning.

At first Winnie was glad to see that I had arrived home safely. You can imagine the dissertation that an irate woman can deliver. It didn't last too long, for I fell asleep from exhaustion sitting on the living room sofa.

The next day I was up at 7 a.m. At 8 o'clock I was on my way to work and glad to be away from the harassment that continued in the morning. I knew from experience that by dinner time Winnie, my two children, and I would settle into a normal happy family routine. This serenity was not to last very long, for I was about to embark on the next exciting phase of my golf life.

During the years we were building up Eiben and Irr, my home in Pleasant Hills was three miles from South Hills Country Club. Each working day, I would pass this beautiful manicured golf course. Sitting in my car waiting for the light to change at the intersection of Brownsville Road and Route 51, I could see a green close to the road that looked smoother than my living room carpet. This golf course is one of the most exclusive clubs in the Pittsburgh area. Envy may be a sin, but I sure was guilty of it each time I would drive by, seeing the golfers on the course.

Could it ever be possible that I could belong to this club? Dream on, Mel. You have two children for whom you will some day pay a substantial sum of money for college tuition. You have a car payment, a mortgage, and everyday expenses that are a challenge to pay each month.

After many years of hard work though, I had some extra money and it was finally possible to consider becoming a member at South Hills Country Club.

Having enough money to join is not the simple solution to joining, though. A member has to pledge you, much the same as fraternities in a university.

As luck would have it, John Keppie, the owner of the diamond-importing firm where I bought diamonds asked me to play a round of golf with him at South Hills Country Club. I always look forward to a game of golf, but playing at SHCC would be a special occasion. To add to the anticipation, he could be the key to my becoming a member.

South Hills Country Club

John was expecting me in the men's grill. After a warm welcome, he introduced me to the other two players.

We all ate lunch together and rode down to the driving range. I hit a couple dozen balls, many of which were not hit very well, since I was really excited about this eventful day. We proceeded to the first tee, the very same place that the famous Ben Hogan started his round of golf many years ago. (The club has been in existence since 1920.) John suggested I tee off first. I was so nervous I could hardly hold the club steady. I did manage to get the ball in the air, slicing into the right rough. Once I had relaxed a little, I was able to enjoy the game.

When we were back in the dining room, after finishing 18 holes, John suggested ordering the the club's famous roast beef dinner. With another round of drinks our conversation turned to the jewelry business. Since all three of us were John's clients, it was most certainly the appropriate subject. At ten o'clock, we all said our good byes and were on our way.

I had occasion to be in the Clark Building on business on Friday, so I stopped in John's office to visit with him and let him know what a great time I had at the country club. John was possibly the best salesman I ever met and attempted to sell me some inventory, which I had no need for.

In regard to his expertise as a salesman, one day I was having lunch with John. After a martini with the two of us enjoying each other's company, I said to John, "I am really proud to know you because you are the second best salesman in the world." Looking pleased and after a pause in the conversation, he asked, "Who is the best?" I replied, "You are looking at him."

I was about to leave when he suddenly said, "Mel, why don't you become a member of the club? I would be glad to recommend you and have one of my friends do the same." Trying not to seem too anxious, I replied, "I will talk it over with my wife." I could have made my own decision immediately, for I was sure Winnie would enjoy the amenities the club would provide for my family.

As expected, Winnie was thrilled about joining. The next day I called John, and he set in motion the procedure for becoming a member. John and his friend put my name before the membership committee.

John told me that it was possible that of the 300 bonds, none may be for sale, and I would be put on a waiting list. Sometimes it may be months before one is for sale. After only three weeks, the approval finally arrived in the mail, and the next morning I purchased a bond and became a proud member of South Hills Country Club.

I could not believe that I no longer had to stand in line at the public golf course and envy the golfers as I waited in line for the light to change at Brownsville Road.

My life contained a mixture of other enjoyable activities. I owned a summer home at Deep Creek, Maryland. I also had Steelers season football tickets. As a result, it was not possible to play golf every weekend. I began to think it may not have been such a great idea to belong to the club. If I divided the dues by the number of times I played, each round of golf was extremely expensive. I just had to come up with some plan to make more use of the golf course. I conferred with Bob, and I told him I was leaving work at 11 a.m. each Wednesday to play golf. This day was a tradition for doctors and professionals to play golf, why not jewelers?

As luck would have it, in the middle of the summer three men—Harry Sanders, Dick Koerber, and Bill Sausser— needed me to become part of their foursome. When playing a round of golf with these individuals, much conversation would occur to rattle the opponent. One day on the putting green, I advised Harry how I felt the putt would break into the hole. Missing the putt, Harry remarked, "Beat me with your putter not your mouth." Dick and Bill were experts at conversation to disturb the opponent. This made for very interesting rounds of golf. On one particular day, I lost my wager to Harry. When he came in from the men's room, he found his winnings in a glass of water. I said to Harry, "I am not a hard loser."

It became a tradition with me to stay at the club for dinner. I usually arrived home about 10 p.m. However, this was about to change. My three friends would always play gin rummy after golf, so one day Dick asked why I didn't play? It was because I had never played the game. Dick said it was simple to learn. He was right. However, playing it well was another issue. It wasn't long before I became a gin rummy addict, losing more money than I would win. As time went on, losing and winning seemed to balance out. As soon as we would finish golf, I would play gin rummy, stopping only to have dinner. These games would sometimes last well into the night, finishing as late as 2 a.m. Each Wednesday, I would say to myself never again would I stay that late, for it was no fun getting up the next day at 7 a.m. Nor was it a joy to listen to my wife's disparaging remarks in the morning.

One drawback to playing golf in Pittsburgh is that the weather after Labor Day is not very conducive to golf. The second year of my membership, I noticed that a group of about seven members with whom I occasionally had a round of golf played well into the winter. George Raynovich and George Haddad, coming in after one of these winter games, asked me to join their group. I asked how they could possibly hold the club with their hands being so cold. They informed me that they all use charcoal hand warmers. The device was very temperamental, for it was difficult to keep the charcoal burning. The plastic pads holding warming chemicals were not yet invented. He also advised me to buy red balls that would be easy to see in the snow. We were able to play most of the winter. I have to admit that at times we carried winter golf to the point of being ridiculous. On occasion John Micklege came out with a small shovel to clear off parts of the tee and the green. At other times, the green would be frozen, and the balls would fly into the air as if landing on concrete. These rounds of golf were different, creating lots of laughs dealing with the unexpected.

One day my gin rummy friends decided on a golf trip to Puerto Rico to the golf resort known as Dorado Beach. This seemed exciting to me, for I had never before visited any of these tropical islands. The group that decided to go was an assortment of the most conservative and the most exuberant individuals that could be assembled. Art Liebler and George Hagerty were on the moderate side, with Dick Koerber and Bill Sausser on the extroverted end, with the rest of us falling somewhere in between.

It's hard to describe the excitement of meeting at the airport, each one of us carrying a golf bag and a piece of luggage, anticipating the week ahead. Arriving at our destination I discovered the distance from the San Juan airport to Dorado Beach was very long, so one had two choices: go by bus, a tortuous two-hour ride, or by airplane. A few of the individuals had been here before, and I could not understand why they decided to take the bus. It was immediately evident. The year was 1976; however, the single-engine aircraft looked like it must have been manufactured in the late thirties. Much to my surprise, the plane only carried six passengers. There were seven of us, so Bill Sauser jumped at the chance to be in the co-pilot seat. The pilot seemed to be very careful as to how he distributed the golf clubs and baggage into the cargo space. I became more concerned when he then recommended the passengers be distributed according to weight on each side of the plane. I breathed a sigh of relief when we arrived safely at the Dorado Beach Resort.

As a person who had never been at an island resort, I found the surroundings and accommodations overwhelming. I eagerly anticipated an enjoyable week. We all met at the lounge. After dinner, we arranged foursomes and wagers for the next day's events.

The week passed quickly. There was the usual stretching of the rules of golf, causing arguments that added some extra excitement to each round of golf. After dinner, most of us would go to the casino and play some blackjack. Dick Koerber, Bill Sausser, and John Roth fashioned themselves as experts at the dice table. The game seemed much too complicated for me to participate. The next day, they were bragging about how much they won. I have always been suspicious about my pals who like to gamble, since they never tell me about their losses.

Like all golf vacations consisting of exciting games of golf, swims in the hotel pool, excellent food, and then moving to the bar for some drinks and relaxing music, it had to end. There is one thing that never ends, and that is the reminiscing about the happenings of an eventful golf vacation.

In 1977, it was decided by the "decision-makers" in our

group of golfers that we should go to the Doral Golf Resort near Jacksonville, Florida.

This golf course is famous in that it hosts one of the first major golf events of the season for the touring professionals. Bill Sujanski loved all the aspects of the game, so he thought it would be a great idea to book our rooms one week before the event.

Much to our surprise, they booked us for the same week as the tournament and at the same price. After our round of golf, we would be able to watch the professionals compete in this major tournament. This seemed too good to be true.

We arrived at the Miami airport and proceeded to the golf course. Major golf resorts have beautiful grounds and accommodations. Doral is in a class by itself. Coming away from the cold, dreary climate of Pittsburgh, the warm air and sunshine were especially inviting as we anticipated the week that was about to unfold.

The next morning, we teed off at 10 a.m. No need to go into detail of the fun of playing golf in the middle of the winter in this climate. We had our usual wagers and arguments. Thursday, the first day of the tournament, we had lunch at the 10th hole, so as soon as the game was over, we were able to observe the professionals playing in the tournament. To be able to stand next to a tee and see such famous golfers as Arnold Palmer, Jack Nickalus, and Gary Player was indeed a thrill.

When I spoke to my wife on the phone the night before the last round of the tournament, she said, "Why don't you get yourself on television?" I informed her that it would have to be pure luck for it to happen.

The next day, the leaders were going into the last hole, known as the blue monster. I was behind the rope and able to see the green in the distance. Tom Kite was the leader going into this hole. His ball landed very close to where I was standing. He was looking at the green in the distance, about to select which club to hit to the green. There was much TV equipment in the vicinity, so I thought it could be possible that I would be picked up on one of the cameras and sure enough I was.

I called Winnie that evening. I could not imagine why she was laughing even before we spoke. "You did it Mel; you were on Channel 11 news at 7 o'clock. I saw you just before Tom Kite hit the shot that won the tournament."

As the years passed, I continued to play golf, and take part in the yearly trips. Then one Wednesday while attempting to hit the ball out of deep rough, I got a severe pain in my shoulder.

In the clubhouse, I noticed Dr. Tom Saracco at the bar. I related to him the nature of my pain. With a sad look on his face, he said, "It could be serious. It's probably your rotator cuff." The obvious question was, what do I do about it? He recommended a doctor at Jefferson Hospital nearby to examine me. By luck I was able to get a copy of my X-ray the same day.

Tom said he would read the X-ray under his kitchen light. In the kitchen looking at the film, he gave me the bad news. It was a rotator cuff problem. He said it might not be too serious, and a ray of hope arose that I would be spared an operation and the possibility of never playing golf again.

I had an appointment with a specialist on Friday and the doctor examining the X-ray gave me encouraging news. He felt a cortisone shot may help me. Lucky me. In two weeks, I was back playing golf.

Ten years later I developed the same problem. This time I was advised that only an operation would solve my problem. At age 81 this was not an option, and I resigned myself to the fact that my golfing days were over.

A friend of mine told me that a Dr. Lewis in Portersville was successfully treating cases such as mine with prolotherapy, which is a series of shots. The results seemed questionable, but after four months of treatment, I was playing golf again. However, I was not allowed to take a full swing. It was like learning to play golf all over again. I went from an 18 to a 35 handicap. But it did not matter, for I was back on the links.

As years go by, many of my friends have passed away, no longer golf, or have left the club. I am very fortunate to have two golfing gentlemen who put up with my lack of talent, Ray Dodson and Joe McNally. They both have a subtle sense of humor that makes my Wednesdays very enjoyable.

I am now 84 years old, playing golf twice a week, and enjoying it as much as ever. South Hills Country Club is still a big part of my life.

CHAPTER 20
NEW BUSINESS - EIBEN AND IRR

Little did I know that on a day in late January 1952, a momentous event in my life was about to take place. It is hard to say which fork in the road affected my life the most, but I have to say that this event was as important as any that occurred up to this time.

I was on the bus, headed to work around eight o'clock in the morning. A few blocks later, an old fraternity brother of mine, Bob Irr, got onto the bus. Bob managed a luggage store and he and I occasionally rode the bus together. On this particular day, neither one of us was happy about our job. During our 45-minute commute to work, we tossed around the idea of having our own business together. Using our combined experiences we could open a retail store selling merchandise other than jewelry.

That evening I spoke to Winnie about my meeting with Bob on the bus. He was no stranger to my wife; she had been with him at many social affairs at Duquesne University. This was the first time I had told my wife about my concern for my future as an engraver. Engraving machines were entering the jewelry industry. The machines could do just about every type of engraving. It wasn't nearly as professional a job as hand engravers did, but certainly it was more than adequate. The big problem for me was that the machines could engrave trophy plates just as well as I did. Without the trophy work, my income could be cut by as much as 60 percent. The future of my career in that area looked bleak.

This was not my only concern with remaining in the engraving business. I was afraid the long hours were affecting my health. All those long days of sitting hunched over the engraving bench were giving me back pain. Not only was the job physically tiring, it was affecting my nerves as well. With every job I did, there was a danger of destroying a piece of jewelry. The mental aspect was overwhelming, and my eyesight was starting to bother me because of staring through the magnifiers for so long. Plus, due to the long hours, our social life was very limited and I often fell asleep while Winnie and I visited with other couples.

After discussing all my concerns, we decided to pursue the possibility of Bob and me becoming partners. On Saturday morning, January 26, 1953, Bob and I met to go over the details of making our partnership a reality. One major hurdle was already out of the way. I had a retail license to buy and sell merchandise, and it actually gave us the right to sell all types of consumer products in Pittsburgh. Because of that, instead of opening up a new venture, Bob would join me in my existing business, and we would expand on it. Instead of it being C. Mel Eiben Engraver, the name of our company would become Eiben and Irr.

On February 3, 1953, the Eiben and Irr partnership became reality. To start our new business, we both contributed $300. This obviously wouldn't go far. I agreed to continue to engrave, and all of my earnings would become part of the assets of the business. When I told Winnie about this, she wasn't so sure that our partnership was such a great idea. After reminding her about my doubts regarding my future in engraving, she was once again convinced that this partnership could be a key to our future.

Bob and I calculated the amount of money we needed for our families to exist on. I would have to reduce my earnings by 25 percent. With my engraving income plus anticipated sales, we knew there was a chance to be successful.

At that time my engraving office in Room 217 of the Clark Building was a desk in the corner of a room occupied by Al Brown and Harvey Kuni Manufacturing Business. We contacted the building rental agent and leased half a room on the sixth floor. Our first display of merchandise was a few pieces of luggage, a toaster, and a food mixer. They took up a lot of space, and it looked like we had inventory. As far as jewelry was concerned, we depended on memos from wholesalers in the building to complete our sales.

Only our integrity as individuals made it possible for our early survival. Wholesalers and manufacturers expected to see a profit and loss statement with a bank account to justify allowing us to have credit. By our paying cash promptly, they became liberal with shipments of merchandise. The business grew at a rapid rate despite our lack of inventory. When we got orders for a small appliance, Bob hopped in the car and picked it up at a wholesaler.

With each month that passed, my knowledge of the jewelry business increased. I had many contacts in the building with wholesalers and manufacturers since my profession as an engraver put me in contact with all phases of the industry. Bob's strength was his knowledge of the leather goods business. Both jewelry and luggage retailing were different from many other types of merchandising. Take the small appliance business for example. There were only four or five types of toasters for sale, and the quality of the product was well documented. Buying jewelry and leather goods is much different. A person buying one of those items needs an expert to help him pick the best product. Back in 1952, the only place to buy quality jewelry was in a jewelry store or a major department store. And only in a leather goods store or the department store could you hope to find a quality briefcase or luggage. Our combined knowledge in these fields of retailing gave us an edge over other general merchandise establishments.

After about a year of occupying a half room, we doubled our space and acquired our first showcase. Now it was possible to display a section of jewelry. As the selling activity increased, we hired our first employee. A good part of my time was still being consumed by engraving and the capital created by my efforts was still much needed for our personal expenses.

In 1955, we needed even more space and kept adding more types of merchandise. Three years later, we had a huge showroom at the end of the hall. By this time, we were in many phases of retailing. We had a gift department that sold a variety of merchandise including clocks, dishes, lamps, pewter, and silverware. Televisions, stereos, and record players were a big part of sales, and we eventually added a record department.

We soon became a major dealer in refrigerators, washers, and dryers. We also added a camera department. When the Polaroid camera craze hit the market, we sold hundreds of them. We had a large sporting goods department that turned out to be very important to our operation. Naturally, I was involved in procuring the golf equipment. Arnold Palmer made the sport more popular than ever and Wilson Sporting Goods had his name on many of their products. In fact, I did the engraving for the wholesalers who distributed those products. At that time, Kaufmann's department store had an exclusive deal with the Wilson Company. Their clubs were sold only at Kaufmanns. Every time I picked up the engraving jobs at Wilson's, I would beg the owner to sell me his clubs for our inventory. Finally, after much harassment, he gave in, and we eventually had a franchise for Wilson golf clubs. The reason he agreed was that we were blocks away from Kaufmann's, and he felt it would not create any problems. Our sporting goods department became very popular because we were the only other retailer to carry Wilson products.

One day, Arnold Palmer came into Eiben and Irr and asked to see his new clubs with the special grip. Much to my surprise, Arnold said, "I wondered what the clubs looked like." I honestly feel he had never seen the clubs before. The grip had a shape about it called a "reminder grip" which never caught on and after a short period, this style of club was no longer manufactured.

In 1961, we decided to move Eiben and Irr from the Clark building to a spot across the street. The Clark building did not have freight elevators or loading docks, and it was difficult for us to deal in major appliances. At the time, we were a major buyer of Hamburg Appliances. We sold and carried so many Hamburg items, a deal was made with the help of Hamburg Company for us to occupy a building across the street. It turned out to be a successful move.

Moving time for Eiben and Irr was done in a very unusual manner. We did not use any trucks at all since all we had to do was go across the street. We filled dollies and clothes hampers with our merchandise and pushed them across Wood Street and Liberty Avenue. We hired a police officer to control traffic, and we completed the major move in one weekend. We started on Friday, and by Monday morning we were open for business.

New Store - 606 Wood Street

After the move we were located on street level, giving us more exposure to walk-in business. A large wholesaler, Grafner Brothers, was located a few buildings down from our location. One of the owners, Jim Lloyd, became a personal friend. We decided to put in a direct phone connection to Grafner's and made them part of our phone system. We would place an order, and their messenger would immediately deliver the product as if it was coming from our own stock room.

Our jewelry department was different from most mass merchandising stores. I designed many one-of-a-kind pieces of jewelry for our customers when what they were looking for was not available. One piece in particular that I created was a tie tack. Tie tacks were very popular at the time (1961), and although most were inexpensive, some occasionally sold for a considerable amount of money, even as high as $1000. The tack fastened to the tie with a simple spring-operated clutch, and many customers were hesitant to buy an expensive one for fear of losing it. I believed there must be some way to assure them it was impossible for the tie tack to be lost.

As a result of my concerns, I invented a loss-proof tie tack. The back portion of the tack, the part that goes through the tie, has an opening like the top of a needle. Through this hole, a hook with a chain attached is positioned in place. The chain is then attached to the buttonhole in a shirt. If the clutch comes off, the pointed end of the tie tack is still in place. (See the following drawing showing the details of the patent.)

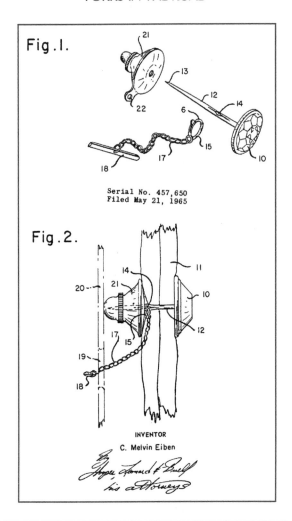

Fig.1.

Serial No. 457,650
Filed May 21, 1965

Fig.2.

INVENTOR
C. Melvin Eiben

his attorneys

Loss-proof tie tack

The solution seemed so simple and at the same time a sure way not to lose a tie tack that I decided to hire a patent attorney. This became a very intriguing experience. I thought you just sent a sample to the government, and they would grant a patent if they thought it hadn't already been invented. As it turned out, it wasn't so easy. Part of the application involved the government sending me about 40 pictures of tie tacks, and it was my job to determine if I infringed on other patents. None of them was close to my design, so I applied for a patent, and it was granted. This gave me a great feeling of accomplishment. I contacted Ballou Findings, a large manufacturer specializing in the manufacturing of findings in Providence, RI. The nature of a findings business is to make the basic part needed to assemble pieces of jewelry. In this case, they would manufacture the back part of my tacks. Upon seeing the pictures of my invention, they asked if I would visit their plant, which I agreed to do.

A close friend of mine, Martin Gluek, who was the owner of a major wholesaler jewelry company was located in the Clark Building. I decided to visit with him to show off my patent. He was very impressed with the design, and much to my surprise, he decided to call a friend of his who was the owner of Swank and Co., a major manufacturer of men's jewelry. He turned the phone over to me to explain my design. I was asked if I would visit with him to show my samples. I explained that I had an appointment with Ballou Findings in Providence. He said to check with my airline, as I probably had a layover in LaGuardia Airport, and he could meet me there. I said it would seem almost impossible to find him in such a large airport lobby. He said it would be no problem, and explained why.

He said he would be dressed in a dark blue suit and his chauffeur would be dressed in a blue uniform. I said that did not seem like enough to identify him. He went on to say that the chauffeur would have two Doberman Pinschers on a leash. Sure enough, upon arrival at the airport lobby, I had no problem identifying him. I showed him my sample. He was very much interested in the product and said that I should meet with his production manager the next day. I had to say I was sorry but I had the meeting in Providence with Ballou Findings.

The next day the finding manufacturer decided to use my invention and offered me $3000 for the patent. I declined the offer and told him I would rather have royalties from each piece sold. He agreed to this, and I was to get 10 percent for each one. This had to be a better deal than what Swank could have offered because my finding would be sold to Swank from Ballou for the back of his tie tacks. I should have taken the $3000. For some reason tie tacks, as popular as they were, suddenly became a dead item. Oh well, it was a wonderful experience and gave me great pride to be an inventor.

At this time in retailing, there were fair trade laws. Manufacturers could dictate the product be sold at only a certain retail price. Sunbeam appliances and Hamilton watches are examples of such companies.

The Hamilton watch distributor would not sell to me, for he knew I would sell his watch at a discount. My friend owned a jewelry store, and he placed my order for watches along with his. He'd add 10 percent to the cost for his part of the deal. We didn't make a lot of profit on them at Eiben and Irr, but we were able to sell a prestigious watch which helped our store image. Word got back to the Hamilton Watch Factory that we were in violation of the fair trade law. As a result, they sued us. The case went before Judge Weis. After hearing the testimony, he put his arm in the air and said, "See this watch? I bought it at a discount store. However, I have to interpret the law. Eiben and Irr can no longer sell Hamilton watches." We weren't surprised by the ruling. Eventually, free trade laws were declared illegal. I like to believe that Eiben and Irr had something to do with that decision.

As Eiben and Irr's sales volume became larger in many categories of merchandise, the customer base for the jewelry department greatly expanded. To keep informed of the latest trends, I was making a yearly trip in the fall to the New York jewelry show. Only if you'd been to this event could you visualize its huge number of displays. The show took place at the New York Hilton Hotel. The many booths displaying merchandise would fill the main ballroom and many large secondary party rooms. It made me wonder how there could possibly be so much beautiful, expensive jewelry at one location. In addition, all the major suppliers would have a suite to take orders and display their entire line. Food and drink were plentiful at these locations. Most of my time would be spent visiting the displays of my traditional suppliers. However, on each trip I would find one or two new manufacturers with some products that would intrigue me. One such company was the American Diamond Syndicate. It had a close relationship with the DeBeers Trading Company, which at this time in the diamond industry, had almost complete control of the rough diamonds mined in the world. In the ensuing years, they became my main supplier.

One year, the owner of the company was retiring, and they had a huge affair at the Twin Towers in the Main Ballroom on one of the top floors. Winnie never went with me on these trips, and as a result, I was all alone and felt a little out of place. Not for long, because one of the sons of the owner put me at a table with four beautiful ladies who were in their employ. As my friends who know me might suspect, I quickly became at ease. I put my dancing talents to good use and had a wonderful time that memorable evening.

In this same time frame, Bob approached me about incorporating our business. I had no qualms about this idea until he said he was going to be president. I was against that idea. Then he came up with another real shocker. He said as president, he felt his wage should be higher than mine. I became irate at this suggestion and told him in no uncertain terms there was no way this was going to happen. However, there are times in our lives when compromise is necessary even though hard to accept. What would the future of our company be if we were at odds with each other? How would Winnie feel about my decision to give in to Bob? At the time of all these major decisions, Winnie was having one major health issue after another, which left me vulnerable to Bob's decisions. The timing was bad to risk going separate ways. I finally did decide to let him be president, and our wages were not as different as he had first proposed.

Our business continued to thrive, and once again, space became a problem. In 1964, Bob negotiated the purchase of a building at 808 Liberty Avenue. This building had double the floor space of our current location.

About the same time as our move to Liberty Avenue, a deal was negotiated where we became part owners with a store called Bernie Glenn in Wheeling, West Virginia. We moved some of our merchandise down there for inventory. Eiben and Irr's credit rating and reputation made it possible for Bernie Glenn to prosper. In 1964, we made a similar arrangement with Tony Computo in Beaver Falls. This operation was also a success. As a result, Eiben and Irr now conducted business at three locations.

As overwhelming as all these changes were, I was not quite prepared for the next major decision.

CHAPTER 21
BOUGHT OUT

By 1966, Eiben and Irr was as well known a retailer as the major department stores in Pittsburgh. We were part owners of a store in Beaver Falls, Pennsylvania, and another one in Wheeling, West Virginia. At the time, we were at the height of our popularity and had a large, beautiful store at the corner of Wood Street and Liberty Avenue.

One important customer was Frank Rath, President of Spang and Company. At one point, I noticed that Frank was making more frequent visits to our store without buying any merchandise. It seemed odd, but I didn't think it was significant in any way. It turns out that I was wrong.

Surprisingly, one day Bob walked up to me and told me that he had decided to merge Eiben and Irr with Spang and Company. I could not believe what he just said and was shocked to say the least. I was traumatized by his announcement. Now all Frank's recent visits to our store made sense to me. Why should his wanting to merge surprise me?

When Bob and I talked about his decision, he told me of the benefits of our merger. There would be a financially advantageous stock transfer to us, but it was difficult for me to comprehend the terms of the agreement since I was not privy to all of Bob and Frank's meetings. There was no question of the significance of the deal; it did mean a large increase in our net worth. However, one very important issue that was never mentioned to me was whether there would be a change in my annual income or job status. I didn't have time to think about the terms since the official merger signing was just a few days away.

I talked it over with Winnie, and we both decided I had little choice in the matter. Since Bob committed our company to the merger, I agreed.

A bit of history about the man who had controlling interest in Spang and Company. Frank Rath became owner of Spang, after marrying the daughter of the original owner. When he first became president, it was called Spang Fishing Equipment Company. That company manufactured the equipment used to remove parts of machinery that broke off in the process of drilling oil wells. The engineering division of the company developed a technique to remove steel from slag dumps and found many uses for other ingredients found there. This became a huge and profitable division of the corporation, so much so that they had excess capital to acquire other companies. The parent company eventually bought into and controlled companies such as Magnedicts, Sun Drug, Wolverine Toy, and Fort Pitt Bridge. Frank continued to search for other companies to buy or merge with, and as a result, Eiben and Irr became part of Spang and Company.

The attorney Bob hired to represent our side of the deal inspected the merger contract and assured us that everything was in order and it was safe for us to sign the agreement. Unfortunately, there was a major part of the document he overlooked, which caused me to be swindled out of a large sum of money later on.

Bob and I met with Frank Rath and the Spang and

Company officers at the Duquesne Club and signed off on the merger. After lunch, we said goodbye to Frank and his associates. As I left the club, I was very depressed about our merger. I just knew that it was not going to be a good deal for me. After this, I no longer had the same enthusiasm for my work as I had before.

Frank made Bob president of both Eiben and Irr and Sun Drug. Frank gave me the title of Vice President. It was just a title. My job at the time was to manage the jewelry department. At least it was Eiben and Irr's most important money-making division.

In 1966, Spang & Company purchased a building on 10th Street and Fort Duquesne Boulevard. Here, Eiben and Irr opened a furniture store. The building itself was to become a very important part of Eiben and Irr's future.

At huge expense, Frank installed an elevator and made massive renovations to the building. Then a mere year later, Frank decided to have Eiben and Irr in all the Sun Drug locations. Another move was to have Eiben and Irr become a catalog showroom-type business. At this time in retailing, a single store could join a group of stores that were in no way connected, and could buy catalogs with their names printed on the cover.

Every year I would go to New York to help decide what merchandise would be in our annual catalog. Most of the other stores involved wanted to sell merchandise of a lesser quality than I was accustomed to stocking. Actually, most of the merchandise in the catalogs had inflated prices considering its quality. As a result, the prestige of Eiben and Irr's jewelry department was deteriorating. I already had an extensive inventory, and my purchases were controlled by an "Option to Buy," which allowed me little money to buy the catalog merchandise. That meant that almost all items in the catalog had to be special ordered, a further complication.

My trips to New York were always in February, which made for some interesting flights. Air travel in the 60s was a lot different from today. Back then, we flew in airplanes propelled by turbo-prop jet engines. On one particular trip, the pilot, who obviously fancied himself a comedian, told us there was plenty of fuel to make it to New York. Down the runway we went, and it seemed like a normal takeoff. I had a seat next to the wing. Suddenly, I looked out and noticed that part of the cowling of the engine was peeling off. This obviously made me very concerned for my safety. The pilot said to us, "Remember all the fuel I bragged about? Well, I have to jettison it before I land back at the airport."

The airplane made a turn, and we were now circling at a low altitude over the bay. The pilot came out, looked over my shoulder and said, "I often wondered how it looked when fuel was being released from the wings." With most of the fuel gone, we landed at the airport. We all thought we would disembark and go to another plane. This was not the case. Instead, we were not permitted to leave the plane.

A truck with an elevation device pulled up along side the plane and a mechanic secured the cowling of the engine with some kind of tape. While this was going on, one of the passengers began to scream, "Let me off this plane!" Finally, the flight attendants let the screaming passenger off, and the rest of us sat around like idiots and didn't say a word. With the plane refueled and the tape in place, we took off again. I spent most of the trip with my eyes glued to the engine, wondering if it would hold long enough for us to land safely in New York. We did arrive safely, and I was on my way to the hotel.

Back at the store, or catalog showroom as Eiben and Irr was now known, management came up with another idea. It was bad enough buying merchandise in the catalog that was hard to sell; then he decided to computerize the catalog operation. By now, half of our merchandise was still non-catalog jewelry, complicating the process.

At this time, computers were in their infancy. The mainframe for his conglomerate was in Butler, PA and it occupied a large room that had to be kept at a constant temperature. The system used punch cards to input the data. Due to the large variety of inventory in the jewelry department, we spent most of our time punching cards instead of selling the merchandise.

Management's next idea was to close the Liberty Avenue and Wood Street location and move us down to the furniture storefront at 10th Street. This was a huge mistake. The Liberty Avenue store had a great layout, beautiful décor, and stunning showcases. It was by far one of the nicest retail stores in Pittsburgh at the time. A fortune was spent renovating the 10th Street location. The results of his revamping were disappointing; it still did not have the class of the former location.

New Store - 808 Liberty Avenue

The Liberty Avenue location had been far superior, as we were within walking distance of other major retailers such as Kaufmann's and Gimbel's. In the new location, walk-in traffic was greatly reduced because it was out of the heart of Pittsburgh's retail district. The 10th street move was the kiss of death for Eiben and Irr.

New Location - Corner of 10th & Penn Avenue

As profits declined, we were ordered to increase prices and cut advertising expenditures. Employees were laid off to try to save money. It was only a matter of time until Eiben and Irr would go under. I could sense it. One day, Bob walked into my office and told me he was resigning as president of the retail division of Spang and Company. I asked him why, and he told me that working for Spang and Co. was more pressure than he could stand.

Six months before the official closing, I was informed that I was no longer part of Eiben and Irr. Finally, the store closed in 1979. The Eiben and Irr operation certainly was an important part of my life financially and it was also enjoyable. Bob and I, through hard work and dedication, brought a major retail store into existence. Its demise was a combination of poor judgment and simultaneous modifications in all phases of retailing.

Although the news concerned me at first, it came as a huge relief. I felt like a man just released from prison, eager to create a new beginning. I began the process of seeing to all the details that go into opening a new business.

CHAPTER 22

C. MEL EIBEN vs. SPANG AND CO.

In order to put myself back into business as an
independent jeweler, I was counting on using money from
the Eiben and Irr stock I received as a result of the buyout
by Sprang and Co. The money would not only set me up in
business, but it would help keep Winnie and me afloat until
such time as the business started to show a profit.

The stock I retained in Eiben and Irr was worth $550,000,
but their controller said that my holdings only totaled
$350,000. I asked how this could be possible; it was a
tremendous reduction in value. I understood that the stock's
value could not change without the Board of Directors
agreeing to a reduction. It seemed strange to me that the
Board members, who were also stockholders, would approve
such a huge decrease in the value of the stock. It turns out the
Board had no choice because Frank Rath, the president of
Spang and Company, replaced all of them with a new board.
He now had free reign to do anything he wanted.

The old adage "being caught between a rock and a hard
place" rang especially true in this case because it seemed I
had no other option but to accept the lesser amount; however,

I decided to call an attorney to find out if I had any legal recourse. The lawyer advised that I might be able to win in court, but I was not in a strong position, and the firm would not take my case. Disheartened by the news, I went to another law firm and unfortunately received the same opinion. After being turned down twice, I decided to contact Jack Luke, an attorney who had done some estate work for me.

Jack's operation was small; his firm had only two lawyers. I made an appointment with him to discuss my dilemma. At the meeting, I turned over all the information I had regarding my stock and told him everything I knew about the situation. Jack said he would review the paperwork and call me in a few days to let me know if he would try to help me recover the full value of my shares. True to his word, Jack phoned two days later and said he would handle my case on a contingency basis, retaining one-third of the settlement if we won. This seemed fair considering the effort involved in this lawsuit.

Reed, Smith, Shaw and McClay, the largest legal firm in Pittsburgh at the time, represented Spang. As the proceedings moved forward, I felt confident my attorney was at least equal, if not superior, to the representation the larger firm provided. I also received tremendous help with my lawsuit from Sam Greco, a former executive with Spang and Company. Sam supplied much of the information that Jack needed to try my case. The proceedings lasted several days, and I testified for what seemed like hours. I was no stranger to appearing in court. I did so when I was involved with the fair trade laws at Eiben and Irr. I also had my share of dealing with the legal system when I helped my daughter through her divorce, and I felt well prepared not to let the opposing attorney intimidate me regardless of his experience.

There is one particular incident when I was on the witness stand that I will never forget. The defense was trying to establish that I lacked dedication to my job and asked me to recall the time during a sale at the store when I went to play a round of golf. I replied by saying the owners were well aware of my Wednesday afternoon golf habit because it was established when we merged the two companies. I looked out over the people in the courtroom and said, "I am sure that many of you play golf. Please raise your hand if indeed you play?" I felt a little foolish to make such a request in a courtroom, but much to my surprise, a fair amount of men acknowledged that they played. "Then it's obvious you know the importance of showing up for a foursome of golf," I replied. This brought a bit of laughter into the room, and I hoped that the interrogating attorney would feel he was dealing with someone who was not easily intimidated.

Judge Finklehorne decided the testimony on both sides was complete, and after reviewing the proceedings, she would render a verdict. A week went by. It was now beyond 30 days, and I received no news as to the final ruling on my case. I called Jack, and he said the judge had a reputation for being slow and that she would eventually let us know the results.

After three months, I again called Jack, and he assured me he would see what he could find out. He told me that Judge Finklehorne was irritated at his calling her office regarding a verdict. Jack said it was hopeless to push for a decision, since pressuring her would only have a negative effect on the outcome. I decided to put this matter in the recesses of my mind.

A year later, with my case still undecided, I stopped in at my attorney's office, and Jack reiterated that there was no way to force a verdict. It was very frustrating for both of us because of the time we had invested in the lawsuit.

It is hard to believe, but it was *nine* years later that Judge Finklehorne rendered a verdict! I was entitled to the full value of my stock. It goes without saying that I was elated at the news, but the euphoria did not last very long. Spang and Company appealed the verdict, and my case went to the Commonwealth's Supreme Court.

The Supreme Court Justice reviewing the appeal was only on the bench for a few months at the time. When he took office, he announced he would process the many undecided cases before him in short order. He was as good as his word in this regard. Three weeks later, he ruled my favorable decision was not valid and dismissed my case on a technicality.

Mr. Luke, being a determined man, decided to challenge the Judge's decision. Back to court we went, but to no avail. The $200,000 dollars I lost when Frank Rath manipulated the stock value was gone forever. My original agreement with Spang and Company did not have the safeguards needed to protect my stock from a reduction.

My case also proved to me once again that judges have tremendous power. Fortunately, I had the ability not to let adverse circumstances get me down.

CHAPTER 23
DEEP CREEK

From the time I started my engraving business in 1946, for the next ten years, we did not have a vacation. Once Eiben and Irr was in existence, having a partner made it possible to have time off for vacation. Don Jones, a neighborhood friend, suggested we join him on a vacation to Grandview Lodge on a huge lake in Canada. When he described the amenities, a cottage and three meals a day included, I felt for sure we could not afford it. There was golf, tennis, water skiing and fishing. I was afraid to ask the price. When he told me it would be $250 for the whole family I could hardly believe it. We had a wonderful time at Grandview and continued to go for many years.

When the girls became teenagers they felt they needed to be where there were more people their own age. We then started vacationing at Geneva on the Lake, which is where I first became intrigued with sailing.

In the foreword, I mentioned how small seeds of our existence can become a large part of our lives. Well, the following is a seed that greatly influenced mine. In 1965, Sunbeam Steam Irons ran a promotion at Eiben and Irr. If we sold all the irons they put in a Styrofoam sailboat, we would own the boat.

It wasn't too long after the promotion started that an empty 8-foot sailboat sat on our salesroom floor. Bob didn't want it. I had no idea what to do with it at the time, but I decided to haul it home anyway. Two weeks later we were going on vacation to Geneva on the shore of Lake Erie. Each day I would come home from work and look at the boat sitting in my garage. I said to myself, "Why not buy a rack for the roof of the car and take the boat to the lake?"

Of course, it seemed like a good idea to me, but I didn't really know how to sail. Captaining an LCT required a much different technique and set of skills than sailing does. The boat came with an instruction book, but that didn't ease my mind very much. I was to find out that sail boating is not as easy as one may think, especially the part about sailing into the wind. It was hard to comprehend how this was possible. The book had all sorts of warnings about how treacherous this maneuver can be. Despite the warnings, I decided to give it a try on our vacation.

We arrived at Geneva on a Friday afternoon, and I anxiously prepared my new craft for sailing. I carefully removed it from the roof of the car, put the mast in place, and attached the ropes and sail. The following morning, a neighbor helped me carry it down to the beach. As soon as I hit the shoreline, I was very eager to get it into the water. My enthusiasm was somewhat dampened when I realized there was no wind. In fact, I never saw the lake so calm. I sat around all day waiting for the slightest breeze, but none came. To make matters worse, there was no wind on the three days that followed either.

Finally there was a steady gusting of wind that seemed perfect for sailing. The lake looked awesome to me, so I had some trepidation about launching the boat.

I brushed aside my concerns and quickly pushed the boat into the water, past the small breakers, and hopped on board. The sail suddenly picked up a stream of air, and I was on my way. The speed I seemed to be traveling was surprising. The whole experience was quite exhilarating. In no time at all, I was a great distance from shore. Then of course, I realized I had to sail back to where I started. How on earth was I supposed to turn this baby around? I vaguely remembered something in the sailing book about making a turn; I knew I had to be on the other side of the boat. I also had to be very careful not to get knocked overboard or capsize the boat.

The Styrofoam Sail Boat

It then occurred to me that I didn't even have an oar or life jacket with me. I was so far out in the lake that Winnie and the girls looked like tiny specks on the horizon. To complicate my predicament, the wind became very intense, and a storm was on its way.

The exhilaration I felt heading out onto the lake quickly turned into a deep panic. I attempted to turn the sail over to the other side, but it was hung up in the middle and intensely flopping in the strong breeze. The adrenaline took over, and I got control of myself and forced the sail out of the center position. Now the sail swung over to the other side, and the boat leaned at a very dangerous angle. I positioned the sail in a stable position and continued to sail back to the shore.

The speed going back to the beach was three times as fast as going out. I was riding up and down on huge waves. Near the beach the breakers were as high as five feet. I was thrown onto the beach and the mast broke off. I found myself under the boat and yelled that I was okay. And added, "Sailing sure is a lot of fun!"

The next year was the year we went on vacation to Deep Creek, Maryland. Deep Creek is a huge lake and is a popular place for sailing. I took my little Styrofoam boat with me and sailed it everyday. The most popular boat on the lake was the Flying Scot. The Flying Scot was manufactured in Garrett County, a short 10 miles from the lake. I sure would like to own a Flying Scot someday. Of course, due to its price, that dream was just about as impossible as my buying a Corvette.

The Glendale Bridge
Entrance to Deep Creek Lake

After several years of renting a cottage at Deep Creek, we decided to stay at a home located at Four Hooppole South. Bill Weisgerber was the rental agent.

It came time for us to leave, and we stopped at the real estate office to say goodbye to Bill on our way out of town. He suggested we buy one of the homes over on Four Hooppole South. This idea seemed as wild as my ability to buy a Flying Scot. Like all good salesmen, Bill planted a seed of desire to someday have this dream come true. It was hard to get the thought of a home in Deep Creek out of my mind, especially during the long cold winter months in Pittsburgh.

It was the summer of 1974, and we were on our way to Deep Creek. This time, there was no doubt about where we were staying. Four Hooppole South. What a weird name for such a quality location.

Bill Weisgerber handled the rental, same as the year before. he again approached me in regard to buying one of the units. I had sold my share of Eiben and Irr to Spang and Company, and I had a substantial amount of value in their stock. Why not use some of this money to buy a unit at Four Hooppole South? It would be a combination investment in real estate and a place to go on the weekend the year around. When Bill got an inkling that I might be interested in buying a unit, he was on the phone or would come visit almost every day. He would tell me which homes were for sale and their asking price.

Finally, on the Friday of our last day at the lake, I caved in. We had found one with an excellent price and all the furniture and kitchen equipment, glasses, pots and pans were included. We had no furniture to buy. Just turn the key in the lock and we had a resort home ready to live in. The Eiben family was the proud owner of a summer home at Four Hooppole South, Deep Creek Maryland. We now spent almost every weekend at the lake. It was home away from home for the family.

Several years later, Winnie, Suzi, Cindy, and I visited Bill's Marina to purchase an inboard/outboard motorboat. I bought a two-year-old boat for $3200. The boat was 19 feet long and had a 150 horsepower engine. This was more power than most craft of this size.

I already knew how to water ski, so teaching Suzi and Cindy how was a lot of enjoyment for the whole family. Everything is easy when you know how, so after a few spills on their part and complaints about me being either too fast or too slow on the tow, they both learned. Winnie had no desire to learn; she said she just liked to watch.

As much as I liked cruising around the lake in the motorboat, the Flying Scot was never out of my mind. I became intrigued with watching them gracefully sail over the lake with no engine, just the wind to create the direction and movement of the sailboat. Winnie would see me reading

The Flying Scot

the advertisement time after time. One evening she suggested we go visit the factory in Oakland and find out the price.

On Monday morning, inside the office of the manufacturing facility, we met the representative of the firm. You could tell he was very proud of the operation. Before even discussing the price, he insisted we go into the plant. He described the method of manufacturing one of the boats.

I can see why he had me visit the factory and share the process of manufacturing the craft. He knew that most customers had no idea of the selling price, and this was his way of reducing the shock when he said the price. I had a number in my mind of about $2800. Holding my breath, I asked the price. It hit me like a bombshell. $4200! I thought how could this be? A sailboat does not even have a motor. We left the office saying we would let him know after we thought it over.

Back at our unit, Winnie could see I was very depressed. I was thinking Winnie would never agree to such a large expenditure. She looked me in the eye and said, "I know how badly you want to own a Flying Scot. If you can find a way to pay for it, then just go ahead and buy one now." The next day, we were back at the plant and closed the deal.

Boats are made according to customers' specifications. As a result, I would not be able to take possession until the spring of 1976. As I was writing this book, I decided to call the boat factory to ask today's prices. Would you believe the price is now $12,000?

I received a call at my office that the sailboat was finished. The call came through in April, far too early to do any sailing. The next week, I just had to see the boat arriving at the storage area of the plant. There she was, sitting on a trailer. What a thing of beauty, painted white and highlighted with blue trim. Its number was 2605, indicating mine was the 2605th boat manufactured.

Included with the purchase were sailing lessons that lasted until the instructor felt you could safely operate the craft. My vacation was the first week in July. We arrived at our summer home on Friday night. On Saturday morning, I was in their office to find out when my first sailing lesson would be. I was informed that on Monday afternoon, one of their representatives would meet me at the cove that is used for launching new boats. A gentleman walked into the office, and I was introduced to Sandy Douglas.

His name is on all the folders advertising the Flying Scots. What luck that I should actually meet the man who designed the boat. I said to him, "What an honor to meet you; you are to sailing what Jack Nicklaus is to golf."

I will never know if he just wanted to go sailing on Monday or whether my statement about Jack Nicklaus influenced him. He said, "I will meet you at the company's anchorage on Monday at two o'clock."

I thought Monday would never arrive. I drove down to the cove and sat at the edge of the dock.

I will never forget the sensation of seeing the boat anchored to a buoy about 20 yards from the shore. It was a warm summer day, a few cumulus clouds settled overhead, and I felt a warm, gentle breeze on my face. This was a perfect day for sailing.

What a thrill to know that my dream of owning this boat was finally realized. It looked so beautiful sitting out there in the water. I was surprised to see it anchored. I thought all you did was get into it at the dock and sail out onto the lake.

At exactly two o'clock, Mr. Douglas arrived. He looked much younger than his age. He had a sparkle in his eyes that seemed to indicate he was about to enjoy this day as much as I would.

The afternoon progressed as we went through every possible sailing maneuver. Undoubtedly my experiences in my little Styrofoam boat had taught me a lot, because after a few hours Sandy pronounced me a student at ease in his Flying Scot and said I was now on my own.

Sandy asked me where I was going to anchor the Flying Scot. He said one of the men from the plant would place the buoy and deliver the boat to Hooppole in the morning. I said goodbye to Sandy and could not thank him enough for teaching me how to sail. I have to think that my sailing the small Styrofoam boat taught me the basics of sailing.

The next morning, I was out on the patio looking for the Flying Scot. There it was anchored at the buoy in the exact location I decided on. This particular week, Suzi and Clyde, her husband, along with Cindy and her husband, Tom, were at the lake. After admiring the boat for a few moments, I went back to the unit anticipating my first solo sail in the Flying Scot. It was akin to the sensation one would have for their first solo flight in an airplane. I told the family I was going to take the boat out for the first time. All four of them immediately expressed a desire to go along. I said maybe only Tom and Clyde should go in case we turn over. The girls would have none of this plan.

So off we all went, the five of us. As far as Winnie was concerned, she wanted no part of sailing. She had to have a motor on the back of any craft before she would get in.

The passengers were as delighted as I was to be moving down the lake at what seemed to be remarkable speed. I never gave a thought to how far we traveled. Suzi finally said, "Dad, maybe we should turn around and sail back." I was so enthralled with the fun we were having that it never occurred to me to turn back. Great idea, Suzi.

Motorboats are able to go in any direction at any time. The trouble with a sailboat is that God made the wind, and all of a sudden the wonderful sailing wind was no more. We were dead in the water two miles from Hooppole, and Sandy Douglas was not here to tell me what to do in a situation like this.

I found out that the craft could sail in very little wind. We made our way back at a snail's pace. We secured the sail to the spar and cranked up the centerboard before pulling the motorboat along side. This gave Winnie enough time to be at the shoreline to yell at me for being gone so long. I could certainly understand her concern. Four hours is a long time not to know where we were or what may have happened.

From that day forward, I never sailed more than a mile from Hooppole. Most of the time, I sailed by myself, and I had many thrilling moments out on the lake alone. I never became bored sailing the Flying Scot.

I continued to sail the Flying Scot for the next 20 years. It was sad when I sold the Flying Scot, knowing I would never sail it again.

The reader may be interested in knowing what happened to the little Styrofoam boat that started all this. I always stored the boat on a canoe rack near the edge of the lake at Hooppole. Many times, I would take my young nieces and nephews out in the small boat. Older friends and relatives liked to sail it themselves. Even after I had the Flying Scot, I had many hours of fun in the craft.

One Sunday morning in late August 1980, I went down to the boat rack, and couldn't see the craft in its usual place. A few yards away were many small Styrofoam pieces lying on the lawn next to the lake.

Apparently, a group of young teenagers having a drunken binge decided to jump up and down on the sailboat. What a sad way for this beautiful craft to meet its end. The boat may be gone; but, there is one thing the vandals could not take away, and that is the wonderful memories I have that I will treasure forever.

In 1976, as things were going downhill in my business life, I faced another major fork in the road. One night when Winnie and I were enjoying the music and dancing at one of our local nightclubs Bill Weisgerber, who had sold the condo to us at Deep Creek, came over and sat at our table. He bought us a drink, and told us about a local grocery store and gas station for sale. I asked, "Why are you telling me? What interest would I possibly have in owning a grocery store and gas station?" I told him in no uncertain terms I wasn't interested.

I thought for sure I had convinced him to stop bothering me about any more real estate, especially this type of business. Back in Pittsburgh, I settled into my job at the store. At this time, I was becoming more and more disenchanted with my work. Each month, depressing profit and loss statements indicated that no money was being made in most of the departments. The jewelry department was the only part of Eiben and Irr showing a profit.

Winnie and I were at Deep Creek that September, enjoying the fall weather and the turning of the leaves at this mountain resort. Looking out over the lake with its panoramic view of glorious color on the hillsides was a relaxing relief from the depressing conditions at Eiben and Irr.

Of course, you must know who suddenly arrived at our residence on a Sunday afternoon: none other than salesman Bill. This time he had with him records showing the volume of business at the grocery store. The gas station sold an impressive amount of gasoline and oil. The location was at the main crossroads of the lake and the only such operation at the resort. The nearest gas station was many miles down the highway. There was no real estate agency involved, and it would be a straight deal with the owner.

I told him that although it looked like a very good investment, he was talking to the wrong person. There is no way I wanted to get involved. He continued to give me his sales pitch, and I finally got him to be quiet by replying with an emphatic "No!"

However, back home, Winnie and I could not get the Deep Creek business out of our minds. I knew Eiben and Irr would soon be history. Both Suzi and Cindy were married, and life for Winnie with the children gone had grown monotonous. Her married life had been dominated by her devotion to the family. She taught school for only one year and up until now had never had a job.

Winnie and Evelyn, Bill's wife, were very good friends and spent much time together at the lake. I thought it might not be a bad idea to give some serious thought to the Deep Creek business after all. Why not a partnership with the Weisgerbers? This could give Winnie something to be involved in, helping to manage a business.

Much to my surprise, not only was there no objection to our involvement, Winnie was very eager to consider a deal. So in early October, we were off to the lake to see what kind of arrangements we could come up with as partners with the Weisgerbers. On October 16, 1976, the complex became owned by our two families.

The following Monday morning, Evelyn and Winnie were at the store anxiously awaiting their first customer. Suddenly a huge gasoline trailer truck drove up and asked the ladies how much gas to leave at the station. The two of them looked at each other, having no clue what to answer. After a quick discussion, they said, "Fill them up." What the ladies did not know was that payment was due upon delivery. The little detail of having a business account at the local bank with a reserve fund had not been arranged. The man had his hand out expecting to receive a check in the amount of $2800. He could not very well empty the tanks, so he drove off shaking his head in bewilderment, with no payment.

The first customer arrived and made a purchase, and some change was needed. Guess what! There was no change in the register; in fact, there was no money at all. That was the first hour of business for the Eiben and Weisgerber partnership. Certainly it was not a very professional beginning.

I was at my job in Pittsburgh, and Bill managed to arrive at the business that afternoon and iron out all the difficulties. The Weisgerbers had a son, George, about 26 years old, who was hired to run the business. His younger brother, Bill, was to be a part-time employee. George, a very astute young man, managed to get the operation running smoothly in a short period.

Next to the grocery store was a tavern that had a tradition of serving home-style cooking for many years. The establishment also had a bar with a liquor license. Bill informed me that the owner was about to retire, and the restaurant was for sale. He laid out before me the records showing the dollar volume of the business. The records indicated a successful operation.

By now, I am sure the reader will remember that in the foreword I made mention of how many of my decisions were made in a very short period of time, unfortunately with no regard to the possible consequences. I was about to make a rapid one that would make the next five years very exciting in many different ways.

I knew my position at Eiben and Irr had no way to improve. I also had to think that Spang and Company, the owner of Eiben and Irr, was not going to look at red ink forever. I had the happy thought that Deep Creek, Maryland, was where my new future lay. What a life this could be. Being there was like being on vacation all the time. I contacted Bill, and the four of us put up the money needed to purchase the restaurant. Less than a month after buying the gas station, Winnie and I became half-owner of a restaurant and tavern. We were fortunate in that Mary, the chef of many years, decided to continue to work for us. The bartender also decided to stay on.

As I was still occupied with my job in Pittsburgh, Bill and his son were making most of the decisions. Someone suggested we add pizza to our new menu, so we became involved with a franchise operation known as "Fox's Pizza." The franchise provided all the dough and condiments and

Bill's younger son, along with the cook and bartender, were trained by the franchise employee on how to prepare the pizza.

The upstairs of the restaurant had a big empty room. In the spring of 1977, Bill and I looked around the room and decided that we should consider turning it into a nightclub. There were restrooms on the same floor, which solved one big problem. Getting it painted, purchasing some tables and chairs, and building a bandstand meant we would be in business. Why not, I thought, and another one of Mel's fast decisions was made.

My hope that Winnie would take a keen interest in the business did not materialize. As a result, I had no choice but to leave the day-to-day decision-making up to Bill.

Winlyns Gas Station - Restaurant - Fox's Pizza - Night Club

By June 1, 1977, the room was completed. One night, Winnie and I happened to see a five-piece band with a female singer at a local nightclub. Their music was relaxing

302

and wonderful to dance to. What really made them so terrific was their singer. I asked Winnie if she thought we could hire them for our nightclub. At their break, I spoke to the leader about playing at our tavern. He informed me he would be interested, and he told me how much the band would cost for two nights. I had no idea if the price was the going rate for this type of entertainment. I said I would talk to my partner, and let him know if we decided to hire them.

The next day, I called Bill and he said he would check around the lake and see how much other nightclubs were paying for bands. He called back the next day and said the rate was a fair price. Arrangements were made with the band to play the second week in January.

We put a notice in the local newspaper that Winlyns was ready to open with a band called "The Blue Notes." (If you wonder where the name "Winlyns" came from, it was my wife's idea. She combined the two names Winnie and Evelyn.)

Our opening was a huge success; everybody thought the band was terrific. Bill, Evelyn, Winnie and I had a meeting and discussed the possibility of having the Blue Notes for the summer. We immediately decided to see if the band would be interested. The next day, a contract was signed for the whole summer.

Winlyns immediately became the place to go for enjoyable entertainment at the lake. The patrons could not get enough of the band and Laura's wonderful voice. These were happy times for the Weisgerbers and Eibens, for we could not help feel proud of our business venture.

Since Winnie took no active interest in the business and I had no opportunity to be sure of the integrity of my partner and the employees, I became concerned about the operation. All the transactions were in cash. How easy it would be for the many employees to line their pockets with partnership money. I thought of all the cash being pulled from the gas pumps, grocery store, restaurant, pizza operation, the bar, the gaming machines, and the nightclub. How could Bill possibly have hands-on control of all this money exchange? I had to think that selling real estate would occupy most of his time, especially since the summer months were his best selling season.

No money was coming my way despite large crowds at the club. All phases of the business seemed to be busy. Bill kept telling me that we were paying off capital expenditures. The profit and loss statements were indicating this, but anyone in business knows how numbers can be manipulated. Oh well, I got myself into this business; I had to hope I was dealing with a man of integrity.

"Fast decision Mel" is also beginning to understand the resort business. Too bad his awareness is coming after his deep involvement in it. With Oakland being Deep Creek's major city, all of the commerce in the area is heavily dependent on tourist trade. The area is advertised as a four-season resort. The problem is the lake area is primarily a summer resort. The peak of its activity is June, July and August. In November, the ski season begins. This is better than the autumn, but still has only about one-third the activity of the summer, and most of it occurs at the other side of the lake from where our tavern was located. The early spring is the least active of all the seasons.

Our operation was open year round with enough activity to keep the club open on Friday and Saturday nights in the off season. The other section of the business was open every day. People from the local communities and some condominium owners would visit many weekends throughout the year. The restaurant and the bar were a hangout for many of the local people. This, combined with the grocery store and gas station, provided enough activity to just about pay expenses in off-seasons. Little did we know that a decision by the county was about to have a major impact on our tavern.

Bill told me that the health department was to make a "perk test" on the land near the restaurant. I had no idea what this could mean.

The lake area had no sewer system. As a result, all businesses were dependent on septic tank systems to disperse the wastewater. If the soil could not absorb enough of the wastewater, our operation would be shut down by the county health department. The news was bleak. We were told to close our tavern. Our only way to keep operating was to hire a company that would haul away the waste by a tank truck. This would put a big hole in our profits, but we had no other recourse.

The land next to us was not for sale, and on the other side was a miniature golf course. We seemed to have no solution for our predicament. The only land that was sure to perk was across the highway. The land was for sale, but how would we get across the road? I asked Bill if it was possible the highway department would allow us to burrow under the road. He said it was not very likely, but he would give it a try. He was a native of the area, and being in real estate was often in contact with politicians. He had a meeting with the highway department, and the answer was that it was possible and they would think it over.

Finally, in the fall of 1977, the county agreed to allow us to dig under the road. Many delays occurred as they rejected one burrowing plan after another. In March 1978, we were given permission to proceed with our project. The land was still for sale, and I had a meeting with Bill about financing the purchase. He had no funds available to help buy the land. The parcel of land did not extend out to the lake, and as a result, it was a reasonable price. Being reasonable did not help our situation. I still had the wild dream that my future was in Deep Creek. I had bought the land as an investment. The only way I could come up with the money was to sell more stock.

Up to this time, Spang and Company had never refused my request to sell a portion of my value in the corporation. It had never occurred to me that I did not have the right to sell at any time. I was in for a rude awakening.

Earlier in my book, I mentioned the fact that the attorney representing Eiben and Irr made a big mistake in our merger agreement with Spang and Company. He made no provision for our right to sell shares of stock at will. The owner of the parent company had complete and total control over the stock. I visited various banks in Pittsburgh, and none of them would allow a loan based on Spang stock.

It looked like we were in a no-win situation. There was no way we could continue to operate, hauling the waste away by truck. Weeks went by and my pleas to the controller to release funds from the sale of stock continued to be refused.

Winnie had some relatives living in Frostburg, Maryland, where she was born. The boyfriend of a relative of Winnie's by the name of John Hauser happened to be an executive in a small bank. I had no idea what his position was at the bank. In fact, the thought never occurred to me that he might be able to help me with a business loan.

When we went to visit one evening, I was telling him about my Deep Creek business and the stock I had at Spang and Company. He said, "I don't know if I can help you get a loan at my bank, but stop by Monday, and I will see what I can do. Bring as much information as you have available."

On Monday morning, I walked through the door of the bank. Much to my surprise, a deal was made using Spang stock as collateral. I now had the $20,000 needed to purchase the land. This amount also made it possible to build the septic system to remove the waste from the tavern. On July 20, 1979, the land was purchased, and in early August, work began on getting the pipeline under the road. In late August,

I found myself facing a one-way fork in the road.

As luck would have it, the diggers hit solid rock, and it was more expensive and difficult to put the pipeline in than expected. It was well into September before the work was completed. The operation had to absorb the high cost of removing the waste by truck all summer. We now had to struggle through another difficult fall, winter, and spring before the tourist season would again arrive. In early March 1980, I was spending my usual weekends at my condominium in Deep Creek. I went over to visit with George Weisgerber, Bill's son, to see how business was doing in the winter months. I said to him, "I haven't seen Bill or heard from him in over a month, and I can't understand why."

George replied, "You mean Dad didn't tell you he is in Florida?" "Well," I said, "Lucky him, while you are doing your best to get us through the winter." After this I became very concerned about the operation of the business.

To complicate my existence even more, the Frostburg bank was exerting pressure to pay off the loan. It was a short-term loan to be paid off as soon as a block of stock was sold at Spang and Company. I did not make it clear at the time of my loan that I had no control over when I could convert shares into cash.

Talk about a man having major problems on his mind. I had just started my new jewelry business and was not generating enough capital to show a profit. In fact, it was growing at such a slow pace that I feared it would not succeed. I had no choice but to continue to operate the Winlyns Complex.

Finally, after three months of delay, I did manage to convert shares of stock into cash to pay off the loan. We continued to operate the business until July 31, 1980 when we dissolved the partnership and put the business up for sale. There were no immediate buyers for the operation because major changes were about to occur at the lake.

Garrett County was about to make a major change in the lake community, and plans were being made to install a sewer system along the lakefront. The exact date of construction and completion was not yet established, but there was no doubt that it would be done.

This would make it possible to construct major entertainment centers near the lake, making our nightclub less desirable. It would be just a matter of time until a major grocery store would be constructed near our location. There would be no need for our small store. As a result, the market for our operation was very limited. After several months, it was finally sold at a loss to a developer of a mini-mall.

This was the end of my dream career in the resort business. My philosophy of "nothing ventured, nothing gained" had the unfortunate result of nothing gained. But the years of operation did have some exciting experiences, which I will long remember. One could compare it to an exhilarating romance with a beautiful, intelligent woman suddenly coming to an end.

CHAPTER 24
C. MEL EIBEN JEWELERS

For the last couple of years I worked at Eiben and Irr, I was thinking seriously about doing what I should have done earlier. When I was an engraver, I should have expanded my business into a jewelry store. As I look back on my business life up to August 29, 1979, the happiest times were when I had been the one in charge.

Back in 1941 when I was a lifeguard for the city of Pittsburgh, I had the head lifeguard position. In the Navy, I was captain of my own ship and immediately following, in 1946, I was in control again when I opened my engraving business. Only a person who has been his own boss can understand how important it can be to have control.

When Eiben and Irr was formed as a partnership, I began to realize how much I missed being my own boss. As my business career continued, I became nothing more than an employee of a large corporation. If you consider being financially secure a success, then I had accomplished that. I lived in a beautiful, spacious home in an upscale neighborhood, belonged to a country club, had a summer home, and a sailboat. I was married to a wonderful woman;

I fathered two lovely children and had many quality friends. But losing control of my business life was a definite minus.

On a Friday in late August of 1979, I was out of a job and came home with a box full of personal belongings. It was not exactly a happy time breaking the news to Winnie; this obviously depressed her. I would be lying if I said that after all the years of working at Eiben and Irr it did not have a negative effect on me as well. I tried to soften the blow by telling her how upbeat I was about starting over. This did not help much; Saturday and Sunday were two very gloomy days, but it did give me time to think about how I would go about opening a new business.

At the age of 56, I felt born again, knowing I was about to live my dream of the last ten years. It felt great embarking on this new endeavor, and I knew I would have knowledge and experience far superior to most of my competition in similar businesses. I had recently finished preparing a sales book entitled *The Key to Your Understanding of the Mineral Known as Diamond*, and had it copyrighted. This book was to be a very effective tool in my selling procedure, since I believe in educating customers so they can feel confident about their jewelry buying decisions.

I also planned to use my artistic talent to design special one-of-a-kind jewelry for the discerning customer. Because of my many years in the jewelry business, I would have excellent sources of supply. My diamonds would be purchased from cutters, so I would be in the same position as a wholesaler. All my mountings and most of the other jewelry could be obtained from a manufacturer, so I would have no need for a middleman.

The other big edge that would help me be successful in my new venture was my operating costs. They would be low by comparison to other operations since I did not intend to have a large store—400 square feet was adequate—and I would have only one employee. With a smaller store in an off-street location, insurance costs would be at a minimum. There was one very important ingredient I needed, though, and that was customers. I knew that if I could make people aware that I was back in business, there was a good chance they would come to my new store for their jewelry needs.

Monday morning, September 1, 1979, I was up at seven in the morning. I showered, shaved, and dressed up in my favorite suit and was off to the Clark Building in Pittsburgh. I was no stranger to the building, having spent a good portion of my life there. I already knew the manager of the building and the location of his office; it was on the 22nd floor. Before going to his office, I looked out the window next to the elevators.

The panoramic view of the North Side of Pittsburgh from this vantage point is a remarkable sight. The Allegheny River, railroads, the highways and the many office buildings, apartments and homes that occupy the North Side of Pittsburgh create a stunning view. While looking out I saw a sight that was hard to believe. A tugboat was pushing 15 barges loaded with coal. Seeing this many barges being pushed by one tugboat staggered my imagination.

My eyes moved to the hillside above the river. Here I noticed a train that appeared to stretch out at least a mile and a half along the side of the hill. You never get a chance to see a sight like this at street level.

To the left of the elevator was an unoccupied office space. This room would have the same view as the windows I had just been looking out. If I could rent this space, I could enjoy this fantastic view everyday. The space was small but had enough room for the layout of my new store. I said to myself "Wow! I wonder if this space is available for rent."

I walked into the manager's office and told the secretary why I was there. Frank Heisler immediately agreed to see me since I was no stranger to him; his wife worked for me at

Eiben and Irr for several years. Before getting down to the reason for my visit, we exchanged memories of Eiben and Irr.

Finally, there was a break in conversation, and I was able to ask if the room was vacant. It seemed like it took him forever to answer, but he said yes and there was no reason I could not rent the space. What a relief to know it was available. Frank informed me the rent was $325 a month, which seemed to be a reasonable amount, so I authorized him to prepare a five-year lease. He said I needed one month's rent up front and asked for my bank's name and my account number. Frank went on to ask me exactly what type of jewelry store it would be and if there was any need for alterations to the space. I told him I would have to come back the next day to give him the information, since I had to finalize those details.

I had a personal account at Mellon Bank, so after lunch I went over to open my business account at their downtown branch. I made myself known at the desk of one of the bank's employees and told her I was the former owner of Eiben and Irr, and I was starting a new business and wished to open another account. Eiben and Irr was a major retailer in the city for many years, and the receptionist probably thought mine would be an important account and decided I should meet with one of the bank's executives. I did not expect this, and much to my surprise, I was escorted into an impressive-looking office.

I can still remember sitting in this man's office. He struck me as a pompous individual who was impressed with his own position. I told him my plans to open a jewelry store on the 22nd floor of the Clark Building. Instead of opening my account, he gave me a dissertation on why I should not open a store on the 22nd floor. He said, "How could you possibly hope to be successful at such a location?" After hearing as much as I could possibly listen to, I told him that I liked the view and wanted to get on with opening my account.

I was off next to the city courthouse to procure a retail license under the name C. Mel Eiben Jewelers, and I also decided to get a wholesaler license under the name of Certified Marketing Enterprise. (Notice the initials?) After filling out the papers as instructed, I was issued a retail and wholesale license. I was now officially in business and it gave me a feeling of satisfaction I had not felt in many years.

On Tuesday morning, I was back at the Clark Building rental office, and I signed the lease papers. With the key in hand and before doing anything else, I went to my empty store room and looked out the window and viewed the city pulsating below me. I paused and looked at the boats on the river, a train passing by, automobiles and people going in all different directions and saw all the ingredients of a healthy business environment. In a small way, I was about to become part of this picture.

After lunch at Palmer's Restaurant, I headed for the strip district to find a used office furniture store. Going thorough the door of the first place I found, I entered a huge room filled with showcases, desks, chairs, file cabinets and safes. It reminded me of a junk yard and certainly not a place to look for what I needed.

An elderly man approached me. His warm welcome, speech and manner put me immediately at ease. I told him about my plans to open a 400-square-foot jewelry store; I needed two desks, two chairs, file cabinets, a safe, and three showcases that would fit into the small space. With a pleasant smile, he said, "This is not going to be a large order."

He took great pride in telling me about the famous businesses the various pieces of furniture came from, and in fact, the showcases I chose were from a gift shop at the airport. In a relatively short period of time, I picked what I felt would be adequate to open the store. I was pleased with my selections, and the total cost was only $700.

On Wednesday, September 3, I turned the key and walked into an empty office, wondering if I had made the right decisions about the furniture and fixtures. At 11 o'clock, there was a knock at the door, and all of my purchases were sitting in the hallway. It sure looked like a big pile of stuff to fit into such a small room. With nervous anticipation, I had the two men move everything into my new store. Finding a place for the safe was a major decision because once it was positioned, it could not be moved because of its weight. With that decision made, like magic the showcases and furniture filled out every inch of space just as I had envisioned.

Placing a desk, safe, and showcases in an empty room does not constitute being in business. I did, however, sit in my office chair and relax for a few moments enjoying the wonderful feeling of entering a completely new phase of my life. My new seat was a huge black leather chair, probably owned by some prestigious executive at one time, which made me feel very important. I looked around my store at the empty showcases, and my feeling of accomplishment suddenly dissipated. Once one problem was solved, another crept into my mind.

I decided the empty showcases would be my next hurdle. I figured on a budget of $8000, which was certainly not high enough to make an impressive display. I was being very careful about my expenditures. How was I to know if a store isolated on the 22nd floor would be a success?

As luck would have it, the Mercury Ring salesperson was in the building calling on other accounts. I invited him to come see me in my office. This company sold top quality merchandise. They were one of my major suppliers before Eiben and Irr became a catalog showroom business when Spang and Company bought us out. Their quality jewelry was not sold in a catalog.

It was a happy occasion to renew an old friendship. I told him I wanted to place an order for some of his merchandise.

I did not know what his answer would be, since he sold only to wholesalers and very large retail operations. He acted as if he were unsure what to do. It is a good thing I had procured a wholesale license when I got my retail license because that was the key to his writing my order.

I decided on $4000 worth of merchandise that included a mixture of mountings, pendants and earrings. It was then I learned that my order would not be shipped until it was paid in full. Why should they ship when I had no credit rating? Unfortunately, the thousands of dollars I spent at their company in the past did not help me in my new venture. I just told him to hold the order, and I would let them know when to ship it.

Back in my store on Thursday morning, September 5, I decided to devote my time to solving my merchandise problems. The three empty showcases frustrated me. Before buying any more merchandise, I decided to make maximum use of my past reputation with local suppliers. Ordering from a large corporation like Mercury Ring was the wrong way to proceed.

To operate my store as planned, I would need a loose diamond inventory. The cost of this type of merchandise would be enormous. To help solve this problem, I decided to visit John Keppie, the owner of J.C. Keppie Company. I still had a close relationship with John. Despite our age difference, we never ceased to enjoy each other's company. We both still belonged to South Hills Country Club and played an occasional round of golf together.

The J.C. Keppie Company was a major importer of diamonds in Pittsburgh. In fact, he was a "site holder"; this meant he bought rough diamonds directly from DeBeers Consolidated Mines. On Friday morning, I went to his office to see if he could help me with a diamond inventory. After discussing what I needed, John agreed to give me a balanced inventory of diamonds on consignment. Not only would I have this consignment of loose diamonds, I would have access to his entire inventory since his business was in the Clark Building as well. This was a great arrangement, and it solved my loose diamond inventory problem.

I had another "brainstorm" concerning diamonds. Twenty years prior, I sold a huge number of diamonds to an attorney who bought them as investments. I did not know who his clients were, but all of the deals we made were in cash.

I called Allen on the phone and told him of the huge increase in the value of diamonds since he bought them. Their worth skyrocketed when inflation was rampant during President Carter's administration, and they now cost four times more than when Allen originally purchased them. He agreed that selling some of his diamonds might not be a bad idea. The records concerning Allen's inventory had been left at Eiben and Irr, so that afternoon I visited his office and made a copy of his list of which diamonds he bought and the price he paid for them. After so many years, I had lost track of the number of diamonds and the enormous amount of money involved.

Despite his wealth, Allen was very frugal and said he would allow only some of the diamonds in my care at one time. In addition to this stipulation, he made me aware of another major problem I had yet to address—insurance. I told him I was in the process of procuring insurance, and we parted with him saying, "When your store is properly insured, let me know."

Back in the office that afternoon, I called Jewelers Mutual to see how soon they could send out a representative to arrange insurance for my store. The earliest someone could see me was the following Wednesday.

The showcases were a bit shabby-looking, so on Saturday I painted them. Little could be accomplished that day since most of the businesses were closed.

316

With the various mountings, diamonds, and wedding bands on consignment from J.C. Keppie Company and the diamonds from Allen, I would have a very impressive diamond inventory to start with. The mounting selections were not adequate, so I decided to send a check to Mercury Ring Corporation and have them ship my order. This still did not answer my overall merchandise needs, as I needed more variety. Watches, chains, pendants, and other miscellaneous jewelry were still needed.

The solution to this problem I thought might be an old friend of mine, Jim Lloyd. He was a partner of Grafner Brothers, a large wholesaler across the street from the Clark Building. Back when Eiben and Irr was an independent entity, our orders were so frequent we had a direct telephone line to Grafner Brothers to facilitate ordering. We had lunch together at least once a month through the years, and I intended to make him aware of my inventory needs and see if he could help me.

The Clark Building was filled with all types of jewelry-oriented businesses—jewelry manufacturers and repair shops, large and small wholesalers too. In fact, there was a business as large as Grafner Brothers right in the building called Baggard and Company. They agreed to give me a temporary memo to take to my office so I would have more items to show customers. I realized I had access to more inventory than most jewelry stores.

On Monday morning, my first stop was the Grafner showroom. Jim invited me into his office, and I told him my plans of opening my new store. He said, "This is deja vu; we are turning back the clock. I had a similar meeting with you back in 1947 when you had your engraving business." My first request was for a permanent memo. He said it would be impossible because he knew his partners would not agree to it. That being the case, I placed a small order for about

317

$2500. With special prices for an opening order, I was surprised at how many pieces of merchandise it provided. He gave me three months to pay, with one third to be paid each month. This was my first major step in establishing credit.

At Beggard and Company, the owner assured me I would be allowed to take out a temporary memo at any time. We parted with him wishing me luck with my new venture.

On Tuesday morning, I visited a manufacturer named Kuni and Brown, who did the repair work for Eiben and Irr. All jewelers needed an operation such as this to size rings, set diamonds, and do repair work, and they were also able to manufacture my special designs of rings, earrings, and pendants. Kuni and Brown were glad to open an account with me. John Kuni was very tall and slender; Al Brown was the opposite, short and heavy. John was easy going, and Al was very hyperactive. Jewelers, including me, are always in a hurry to get their jobs done, and as a result, Al and I would often be at odds with each other. Al had diamond tweezers I admired, and although I searched high and low, I could never find a place to buy a pair like his. Every time I went into his shop, which was almost every day, I would mention my desire to find tweezers like his for myself. One day, he finally said to me, "Here are the God damn tweezers. I can no longer put up with your aggravation over it." Twenty-five years later, they are still my favorite tweezers for holding diamonds. If I mislay them, my employees and I cannot accomplish anything until we find them.

Before my insurance was in place, Grafner decided to ship my small order. On Tuesday, September 8, I placed my first batch of merchandise on display. That lifted my spirits, knowing I had some jewelry in the cases. On that same day, I made my first sale.

Lou Owens, a fraternity brother from college, heard about my new venture from an employee of Eiben and Irr. He needed a diamond pendant for his wife for their anniversary. We went to Beggard and Company, made a selection, and I had a $325 sale. We both felt good about the transaction, he as my first customer and I with my first sale.

On Wednesday, a neatly dressed man appeared at the door and said he was the Jewelers Mutual representative. We immediately got involved with the business of insurance. There was no small talk about the weather or politics. In fact, he had a look on his face as if he thought my business was a joke. It did not take me long to discover why. He was not very polite in delivering his opinion of the freshly painted safe sitting on the floor. He said the "antiquated hunk of iron" was only secure enough to hold important papers, and it would be impossible for his company to insure my business with a safe like that. He then informed me of Jewelers Mutual's requirements for safes. Opening up his briefcase, he pulled out a catalog showing pictures of various safes; the one he recommended I get for my store was $7000. I was devastated. He also told me I needed a dead bolt on the door and a buzzer system so I could let customers in. In addition, he said that I had no security system. He must have been questioning why I would have had him come all the way from Philadelphia without first having basic safety measures in place. I should have known better, being in the jewelry business all these years.

He went on to tell me to call Jewelers Mutual when the safeguards were in place, and he would come back to Pittsburgh to finalize my insurance package. After shaking my hand and wishing me good luck on my new business, he was on his way.

Sitting down in my executive chair, arms at my sides, I certainly did not have the exhilarating sensation I had the first time I sat on this piece of leather. I told myself to slow down and refine each move in a more professional way. If it takes another week, two, or even a month, so be it. I am in business for myself. With a deep breath and a wave of new enthusiasm, I sat up straight in my chair and prepared my list. This whole experience reminded me of being captain of my ship in the Navy. All the decisions were up to me. As I would say to my coxswain after pulling away from the beach, "Rudder amid ship, engines ahead, full and steady as you go."

The first item on my list was the safe. There had to be a safe company in Pittsburgh. With the Yellow Pages in front of me, I called several companies and asked a representative to contact me, but none seemed anxious to do so. I did not give up and called a business with a small ad that specialized in used safes. The phone rang and the man on the other end identified himself as the owner. After I explained my problem, he said he would be glad to visit my store and see if he had a safe at a reasonable price that fit my requirements.

Exactly one hour later, a man looking like a construction worker walked into my store. He was strongly built, bald, and had a very warm smile. He looked like a man who could be trusted to solve my safe problem. There was no need for me to explain all the specifications for insurance coverage. Bill knew all about them. He said that even a used safe would cost me $3000, but I urged him to find me a less expensive solution. He told me that a few years ago, he had a customer with a similar problem and to fix it, he sold him a small safe that met the insurance company's requirements and bolted it to the inside bottom of his larger safe. He had one in stock for $850, and that price included delivery and installation.

The price sounded right, and I was sure it was worth a try. I called Jewelers Mutual to give them the details of my safe expert's solution. The man on the line happened to be the head of the insurance company, and without any hesitation, he agreed to talk to the safe expert. The two of them spoke at great length, and I anxiously awaited the result. They finally assured me that as long as I could fit 75 percent of the value of my inventory into the small safe, they could write my policy. This would be easy for me to do since most of my inventory was in loose diamonds. He said his agent would not have to come back as long as I mailed him a copy of the mercantile burglar alarm certificate. Talking to the owner was a very pleasant experience I did not expect after meeting with his salesman.

On Thursday morning, the safe was installed, and Bill called Jewelers Mutual to describe the size of the bolts used to secure the safe within a safe, and I was assured that my new safe met all of their requirements. I could not thank Bill enough for his genius idea, and it was such a relief to have another huge problem out of the way. Twenty-eight years later, I still have the same safe arrangement.

The next item for me to tackle was security. On Friday morning, I contacted ADT, and they said a representative would be in Tuesday to analyze my store's needs and give me an estimate. With this out of the way, I decided to get involved with the major problem of advertising.

I decided to place an ad in the Pittsburgh Post-Gazette Business Section, informing the public I was back in business. I chose this section because I felt my advertisement would be overwhelmed by department store ads in any other part of the paper. The cost was $600. I had no idea it was that expensive. OK, old Navy man, you have to stay the course. Now get your thinking cap on and write an ad like you never wrote before.

I thought newspaper ads were expensive until I heard the cost of advertising in the Yellow Pages. I received another dollar shock. My ad had to stand out and be different from other commercials on the page, and even an ad 2 inch by 1 inch seemed small to me, but it cost $250 per month. No way could I justify that much expense for space in the book. I decided on an ad that was $120 per month. Some of the ads in the book were in color, and that difference grabbed my attention. "How much extra for color?" I asked. He said, "$15 per month." I agreed to go with it. I wanted my ad to stand out as much as possible.

After he left, I wondered if I could justify spending $1680 a year for that little space, but then it occurred to me that one major diamond sale a month would more than cover the cost. Television and radio commercials were far too expensive to consider as a means to get the word out. All I could do now was hope that the public would discover that I was back in business.

One of the other details I had to deal with was getting an accountant. A friend of mine from South Hills Country Club recommended Ed Battle, whose office was a mile down the highway from the club. I was told that when it comes to an accountant for small businesses such as mine, there was no one better. Ed had honed his skills by working for the Internal Revenue Service.

I made my way to his office and received a warm welcome and a firm handshake from Ed. We discussed the nature of my business and how he would set up sound business procedures. There is no way I could have found my direction through the accounting maze without his help. In 2008, almost 29 years later, he is still my accountant. Ed and I are both World War II veterans, and both still on the job.

While waiting for my insurance to be effective, I developed a design for my stationery and business cards. It consisted of a diamond shape superimposed over my address and phone number. To this day, the same basic design appears on all of my printing.

On Thursday, September 17, Jewelers Mutual called and told me my insurance was confirmed, and the policy was on its way. With my store officially insured and security in place, I called John Keppie and asked him to prepare my memo on diamonds, mountings and wedding bands. I also informed Allen, the attorney with the investment diamonds, that insurance and security were in place, and I would like to pick up some of his diamonds.

Since Eiben and Irr closed, I knew that Millie, one of the employees who worked in the jewelry department with me, was out of a job, so I offered her a position in my new company. She quickly accepted and, fortunately, she fit perfectly into my new venture with her many skills and talents.

On Tuesday September 22, John Keppie sent over the loose diamond memo, and I was pleasantly surprised at the number of mountings and wedding bands he included with it. Millie and I trimmed the cases with the merchandise, and there was enough on display to make it look like I was in the jewelry business. It felt wonderful to be officially in business. In one month, I had gone from an empty room to once more being Captain of my own ship!

C. Mel Eiben at his desk in 1980

Now all of the basics were out of the way, but I had a very lonely feeling from not having many sales. Maybe the pompous bank executive was right when he said, "How could you possibly be successful on the 22nd floor of the Clark Building?" I have to say the view did not seem quite as wonderful when there were not any customers coming through the door.

Much to my surprise, my business started to have more activity with each passing week. Sales increased and time passed by very quickly. Suddenly I was in the middle of Christmas selling season, and I did an impressive amount of business that year.

Looking forward to going to work was a feeling I began to experience again. Selling diamond engagement rings to couples at the pinnacle of their love life is very rewarding , and seeing the happy look on their faces brought me joy.

The part of my business I still really enjoy is the custom designing. I create drawings in the same exact detail as the finished piece of jewelry. After the customer confirms the drawing and a price is agreed upon, I have the piece of jewelry manufactured. When it comes back from the manufacturer, I am always excited to see the finished product and how close it is to my drawing.

Of course I am always concerned that the customer be satisfied, and when I open the box for them and see their delight, I get a great feeling of accomplishment.

I also enjoy appraising. Each new piece a customer brings in is a challenge and makes me feel like a jewelry detective.

My business was and is everything I hoped it would be. I am my own boss and enjoy happiness and financial success. I never cease to enjoy gaining the trust and confidence of a customer who is about to make a purchase at my store. With each person who enters, I feel like a teacher in a classroom passing my knowledge on to a student. Jewelry has the unique characteristic of being the same but different, and explaining the disparity, to me, is the joy of selling.

If you're ever in the vicinity of the Clark Building, come on up to the fifth floor where I am now located and say hello. I promise I won't try to sell you anything. Unless, of course, you're in the market for a really great piece of jewelry.

CHAPTER 25
EPILOGUE:
LIFE GOES ON

The readers who have managed to make it to this page in my book have probably surmised by now that I could go on and on. And they would be right. Once I got started writing, I could not stop myself. I had many more chapters in which I planned to tell you about my love of cars and boats and all the great ones I have owned or wished I could have owned or had stolen from me. I planned to tell you of all the wonderful vacations I had with my family and give you a blow by blow depiction of my married life with its many adventures and misadventures, not to mention a room by room tour of all the homes we lived in. And I think I could even have come up with a few more golf stories...

But then my advisors said "Enough already, Mel!" Instead they have given me just a few more pages to tell you the rest of my story.

One thing I will tell you is that the many years of my marriage to Winnie were filled with happiness that far outweighed any depressing times. Our disagreements were infrequent and always short-lived and we never seemed to run out of things to talk about. Our two daughters, Suzi and Cindy, brought much joy and laughter into our home and our lives. Some of the happiest times in my memory were the times we were all together having fun.

Though quite unlike each other, both girls were excellent students and never gave us a moment's worry. We were thrilled to be parents of the bride when each found the man of her choice. Their weddings alone would fill a whole chapter. As would, unfortunately, their divorces.

Suzi and her husband, Clyde, broke up in 1980 after Suzi helped Clyde get through medical school. This was an unexpected event for all of us and a very sad time in our lives. Suzi survived, though, and a few years later, with her friend Bill, opened a computer store in Palmyra, Pennsylvania, which she still operates today.

Cindy and her husband, Tom, had three children, Erin, Shannon and Brendan. Having grandchildren was a great experience for Winnie and me and we thoroughly enjoyed the time we spent with them. Sadly, the marriage broke up seven months after our grandson, Brendan, was born and a long, unsuccessful struggle over child support ensued. The children attended Catholic school and although Tom was supposed to provide for their educations, he never completely abided by the ruling of the court.

Cindy worked only part time in order to raise the children; however, she continued her education and acquired an art degree in addition to her teaching degree and later a degree in psychology. I assumed the financial responsibility until she and the children were out of school. It was a difficult time. I continue to help when emergencies occur.

All three children worked part-time jobs to fund their schooling. Shannon at the University of Pittsburgh and Brendan at Duquesne University took out student loans and earned their degrees, while Erin, with her own money received an education in management at Pennsylvania Culinary School. Cindy is a teacher and therapist and works with abused children. I am very proud of all of them.

And now my granddaughter, Shannon, has made me a great grandfather. Two years ago she surprised us all with twins, Winnie and Xavier.

As with others who have been lucky enough to live into their 80's, my life has included many losses along with all the joyous occasions. My brother, Maurice, whom you first met back at Manus Island, died when in his early forties. He fell off a scaffolding while he was working on a ceiling in a school gym and died the next morning. As this was the first death in our family, it was extremely difficult, especially since my brother, Paul and I had to convey the news to my parents.

I do not remember either of my parents having a sick day in their lives. We were very fortunate to have them both live to the age of 84, when they died within two months of each other.

Throughout the years of our marriage, Winnie underwent several surgeries and eventually, from years of smoking, contracted emphysema. As her trips to the hospital grew more frequent, it became apparent to us that this was one health problem no medicine or operation could cure. In 1990, she made her last trip to the hospital and I lost my beautiful wife. Suzi, Cindy, our granddaughter Erin and I were there with her for her final moments. I will never forget the wonderful male nurse who stayed with Winnie and us throughout this heartbreaking ordeal.

I had been married to Winnie for 46 years. After so many years of marriage, it is difficult to see how your life can go on when you lose that person, that other half of you. But go on, it does. With the support of wonderful friends and family, things started to move again. Of course, there was my golf game to pick up my spirits. (Winnie used to like to tell her friends that if she died on a Wednesday, please don't tell Mel until after his golf game is over.) The jewelry store, as always, kept me busy and my mind occupied.

It is now almost 18 years since Winnie's passing. I am still the owner of my own business, enjoying the excitement of meeting each new customer who walks through the door. I still play golf twice a week and enjoy the camaraderie of a game of gin rummy. And now I'm an author!

And, oh yes, along the way I had the extreme good fortune to meet a gorgeous woman who, incredible as it may seem, has put up with me to this day. Not only is she warm and charming, but intelligent and generous as well and I am ever thankful for her companionship and support. It would take yet another book to tell of all the wonderful experiences we have had together.

As I stated at the beginning of my book, I had no idea in the process of writing my memoirs, how much I would reflect on the decisions I have made in my lifetime. I have had a life full of interesting experiences–some enjoyable and some not, but I assure you, I was never bored. Writing this book has been an incredible experience for me, recalling in sequence all the forks in the road of my life. My life continues to go on, and I am enjoying every precious moment of every day.